THROUGH THE HEART OF THE SOUTH

THE SEABOARD AIR LINE RAILROAD STORY

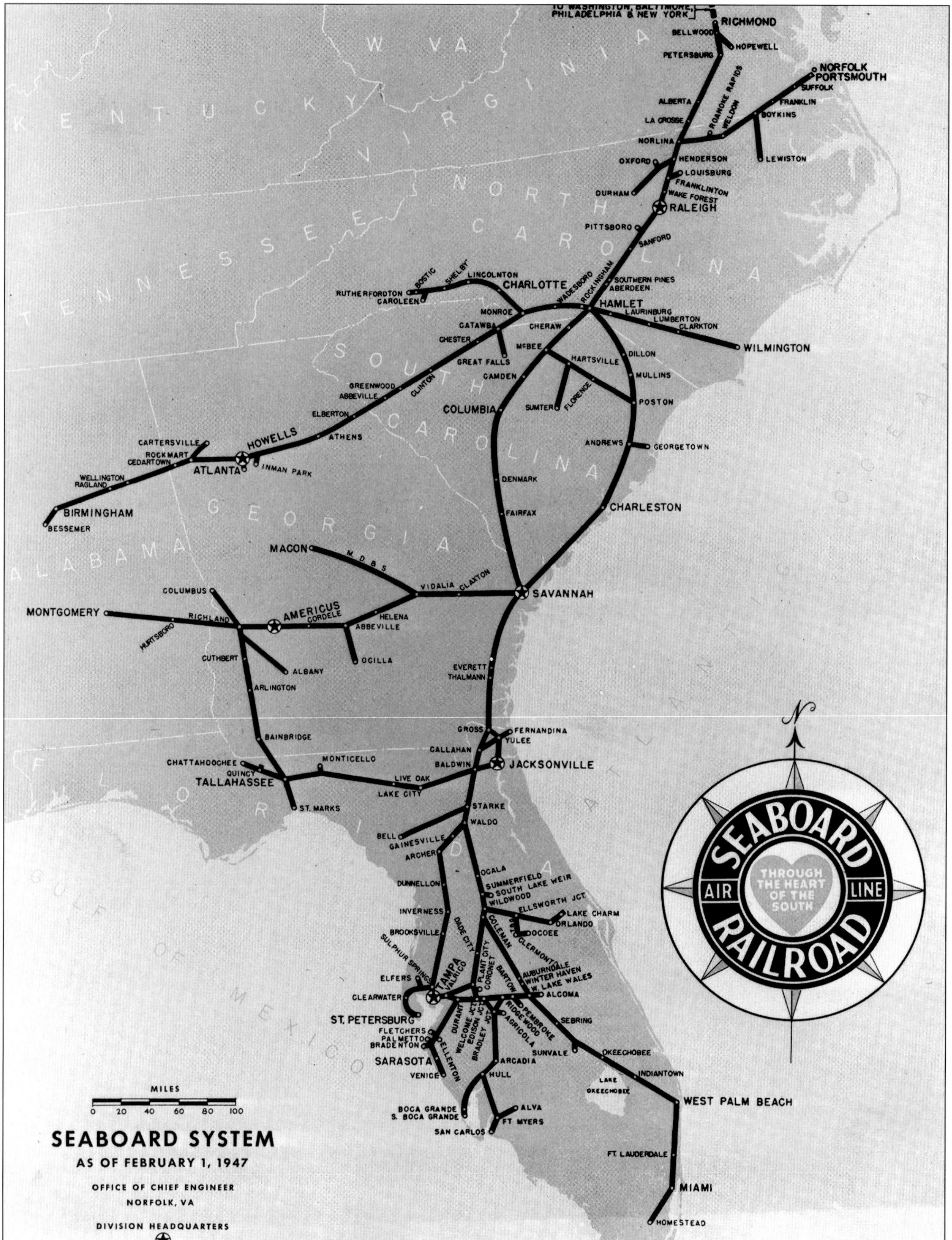

SEABOARD SYSTEM
AS OF FEBRUARY 1, 1947
OFFICE OF CHIEF ENGINEER
NORFOLK, VA
DIVISION HEADQUARTERS
MILES
0 20 40 60 80 100
SEABOARD AIR LINE RAILROAD
THROUGH THE HEART OF THE SOUTH
N
TO WASHINGTON, BALTIMORE, PHILADELPHIA & NEW YORK
KENTUCKY
W. VA.
VIRGINIA
TENNESSEE
NORTH CAROLINA
SOUTH CAROLINA
GEORGIA
ALABAMA
FLORIDA
GULF OF MEXICO
ATLANTIC OCEAN
RICHMOND
BELLWOOD
HOPEWELL
PETERSBURG
NORFOLK
PORTSMOUTH
SUFFOLK
FRANKLIN
BOYKINS
LEWISTON
ALBERTA
ROANOKE RAPIDS
WELDON
LA CROSSE
NORLINA
HENDERSON
OXFORD
LOUISBURG
FRANKLINTON
WAKE FOREST
DURHAM
RALEIGH
PITTSBORO
SANFORD
SOUTHERN PINES
ABERDEEN
ROCKINGHAM
WADESBORO
HAMLET
LAURINBURG
LUMBERTON
CLARKTON
WILMINGTON
BOSTIC
SHELBY
LINCOLNTON
CHARLOTTE
RUTHERFORDTON
CAROLEEN
MONROE
CATAWBA
CHESTER
CHERAW
McBEE
HARTSVILLE
DILLON
MULLINS
GREAT FALLS
CAMDEN
GREENWOOD
CLINTON
ABBEVILLE
COLUMBIA
SUMTER
FLORENCE
POSTON
ELBERTON
ATHENS
HOWELLS
CARTERSVILLE
ROCKMART
CEDARTOWN
ATLANTA
INMAN PARK
WELLINGTON
RAGLAND
BIRMINGHAM
BESSEMER
ANDREWS
GEORGETOWN
DENMARK
FAIRFAX
CHARLESTON
MACON
M. D. & S.
VIDALIA
CLAXTON
SAVANNAH
COLUMBUS
MONTGOMERY
RICHLAND
HURTSBORO
AMERICUS
CORDELE
HELENA
ABBEVILLE
OCILLA
CUTHBERT
ALBANY
ARLINGTON
BAINBRIDGE
EVERETT
THALMANN
GROSS
FERNANDINA
YULEE
CALLAHAN
BALDWIN
JACKSONVILLE
CHATTAHOOCHEE
QUINCY
TALLAHASSEE
MONTICELLO
LIVE OAK
LAKE CITY
ST. MARKS
STARKE
WALDO
BELL
GAINESVILLE
ARCHER
OCALA
SUMMERFIELD
SOUTH LAKE WEIR
WILDWOOD
DUNNELLON
INVERNESS
ELLSWORTH JCT.
LAKE CHARM
ORLANDO
OCOEE
WIT
CLERMONT
BROOKSVILLE
DADE CITY
COLEMAN
SULPHUR SPRINGS
PLANT CITY
CORONET
BARTOW
AUBURNDALE
WINTER HAVEN
W. LAKE WALES
ALCOMA
ELFERS
TAMPA
VALRICO
CLEARWATER
ST. PETERSBURG
DURANT
WELCOME JCT.
EDISON JCT.
BRADLEY JCT.
PEMBROKE
RIDGEWOOD
AGRICOLA
SEBRING
FLETCHERS
PALMETTO
BRADENTON
ELLENTON
SARASOTA
VENICE
ARCADIA
SUNVALE
OKEECHOBEE
LAKE OKEECHOBEE
INDIANTOWN
HULL
WEST PALM BEACH
BOCA GRANDE
S. BOCA GRANDE
ALVA
FT. MYERS
SAN CARLOS
FT. LAUDERDALE
MIAMI
HOMESTEAD

THROUGH THE HEART OF THE SOUTH

THE SEABOARD AIR LINE RAILROAD STORY

Stoddart

ROBERT WAYNE JOHNSON

A BOSTON MILLS PRESS BOOK

Canadian Cataloguing in Publication Data

Johnson, Robert Wayne, 1939–
Through the heart of the south : the Seaboard Air Line Railroad story

ISBN I-55046-I44-3

1. Seaboard Air Line Railroad Company - History.
2. Railroads - South Atlantic States - History. I. Title.

TF25.S4J6 1995 385′.0975 C95-931105-X

Edited by Gordon Turner
Designed by Mary Firth
Printed in Canada

First published in 1995 by
The Boston Mills Press
132 Main Street
Erin, Ontario
N0B 1T0
519-833-2407 fax 833-2195

An affiliate of Stoddart Publishing Co. Ltd.
34 Lesmill Road
North York, Ontario
M3B 2T6

The publisher gratefully acknowledges the support of the Canada Council, Ontario Arts Council and Ontario Publishing Centre in the development of writing and publishing in Canada.

IN MEMORIAM

Robert M. Johnson
Thomas B. Johnson
Fred M. Phillips
My father
My grandfather
My mother's stepfather
Good Men, Good Railroaders All

TITLE PAGE:
Streamlined Pacific 868 prepares to depart Wildwood, Fla., with No. 343, the West Coast section of the Silver Meteor, *in the early forties.* Railway Negative Exchange

THIS PAGE:
FT's 4010 and 4110 at Raleigh, N.C., circa 1946. Sam Appleby, Jr.; collection of David W. Salter

CONTENTS PAGE:
Roundhouse laborers scrub down an A-B-A set of E7's, led by Seaboard 3022, at Howells Yard in Atlanta in January 1947. CSX Transportation collection

CONTENTS

Bracketing RS3 1691, modified RSC2's 1511 and 1517 lead No. 82 near McRae, Georgia, in December 1961. J. Parker Lamb

ACKNOWLEDGMENTS

One of the most delightful aspects of writing this book has been the help I have received from so many people, most of them hitherto total strangers. Without their gracious assistance there is no way this project would have been possible.

First, of course, are the photographers: Sam Appleby, Jr.; Kenneth M. Ardinger; Frank E. Ardrey, Jr.; Hugh M. Comer; Fraser Hale; D. Wallace Johnson; J. Parker Lamb; the late James G. LaVake; L.A. McLean; David W. Salter; Jim Scribbins; Curt Tillotson, Jr; George E. Votava; and Ed Wojtas. It is their talent and skill that have truly created this book.

Others who have generously contributed photographs from their collections include: Laura F. Brown of the University of Baltimore Library; Prof. Herbert J. Doherty of the University of Florida; George Drury of Kalmbach Publishing Co.; Bob Hall of Railway Negative Exchange; Robert Jones of the North Carolina Division of Archives and History; Gene Mathews of *The Bradford County Telegraph*; Bruce R. Meyer; Robert Niesz; Larry Smith of Prototype Pix; and Harold K. Vollrath. Photographs have also been obtained from Alco Historic Photographs, the Delaware State Archives, the Florida State Archives, the Library of Congress and the Railroad Museum of Pennsylvania.

Among the many individuals who have helped with this book in countless other ways are: Linda Bergquist; the late Wiley M. Bryan; Charles E. Cochran of the law firm of Arnold & Porter; the late Johnny Coleman; James Garner of CSX Transportation; Joseph L. Oates of the Atlantic Coast Line and Seaboard Air Line Historical Society; and my editor, Gordon Turner. Most deserving of mention is Ellen Schwartz of the California State Railroad Museum Library. I would especially like to thank R. Lindsey Leckie of CSX Transportation, a man with an impossible job who did it extremely well.

Like Blanche DuBois, a character in Tennessee Williams's *A Streetcar Named Desire*, "I have always depended on the kindness of strangers." In this case, the strangers have responded magnificently. I am grateful to them all.

Finally, I would like to thank my family: Judy Crumley; Helen Johnson; my daughter Karen for not bugging Daddy too much; and especially my wife Ida and my son Adam for showing me how to make the darn computer function.

Robert Wayne Johnson, Pleasant Hill, California, March 1995

INTRODUCTION

The Seaboard Air Line didn't own any airplanes. It was not an airline. It was a railroad—and a pretty darn good one at that. It seems a rather curious name for a railroad now, but the term "Seaboard Air Line" had been used to describe the Seaboard & Roanoke Railroad almost as far back as the Civil War. A number of railroads had called themselves "air lines" during the Victorian era. The implication, whether accurate or not, was that their routes were straight lines. Thus the term "air line" had been applied to railroads when Orville and Wilbur Wright still dangled from their mother's knee. The Seaboard was, however, the last remaining railroad to call itself an "air line."

In recounting the story of the Seaboard, I am concentrating on the diesel era: from 1938 when it bought its first diesel locomotive, to 1967 when it merged with its long time rival, Atlantic Coast Line, to form the Seaboard Coast Line. While emphasizing the 1938–1967 period, I will also relate the history of the Seaboard from its origins to the 1930s. After all, to understand anything we must know something of its history. Moreover, the history of the Seaboard is a colorful one, well worth the telling.

Seaboard was a fascinating railroad, especially during its later years. It was an innovator in many areas. It pioneered the use of articulated steam locomotives in fast freight and passenger service and inaugurated the first streamlined passenger train in the Southeast. Seaboard was also an early proponent of Centralized Traffic Control, automated classification yards and Trailer on Flatcar (TOFC) piggyback service. Its fleet of "Silver" streamliners included some of the finest and fastest passenger trains in the nation, and the railroad also operated some of the fastest freights. Seaboard's diesels were both colorful and diverse at a time when many of its contemporaries contented themselves with monotonous fleets of nearly identical locomotives, all from the same builder and all dressed in doleful shades of black. Moreover, it was a financial success story in an industry noted for all too few. A traditionally weak line wedged between two stronger rivals, Seaboard Air Line flew high during the booming 1920s, overexpanded and paid dearly for its folly during the Great Depression, quickly crashing into bankruptcy. But it soared back after World War II to become a strong and profitable mainstay of the South's transportation system.

My own interest in the Seaboard was virtually inevitable. I grew up with the railroad. My father was a clerk at the West Jacksonville yard. His father was a carman in the shops, and my mother's stepfather a switchman for the Jacksonville Terminal Co. I was surrounded by railroaders. Some of my earliest and fondest memories are of visits to the yard office where my father worked. It was a magic place: a long narrow wooden structure set on pilings out between the tracks, sort of a two-story building without a first floor. It was dilapidated, unkempt, redolent of coal smoke, sweat and grime. It was gloriously railroady and, to a small boy, deliciously male. Best of all, it had a front porch where one could survey the wondrous world of railroading while serenaded by the "dit dit da dit" of the Morse from the operator's window. I could stand there for hours. I felt sorry for any kid whose father had some dull pedestrian job in a factory or store, who wasn't a railroader. When I was in college, I jumped at the chance to work as a yard clerk and crew dispatcher during the summers. Later, after the Navy, I talked my way into a job as a paymaster, promising to learn to type in three weeks in order to get it. Even when I went to law school I still had the Seaboard. In 1966, when I arrived at Emory University, in Atlanta, I was delighted to discover that my dormitory was hard by the Georgia Division mainline. So the Seaboard Air Line has always been my railroad. Not Seaboard Coast Line, not Seaboard System Railroad, not CSX Transportation, but Seaboard Air Line—the real Seaboard. I loved it. I hope the reader will at least share some of my interest, if not my affection.

The Wilmington-Rutherford line was reorganized as the Carolina Central in 1873 and acquired by the Seaboard Air Line in the early 1880s. Sublettered C.C. on her cab side, but sporting Seaboard Air Line on her tender, 4-4-0 No. 416 was built by the Blood Works of Manchester, N.H., as Carolina Central No. 26, the D.W. Oates. CSX Transportation collection

CHAPTER ONE

THE FORMATIVE YEARS 1832–1900

The Seaboard Air Line Railroad got off to a rather inauspicious start. Its earliest predecessor, the Portsmouth & Roanoke Railroad, was abandoned a few years after it was built, and its next oldest ancestor, the Tallahassee Railroad, suffered the destruction of its Gulf Coast terminus when the village of Port Leon was wiped out by a hurricane. Many of its earliest ancestors were devastated by the Civil War and most of its predecessors went bankrupt at one time or another. Notwithstanding these early misfortunes, however, Seaboard eventually became one of the biggest railroad systems in the Southeast.

As it basically existed for over 60 years, the Seaboard Air Line Railroad was created in 1900 when a group of Richmond and Baltimore bankers consolidated three separate rail systems into a new line extending from Richmond, Va., to Tampa, Fla. The three components comprised the Florida Central & Peninsular Railroad which extended from Columbia, S.C., to Tampa; the Georgia & Alabama Railway which ran between Savannah, Ga., and Montgomery, Ala.; and a group of affiliated lines extending from Portsmouth, Va., to Atlanta, Ga., which had been informally operated as the Seaboard Air Line System.

Although it wasn't formed until 1900, Seaboard's predecessors included some of the first railroads in America. The Portsmouth & Roanoke began operation in 1834. The Tallahassee RR, the first railroad in Florida, was built in 1836 even before Florida became a state, when the "Sunshine State" was still just the "Sunshine Territory." Another early predecessor, the Raleigh & Gaston Railroad, was completed in 1840.

The Portsmouth & Roanoke Railroad Co., the first element of what was eventually to become the Seaboard Air Line, was chartered in Virginia in 1832 and North Carolina in 1833 to build a railroad from Portsmouth, across the Elizabeth River from Norfolk, Va., to Weldon, N.C., on the Roanoke River. The impetus for the line was the construction of the Petersburg Railroad which was completed in 1833. The Petersburg RR, the oldest predecessor of the Atlantic Coast Line, opened a line from Petersburg, Va., to Blakely, N.C., a point on the north bank of the Roanoke across from the town of Weldon.

Norfolk business interests feared losing their North Carolina trade to Petersburg. With construction of the Petersburg RR, Weldon traffic which went through the port of Norfolk would be subject to diversion to boats operating on the Appamatox River into Petersburg. Thus, the P&R was built primarily to retain North Carolina traffic for Norfolk.

Construction of the new line began in Portsmouth in August 1833. The road was constructed to a gauge of 4 feet 8-1/2 inches. That gauge dated back all the way to the Roman Empire when it had been the distance between chariot wheels. It had evolved into the distance between English wagon wheels and, ultimately, the standard railroad gauge. P&R's "rails" consisted of longitudinal wooden stringers which were covered with 2-1/2-inch x 1/2-inch strap iron. Although it was intended to use steam locomotives, the ties were notched in the center to provide a pathway for horses. Instead of switches, hand-operated turntables were used at sidings as it was feared that switches would derail the locomotives. Car wheels had cast-iron spokes and wrought-iron rims and flanges.

By July 1834, the line which skirted the western edge of the Great Dismal Swamp had reached Suffolk, Va., 17 miles from Portsmouth, and service began between the towns. Initially the cars were pulled by horses. One-way passenger fare was 75 cents. In September, the P&R's first steam locomotive arrived in Portsmouth on board the schooner *Hand*. The

A young boy and his dog have wandered into an otherwise formal portrait of Raleigh & Gaston 4-4-0 Romulus Saunders, *built by R. Norris & Sons Locomotive Works about 1857. The Lincolnesque gentleman standing on the running board in this photo (believed to be the oldest existing photograph of a train in the state of North Carolina) is railroad president Dr. William J. Hawkins.* North Carolina Division of Archives & History

new locomotive, which was built in Philadelphia, had four wheels and weighed about five tons. It was named the *John Barnett* in honor of the first white man to ascend the Roanoke River above its great falls. The engine began providing two round trips a day between Portsmouth and Suffolk, operating at a speed of about 15 mph and requiring 1 hour 20 minutes for a one-way journey.

Construction continued and the line crossed the Blackwater River and reached the Nottoway River, 42 miles from Portsmouth, by July 1835. A second steam locomotive, the *General Cabell*, was added to the company's roster in that year. By April 1836, the railroad had bridged the Meherrin River near the North Carolina border and service was advertised to Margaretsville, N.C., 62 miles from Portsmouth. In addition, a connection was effected with a steamboat operating on the Blackwater and Chowan Rivers to Edenton, N.C. The P&R crossed the Petersburg RR at Gary's Depot (Garysburg) and reached the Roanoke River by December 1836. The bridge over the river was finished in June 1837 and the line was finally completed to Weldon, a total distance of 79 miles.

Intense competition soon developed between the new line and the Petersburg Railroad. The two roads were each components of competing routes between Baltimore and Southern points such as Wilmington, N.C., and Charleston, S.C. The P&R connected with the Maryland & Virginia Steam Boat Co., which operated boats between Baltimore and Norfolk, to form one route between Baltimore and Weldon. The Petersburg RR was part of a competing arrangement known as the Inland or Upper Route. It consisted of the Baltimore & Ohio RR from Baltimore to Washington; a steamboat from Washington to a connection with the Richmond, Fredericksburg & Potomac RR at Fredericksburg, Va., or, later, Aquia Creek, Va.; the RF&P to Richmond; the Richmond & Petersburg RR between its namesake cities; and the Petersburg RR south from Petersburg. At Weldon both the P&R and the Petersburg connected with the Wilmington & Raleigh RR, a predecessor of the Atlantic Coast Line. The W&R had completed a line between Weldon and Wilmington in 1840 and also operated its own steamboats between Wilmington and Charleston.

The Maryland & Virginia Steam Boat Co. went out of business in 1840, but it was replaced by a new firm, the Baltimore Steam Packet Co., later known as the Old Bay Line, which was incorporated in December 1839 and began operating in 1840. It continued the competition with the Inland Route.

The competition was strenuous. In an 1838 advertisement, the P&R boat route billed itself as the:

Manufactured in England by C. Tayleur & Co. in 1836, the first two locomotives built for the Raleigh & Gaston Railroad were 0-4-0's Raleigh *and* Gaston, *delivered to the Petersburg Railroad, which was leasing the R&G at the time. Although neither of these historic locomotives has survived, the Seaboard built a replica of the Raleigh, which is shown here.* CSX Transportation collection

> Great Central Route...Through from Baltimore to Welston [sic], N.C. in 21 hours—being four hours in advance of any other Inland line—without one moment's night travelling on Rail Roads, without loss of sleep, with but one change of baggage...

Passengers were also assured that no "burthen" cars would be attached to their train.

In 1840, the Upper Route advertised in the *Baltimore American* that its passengers would "avoid being compelled to remain ALL NIGHT AT WELDON, on the Roanoke—one of the most UNHEALTHY PLACES in the Southern Country, where by the Bay Line, they are delayed SEVENTEEN HOURS." The Bay Route on the other hand said that Weldon was a place where passengers could enjoy a "comfortable rest." One suspects that truth in advertising was not a universally honored concept in 1840.

Unfortunately, the P&R soon ran into difficulty. The rails and ties deteriorated rapidly and the heavy locomotives crushed many of the wooden rails. Moreover, the iron straps began working their way off the wooden stringers. Their ends would bend up, forming a "snake-head" which would snag a train, precipitating a derailment. Such a snake-head caused an accident in December 1837 in which two people were killed and eight injured. Thus, by 1838, the tracks had to be rebuilt, albeit again with wooden stringers and iron straps. In addition, four lighter locomotives, as well as better cars, were acquired. In an effort to prevent accidents an "agent" was posted as a lookout on top of the baggage car of each train. His duty was to apply the brakes in an emergency and warn the engineer with a rope that was attached to the locomotive's bell.

The railroad also had financial problems. Basically there just wasn't enough business at Weldon to support both the P&R and the Petersburg Railroad. A serious rate war developed between the rivals which gravely wounded the P&R. To make matters worse, traffic was diverted from the P&R in 1840 when the Raleigh & Gaston Railroad completed its line from Raleigh to Gaston, N.C., where it connected with a branch-line subsidiary of the Petersburg RR. In that year the president of the Petersburg wrote that the Portsmouth & Roanoke could

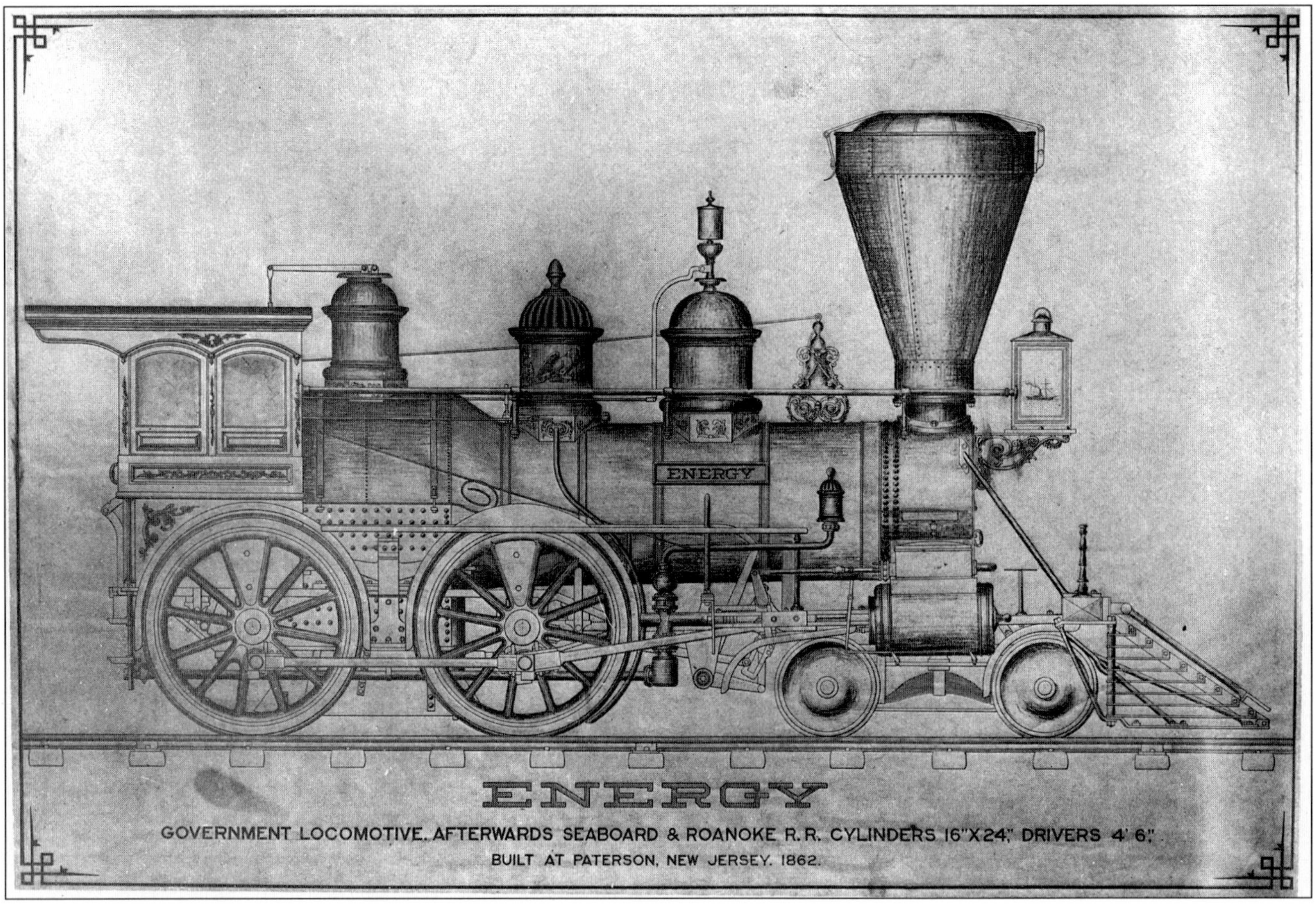

The most common wheel arrangement throughout most of the nineteenth century was the "American Standard" 4-4-0. A typical Civil-War era Eight-Wheeler, Energy *was built at Paterson, New Jersey, in 1862 for the U.S. Military Railroad. After the war, the "Government Locomotive" migrated south to the Seaboard & Roanoke.*
CSX Transportation collection

not sustain itself and that poverty was written on it from one end to the other. In an effort to raise money, the P&R offered to sell a half interest in its Roanoke River bridge to the Petersburg line. In fact, for a brief period the P&R permitted the Wilmington & Raleigh to operate trains over the bridge to a connection with the Petersburg at Garysburg. The Petersburg management, convinced that the demise of its rival was imminent, refused. But the P&R held on, the Wilmington & Raleigh's use of the bridge was soon terminated, and the Petersburg was eventually compelled to build its own bridge in 1842.

The Portsmouth & Roanoke was heavily mortgaged, but through some oversight the mortgage had never been recorded in North Carolina. As a result, the largest creditor of the railroad in North Carolina was able to obtain a judgment against the company, and all of its real property in the state, track included, was sold at public auction on October 7, 1843. The purchasers soon assigned their bid to Captain Francis E. Rives, who was apparently operating in concert with the Petersburg RR. Rives attempted to operate the 17 miles of the P&R in North Carolina. He borrowed a locomotive and cars from the Petersburg and built a connecting track from the P&R to that road. On the night of January 6, 1844, he began to tear up the P&R track south of Margaretsville. When word reached Portsmouth, a train was dispatched, carrying the president of the P&R and his allies. Rives was arrested and fined $25 by a North Carolina court. The damage was soon repaired and train service restored while the judgment against the railroad was appealed to higher courts. Finally, in the spring of 1845, the North Carolina Supreme Court awarded Rives title to the P&R properties in the Old North State, and permitted him to dispose of them as he wished. The Petersburg RR then entered into a contract with Rives, agreeing to pay him $60,000 in installments provided the P&R bridge and trackage remained unused.

The struggling railroad continued to operate the 63 miles between Portsmouth and Margaretsville with connecting stagecoach service provided the rest of the way to Weldon. However, the P&R finally discontinued operations in Virginia and its properties were sold for the benefit of its creditors at an auction held September 5, 1846. The line was purchased by the Board of Public Works of Virginia for $62,000 and the rolling stock was stored in Portsmouth for future use. The brief career of the Portsmouth & Roanoke was ended.

The second segment of the Seaboard to be built in the Carolinas was the Raleigh & Gaston Railroad. It was chartered on the last day of 1835 to build a railroad from Raleigh to a connection with the Greensville & Roanoke RR at Gaston, N.C. The Gaston of the railroad's corporate title should not be confused with the present town of Gaston. The original Gaston was located on the north bank of the Roanoke River about 12 miles upstream from Weldon and several miles west of the present Gaston. The Greensville & Roanoke, which was owned by the Petersburg RR, began constructing a line from a junction with the Petersburg near Emporia, Va., to Gaston in 1834. The G&R completed its line in 1837.

Construction of the Raleigh & Gaston began at Gaston on November 1, 1836. The line was built to the standard gauge and, like the Portsmouth & Roanoke, the rails consisted of longitudinal wooden stringers capped with strap iron. Moncure Robinson was employed as a consulting engineer for the then handsome salary of $3,000 per year. A native of Richmond, Robinson was a distinguished early civil engineer who was instrumental in the construction of a number of railroads. Arrangements were made to lease the R&G to the Petersburg Railroad as it was being constructed. The Petersburg was to supply the rolling stock. Thus, the R&G's first two locomotives, named naturally enough the *Raleigh* and the *Gaston*, were actually delivered to the Petersburg Railroad.

A 1,040-foot-long bridge had to be constructed across the Roanoke and it required 18 months for the first ten miles of the railroad to be built to Littleton, N.C. The next ten miles, to Macon, were completed only one month later. The railroad was originally projected to run through the town of Warrenton, but the shortsighted citizens of that community would have none of it. A meeting of the local townsfolk was called to consider the matter at which one of the participants is reported to have declared, "No railroad's coming through here to kill and scare our pickaninnies to death." The irate citizenry then supposedly loaded their turkey rifles and drove the railroad surveyors away. As a result, the R&G was routed through Warren Plains, three miles to the north of Warrenton. Years later, the people of the town had a change of heart and a connecting short line, the Warrenton Railroad, was completed between Warrenton and Warren Plains in 1884.

Notwithstanding its rejection by the residents of Warrenton, construction of the R&G proceeded apace. The road reached Ridgeway in July 1838 and Henderson, 42 miles from Gaston, in September 1838. Four major bridges were required between Henderson and Raleigh: across the Tar River, Cedar Creek, the Neuse River and, finally, Crab Tree Creek just north of Raleigh. In November 1839 the R&G reached Franklinton and the 84-mile line was completed to Raleigh on May 10, 1840. A three-day celebration was held in that city in joint celebration of the arrival of the railroad and the opening of the new state capitol building. There were parades, speeches, a big barbecue dinner at the railroad station and a total of 85 separate toasts. The hangovers must have been monumental.

The Petersburg Railroad's lease was terminated on December 1,1839, before the Raleigh & Gaston was completed, and the R&G began operating its own railroad. In 1840 the railroad's management was pondering the question of whether to interchange its cars with the Petersburg or transfer freight shipments at Gaston. Fortunately, it opted for the former. Also in that year, the road's chief engineer determined that only eight-wheel locomotives should henceforth be used as engines with fewer wheels placed too much weight on R&G's wooden rails. In addition he opined that the line's trains had been run too fast, stating that they could not economically operate as fast on wooden tracks as on iron rails. He recommended that the speed of mail trains be reduced to twelve miles per hour and freight trains to eight.

Unfortunately, the Raleigh & Gaston proved to be a financial failure. By 1839, the road was in trouble and asked the State of North Carolina for help. As a result, North Carolina endorsed $500,000 in bonds, requiring the R&G to execute a mortgage in the state's favor. The railroad subsequently defaulted and thus became the property of the state in December 1845. By 1846 the condition of the Raleigh & Gaston was described as

> a reproach to the state.... The condition of the Raleigh and Gaston was about as bad [as the prostrate Portsmouth & Roanoke]. The wheezy old engines still drew, painfully and slowly, a

TOP:
Seaboard & Roanoke owned some diminutive 0-4-0 switch engines. S&R No. 23, Hercules, *was built by Taunton in 1885 with 44" drivers, 16x24 cylinders and an operating boiler pressure of 165 psi. Complete with a slope-backed tender, No. 23 tipped the scales at just 52 1/2 tons.* Delaware State Archives

BOTTOM LEFT:
The Georgia, Carolina & Northern Ry., Seaboard's extension from Monroe, N.C., to Atlanta, was built between 1888 and 1892. Near Athens, Ga., the line bridged the Oconee River on a spectacular 885-foot-long steel trestle, shown under construction on July 20, 1891. CSX Transportation collection

BOTTOM RIGHT:
Carrying white flags on her pilot beam, 4-4-0 No. 540 poses with her crew and special three-car train at Portsmouth, N.C., on November 21, 1896. The high-stepping Eight-Wheeler has just made a record-breaking run from Weldon, N.C., covering 76.8 miles in 72.5 minutes, an average overall speed of 63.7 mph. After adjusting the figures to account for some slow orders encountered en route, Seaboard advertised the run as "76 miles in 67 minutes," or 68 mph. CSX Transportation collection

few coaches over the rugged, broken down track. Amid the dust and smoke and constant breaking down, the whole day was generally consumed in passing over the eighty miles between the hamlet at Gaston and the state capital.

The state operated the R&G from January 1, 1846, until October 1, 1851, making some improvements and incurring considerable losses for its trouble. On October 1, 1851, the road was reincorporated as The Raleigh & Gaston Railroad Company with "The" added to its name to distinguish it from its predecessor. The state retained stock in the new company but no longer controlled the railroad. In reorganizing the railroad, the state noted that business was increasing and anticipated that the new company would produce a profit rather than act as a drain on the public treasury.

The state's sanguine expectations were fulfilled. Within two years the road was paying six percent dividends. The new company reconstructed the line between 1851 and 1853, replacing the wooden stringers with iron rails. In 1853, the R&G was extended 12 miles from South Gaston to Weldon, where it connected with the Seaboard & Roanoke (successor to the Portsmouth & Roanoke) and the Wilmington & Raleigh, as well as the Petersburg Railroad. A direct rail route was thus established between Raleigh and Portsmouth. In 1854, the line was also extended one mile at Raleigh in order to connect with the North Carolina Railroad. The NC Railroad was a state- owned line which was constructing a road from Goldsboro to Charlotte, via Raleigh and Greensboro.

Meanwhile, the dormant Portsmouth & Roanoke was resurrected. The town of Portsmouth leased the Virginia portion of the P&R from the Board of Public Works and resumed service as the Seaboard & Roanoke Railroad in September 1846, operating three times a week between Portsmouth and Boykins. This was the first use of the name "Seaboard." The town purchased the road on June 28, 1847, and in July transferred ownership to a new corporation, the Seaboard & Roanoke Railroad Company. Another new company, the Roanoke Railroad, was organized in North Carolina in 1847 to take over the abandoned portion of the P&R in that state. In early 1849, Hershaw & Co., of Boston, acquired the S&R. The Roanoke Railroad, which apparently never actually operated any railroad, was soon merged into the S&R. The line was rapidly rebuilt. The wooden stringers were replaced with the latest iron T-rails imported from Wales, and the North Carolina portion of the road was reconstructed in 1850. New equipment was purchased and the entire road was reopened from Portsmouth to Weldon in 1851.

In the same year, Moncure Robinson, the engineer who had helped build the Raleigh & Gaston, and other principal stockholders of the Richmond, Fredericksburg & Potomac and the Richmond & Petersburg Railroads, bought a controlling interest in the Baltimore Steam Packet Co. The steamboat company, in turn, soon acquired control of the Seaboard & Roanoke. Thus, the two former rival routes between the north and south were brought under common control.

Robinson, the son of a Richmond merchant, had studied law at the College of William & Mary where he was once expelled for refusing to pay some fees which he considered unjust. In 1818, at the age of 16, he accompanied a party that was conducting a topographical survey of the area between Richmond and the Ohio River. After being involved in locating an extension of the James River Canal and visiting the famous Erie Canal, he became convinced of the superiority of railroads over canals. Aware that his technical training was deficient, he went to Europe in 1825 to study mathematics and science. He returned to America in 1828 and began a distinguished career building railroads. He was one of the few pioneer civil engineers in American who had not been educated at West Point. In 1835 he started his greatest engineering achievement, the construction of the Philadelphia & Reading Railroad. He was chief engineer of the Richmond, Fredericksburg & Potomac from 1834 to 1839 and president of that road from 1840 to 1847, having succeeded his brother, Conway Robinson. In 1847 he retired and settled in Philadelphia, where he spent the rest of his life managing his investments. He was followed as president of the RF&P by another brother, Edwin Robinson.

Soon after the Robinson group acquired control of the S&R, Moncure Robinson's oldest son, John Moncure Robinson, was appointed superintendent of the railroad. At that time superintendent was a more important position than president on many railroads.

The Seaboard & Roanoke was almost immediately successful, no doubt helped by the extension of the Raleigh & Gaston to Weldon in 1853. Long freight trains were constantly arriving at Portsmouth with loads of lumber, tobacco, cotton, flour and barrel staves for shipment out of the ports of Norfolk and Portsmouth. Unlike most southern railroads, which mainly hauled cotton, lumber made up the bulk of S&R's eastbound traffic, while lime and guano were important westbound. High charges may well have contributed to the railroad's prosperity. For example, in 1858 the passenger fare between Portsmouth and Weldon was $4.00, a very hefty sum at a time when a skilled worker made only about $1.60 a day.

The happy state of affairs on the Seaboard & Roanoke and the Raleigh & Gaston was soon terminated by the most tragic chapter in American history, the Civil War. Fort Sumter was bombarded on April 12, 1861. The War Between the States had begun.

One problem soon encountered by railroads in the agrarian South was the loss of supplies from the industrial North. Superintendent Robinson of the S&R was especially ingenious in addressing the situation. In February 1862, he reported to the company's stockholders:

> Upon the breaking out of the war between the Confederacy and United States the Seaboard Road, in common with many of the railways of the South, found itself cut off from the source from which it had been heretofore dependent for supplies of almost every description. This led me to attempt the production of many articles from our own resources, and in many respects the attempt has succeeded in a manner which must be most gratifying to you. I have heretofore used exclusively New Bedford whale oil as a lubricating material. The Negroes employed by the company have been fed upon bacon cured in Cincinnati. The company has now erected a large smokehouse, has killed and cured its own pork, from the refuse of which an oil has been prepared answering its purpose most admirably.... The bacon has been prepared at less cost than that which the company has heretofore purchased, and the oil is obtained at so low a rate, and answers its purpose so admirably that I do not propose hereafter to use any other. The engine "Norfolk" is now running upon chilled tires made by ourselves, those purchased by me having failed to arrive in consequence of the blockade. Even the soap used by the Company is now made in our own shops.
>
> It is hoped that the United States may soon be brought to perceive the folly of their attempt at subjugation of the Confederate States, that peace may be restored, and with it a return of the road to its legitimate business.

Unfortunately for the Confederacy, the North did not perceive the folly of its ways. The Union army retained control of Fortress Monroe, and the naval blockade prevented the Rebels from using Norfolk and Portsmouth as seaports. As a result, Seaboard & Roanoke's business soon dwindled to almost nothing.

John M. Robinson was confronted with another problem when the cities of Portsmouth and Norfolk attempted to sequester his father's stock in the S&R as the property of an "alien enemy." But the younger Robinson used his influence in the Confederate Congress to thwart the scheme, arranging the transfer of Moncure Robinson's holdings to himself.

Eventually, the Confederate army evacuated the two cities in May 1862. The retreating Southerners burned the Seaboard & Roanoke's bridges over the Blackwater and Nottoway Rivers. Shortly afterward, however, the Confederates decided to make a stand at the Blackwater. Thus, they returned to the west bank of that river and rebuilt the bridge over the Nottoway. Rail service over the S&R was resumed between Franklin and Weldon for the remainder of the war. Except for the minimal rolling stock needed to operate between those two points, S&R's equipment was leased to other Southern railroads where it was required for military traffic.

The Confederate government ordered the rails on the unused portion of the S&R, east of the Blackwater, removed for use elsewhere. After only three miles had been stripped, the Confederates were driven back by Union troops in a skirmish near Carrsville in May 1863. The Yankees then proceeded to remove the remaining S&R rail between Suffolk and Carrsville. The United States Military Railroad operated the Portsmouth-Suffolk segment for the duration of the conflict. A connection was constructed with the Norfolk & Petersburg Railroad at Suffolk, and the N&P line between Norfolk and Suffolk was converted by the USMR from 5-foot gauge to standard gauge. The Federals thus had a circuitous 45-mile line between Norfolk and Portsmouth, via Suffolk. The Seaboard & Roanoke escaped further significant damage until the closing days of the war when the retreating Confederates burned the bridge at Weldon.

With the S&R rendered largely *hors de combat*, the road's energetic young superintendent, John M. Robinson, was commissioned as a captain in the Confederate army. He made a trip to England in 1863 as a special purchasing agent, seeking equipment for the Confederate government and five Virginia railroads. In May 1864, he was appointed supervisor of railroad transportation between Wilmington and Richmond. He rejoined the railroad after the conclusion of the war and became president of the company in 1867.

After the war the railroads, or what was left of them, were returned to their owners. The US Military Railroad turned over the Portsmouth-Suffolk line to the Seaboard & Roanoke on June 30, 1865. The S&R built a new bridge over the Blackwater River and relaid the track between Suffolk and Franklin. Train service over the line was resumed in the fall of 1865 but traffic had to be ferried across the Roanoke until the railroad completed a new bridge at Weldon in April 1866. The Petersburg RR was granted joint use of the new Weldon bridge. By the spring of 1867, John M. Robinson was able to report, "Seldom do we see in the history of any road so shattered by war—its costly bridges burned, its rails torn up and taken away, its shops rifled—such rapid renovation."

Safely distant from the conflict, the Raleigh & Gaston fared better than the Seaboard & Roanoke, at least for most of the war. Although not as important as some other railroads in the state, the R&G, due to its connection with the North Carolina Railroad at Raleigh, did serve as a link between the Deep South and the Confederate armies in Virginia. With its ports blockaded by the Union fleet, the South was forced to rely on its railroads for transportation. As a result, the R&G was involved in some important mass troop movements. In September 1863, for example, it helped transport General James Longstreet's troops from Virginia to the battlefields around Chattanooga, Tenn.

General Robert E. Lee, for one, regarded railroad rolling stock as more precious even than army stores. Reflecting the importance of railroad equipment, the Confederate government established a locomotive shop at Raleigh in 1862. The shop was intended to repair motive power that had either been captured by the Rebels or evacuated from territory abandoned by the Confederate army. Thanks largely to General "Stonewall" Jackson, the Baltimore & Ohio was an especially generous, if involuntary, donor to the South's locomotive supply. In fact, the Raleigh shop was largely equipped with machinery captured from the B&O.

The Raleigh & Gaston was unscathed until 1865, when the Confederacy was on its last legs. After the fall of Richmond, the Confederates destroyed the line's bridge at Gaston as well as the bridge over Cedar Creek near Franklinton, a structure that was 725 feet long and 70 feet high. However, many of the R&G's locomotives were stored at Gaston for safekeeping. The US Military Railroad began to operate 25 miles of the R&G between Raleigh and Cedar Creek and subsequently built a temporary trestle over Cedar Creek, reopening the road from Weldon to Raleigh. In exchange for the reconstruction, R&G's president agreed in April 1865, after General Lee's surrender, to loan the USMR four locomotives and 40 cars until the war was over. But the surrender of the last Confederate army, under General Joseph E. Johnson, on April 26 obviated that necessity. The USMR returned the Raleigh-Cedar Creek segment of the R&G to the road's owners on May 8, 1865.

The Raleigh & Gaston built a new permanent bridge over Cedar Creek after the war, as the Union army's temporary trestle was considered to be safe for only a few months. However, the road never did rebuild the bridge across the Roanoke at Gaston because it had an adequate alternative connection with the Petersburg RR at Weldon. The Petersburg Railroad finally abandoned its line to Gaston in 1874, and the original town of Gaston eventually disappeared from the map.

The Seaboard & Roanoke prospered after the Civil War. The road had a low funded debt, a favorable operating ratio and paid regular dividends of as high as eight percent, even

TOP:
Modern motive power in the 1890s included the class I-4 Ten-Wheelers Nos. 552-568. Built by Pittsburgh in 1896 and 1898, the I-4's were equipped with 58" drivers and designed for freight service. Later renumbered 1552-1568, they were retired in the 1920s. CSX Transportation collection

MIDDLE:
Raleigh & Gaston 217 was built by Baldwin in 1884 as R&G No. 24. In 1890, she became R&G 217 with implementation of a common SAL numbering system. Renumbered once more before retirement, the 4-4-0 finished her career as SAL 125. CSX Transportation collection

BOTTOM:
Boasting an all-Pullman vestibuled consist lighted with Pintsch gas, Seaboard's premier passenger train during the nineties was the Atlanta Special. *Running from Washington to Atlanta, it was handled by RF&P as far as Richmond, Va., where Atlantic Coast Line took over for the run to the Seaboard connection at Weldon, N.C.* CSX Transportation collection

during the depression years of the mid-1870s. By 1867, the railroad was in control of the Old Bay Line, as the Baltimore Steam Packet Co. began being called. John M. Robinson continued to serve as president of both the railroad and the steamship company, with executive offices in Baltimore. Moncure Robinson, who remained in Philadelphia during the war, and his associates still controlled the Seaboard & Roanoke as well as the Richmond, Fredericksburg & Potomac Railroad. In fact, John Robinson also served as president of the RF&P from 1871 to 1878.

By 1871 the Seaboard & Roanoke had gained control of the Raleigh & Gaston, and John M. Robinson became president of that company in 1875. Control of the R&G was reported to have been acquired through the Seaboard Air Line Agency. This appears to be the first formal mention of the term Seaboard Air Line. The appellation soon came into general use to describe the Seaboard & Roanoke and the railroads that came under its control.

Meanwhile, the Raleigh & Gaston had begun building a new line south from Raleigh, the Raleigh & Augusta Air Line. That line had been chartered in 1861 as the Chatham Railroad to build a line from Raleigh to the coal fields near Sanford, N.C., but little work was done due to the Civil War. After the conflict ended the project was revived, largely financed by North Carolina state bonds. The R&G acquired an interest in the fledgling company in 1868 and, in 1871, a line was completed 28 miles from Raleigh to the Haw River. In December of that year the name of the company was changed to Raleigh & Augusta Air Line Railroad Company as it was intended to build the line through to Columbia, S.C., and Augusta, Ga. In 1872 the road was extended to Sanford. Traffic was light during the depression of the 1870s and the line was not very prosperous. It proved to be something of a drain on the R&G. Nevertheless, the R&AAL was completed to Hamlet, N.C., in 1877, a total distance of 96 miles. At Hamlet, the road connected with the Carolina Central's line between Wilmington and Shelby, N.C. In 1884, the road added a 10-mile branch line extending from Hamlet to Gibson, N.C. The R&AAL had no rolling stock of its own, but rather leased equipment from its parent Raleigh & Gaston.

The next major expansion of the Seaboard system began in 1881 when the Seaboard & Roanoke acquired a large interest in the Carolina Central Railroad. By the summer of 1883, S&R and its affiliates were in control of the CC and it became a part of the Seaboard Air Line.

The Carolina Central was incorporated in 1855 as the Wilmington & Charlotte Railroad Co. to build a line from Wilmington to Rutherfordton, N.C. A few months later the name of the company was changed to the Wilmington, Charlotte & Rutherford Railroad Co. Construction of the standard-gauge line began January 1, 1857, at Navassa, on the west bank of the Cape Fear River across from Wilmington, and at Charlotte. By April 1861, the road had completed 112 miles from Navassa to Rockingham and another 31 miles from Charlotte westward to Lincolnton. Construction was suspended at that time due to the Civil War, leaving a gap of about 71 miles between Rockingham and Charlotte.

Even though Wilmington was the last seaport to remain in Confederate hands, the WC&R was not strategically very important during the War Between the States. As a result, the line's rails between Laurinburg and Rockingham were removed by the Confederates for use on more important lines. After the fall of Wilmington to the Union in February 1865, the Confederate army also burned the road's trestle over Big Swamp, east of Lumberton. The damage was repaired after the war and the railroad resumed operations.

In 1866 the WC&R and the Wilmington & Manchester RR entered into a joint venture, known as the Wilmington Railway Bridge Co., to construct a line into Wilmington. The Wilmington & Manchester, an Atlantic Coast Line predecessor, operated a 5-foot-gauge line from Eagle Island, across the Cape Fear River from Wilmington, to Kingville, S.C. The bridge company built about 2.5 miles of line from Navassa to Wilmington, with bridges over both the main Cape Fear River and the North East Cape Fear River. Presumably the bridge line was dual gauge in order to accommodate both parent railroads. As a result of the project, the WC&R gained entrance into Wilmington proper in 1867.

Construction of the remainder of the Wilmington, Charlotte & Rutherford resumed in 1870 when a nine-mile section of the line was completed from Rockingham to Pee Dee. However, the WC&R failed financially and on April 10, 1873, the line was sold at foreclosure, emerging as the Carolina Central Railway Co. The new CC Ry. resumed construction

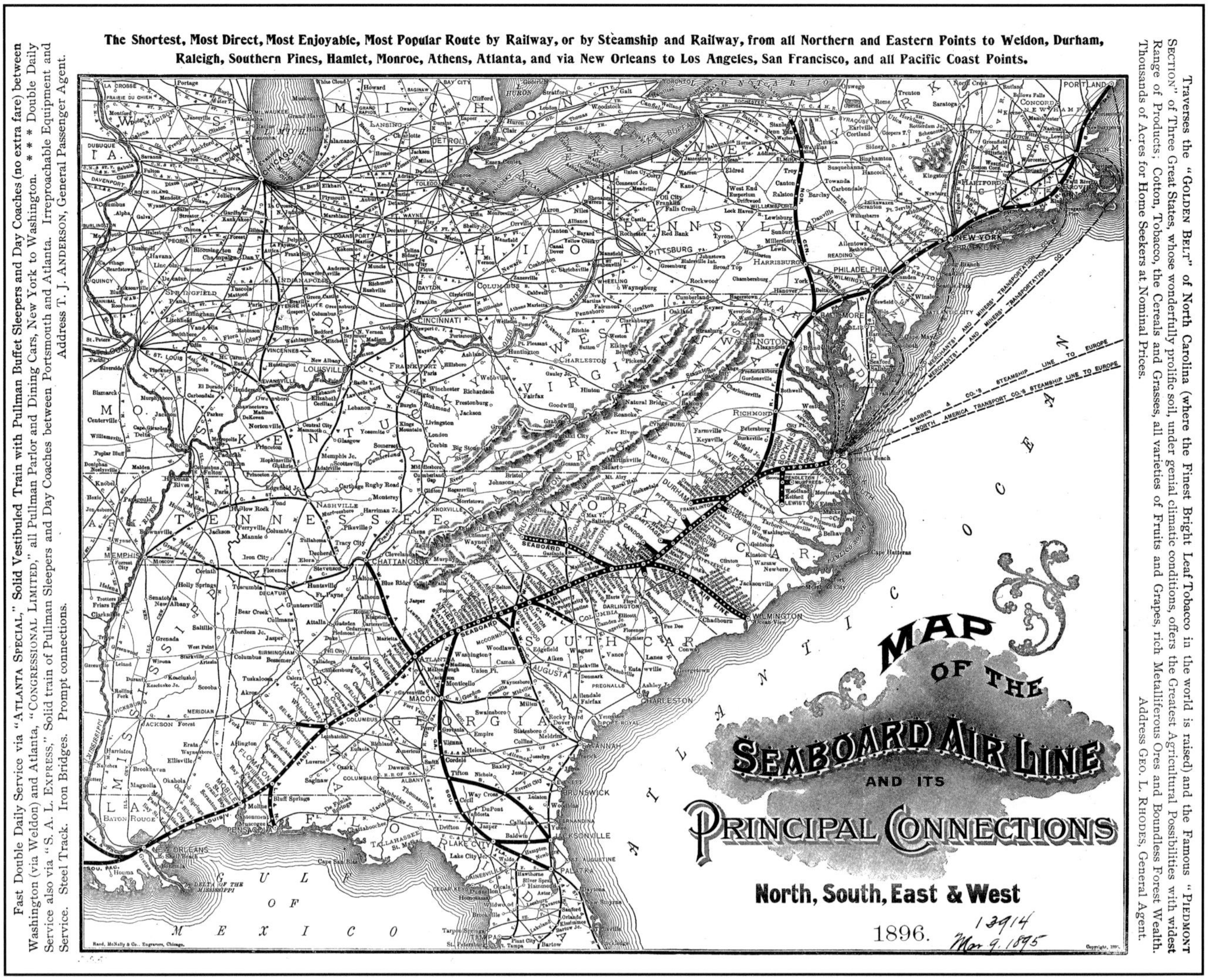

In 1895, the Seaboard Air Line was not yet a formally organized company, but rather an alliance of commonly controlled roads under the domination of the Seaboard & Roanoke. This map, dated March 9, 1895, highlights Seaboard's Portsmouth-Atlanta mainline, as well as the lines of affiliates and friendly connections stretching as far as Portland, Me., and New Orleans. Library of Congress

of the line in 1873 and by December 1874 had closed the gap between Pee Dee and Charlotte and extended the line westward from Lincolnton to Shelby. The CC Ry. also proved unprofitable and it went into receivership in 1876. On May 31, 1880, the Carolina Central Rail*way* Co. was sold under foreclosure becoming the Carolina Central Rail*road* Co. In the next year the Seaboard & Roanoke began acquiring control of the CCRR Co. and the line became a part of the Seaboard Air Line, although retaining its individual corporate identity. In 1887 the last 27 miles of the road were completed from Shelby to Rutherfordton and it finally reached its original goal, 30 years after construction had begun. The total distance of the line from Wilmington to Rutherfordton was 267 miles.

The Seaboard Air Line expanded rapidly in the late 1880s and early 1890s, adding a number of lines to its system. The most important addition was the construction of the Georgia, Carolina & Northern Railway from Monroe, N.C., to Atlanta, Ga. The road was chartered in 1885 as the Chester, Greenwood & Abbeville RR Co. but its name was soon changed to the Georgia, Carolina & Northern Ry. Co. By 1888 the GC&N had laid 45 miles of line from Monroe, where it connected with the Carolina Central, to Chester, S.C. Construction continued through Greenwood, S.C., and Athens, Ga. In 1892 the line was completed to a connection with the Georgia Railroad at Inman Park, on the eastern edge of Atlanta, 266 miles from Monroe. The GC&N was operated by the SAL from before its completion.

An injunction was obtained preventing the GC&N from entering the city of Atlanta from the east. Seaboard overcame that legal obstacle by constructing a belt line, the Seaboard Air Line Belt RR Co. in 1892. The Belt Line, which was probably the first corporation to be legally named Seaboard Air Line, built an eight-mile line from a connection with the GC&N at Belt Jct. near the present site of Emory University. The line skirted the north edge of the city to Wanda (Howells). At that point it connected with the Nashville,

Chattanooga & St. Louis Ry. SAL obtained trackage rights over the NC&StL into the Atlanta Union Station and built a yard at Howells. In later years the original SAL Belt Line came to be considered part of the mainline and the line between Belt Jct. and Inman Park came to be called simply the Belt.

Soon after completion of the GC&N the Seaboard began operating a through passenger service between New York and Atlanta, in connection with the Atlantic Coast Line at Weldon, N.C. SAL called its through train *The Atlanta and Washington Special.*

Several smaller Seaboard lines were also built during this period. The Louisberg Railroad Co. built a 10-mile line from a connection with the Raleigh & Gaston at Franklinton to Louisberg, N.C. Construction began in 1884 and the road was opened for operation in July 1885. The R&G leased the line from its completion.

A more important line was the Durham & Northern Ry. Co. The D&N owned a 41-mile line from Henderson, on the R&G, to Durham, N.C. The line was chartered in 1887 and constructed in 1889. It was jointly financed by the R&G and the towns of Henderson and Durham. The Durham & Northern was operated as a separate component of the Seaboard Air Line until 1893.

The Seaboard & Roanoke added a 35-mile branch from Boykins, Va., to Lewiston, N.C. The portion of the line in Virginia was built by the S&R, but the segment in North Carolina was chartered as the Roanoke & Tar River RR Co. The entire line was constructed in 1887 and 1888. The R&TR was leased by the S&R from 1887. The Roanoke & Tar River also had a 6-mile branch, the Tar River, which extended from Pendleton to Murfreesboro, N.C. However, the Murfreesboro branch was short lived, being abandoned in 1897.

The Raleigh & Augusta Air Line acquired two small branches in the late 1880s, the Pittsboro RR and the Carthage RR. The Pittsboro was chartered in 1885 and constructed an 11-mile line from Moncure, on the R&AAL, to Pittsboro, N.C. The line was leased by the R&AAL when finished in 1886. The Carthage RR built a 10-mile line from Cameron to Carthage, N.C., in 1888, which was also leased by the R&AAL upon its completion. However, the Carthage RR did not remain a part of the Seaboard system for long, as the lease was soon transferred to private parties. The line was operated as the Randolph & Cumberland Ry. Co. for many years and, finally, as the Moore Central Ry. The short line was eventually abandoned in 1948.

Another Seaboard subsidiary built in that era was the Palmetto Railroad Co. It had been chartered in 1884 to extend the Seaboard Air Line southward to Columbia, S.C., and Augusta, Ga. However, all it ever completed was an 18-mile line from Hamlet, N.C., to Cheraw, S.C. Construction began in 1885 and the line was opened on October 1, 1887. Although controlled by the Robinson family, the Palmetto RR was operated as an independent railroad until 1895. It went into receivership that year, was reorganized as the Palmetto Railway Co. and was leased to the Raleigh & Augusta Air Line in December 1895.

In 1890, the various Seaboard railroads established a common locomotive roster and began purchasing their locomotives through the Seaboard Air Line Equipment Trust rather than as individual railroads. As of August 1, 1893, they officially initiated the Seaboard Air Line System as an unincorporated operating association or pooling agreement. However, the different railroads retained their separate corporate identities.

Moncure Robinson, the patriarch of the Robinson clan, had died in 1891 at the age of 89. His son, John M. Robinson, the long time president of the Seaboard, died February 14, 1893. They had a falling-out in Moncure's later years, but fortunately relations were restored before the elder Robinson died. Robinson family names were memorialized by such Seaboard stations as Moncure and Conway, N.C. John was succeeded by Richard Curzon Hoffman as president of the Seaboard & Roanoke.

The Seaboard added two more small branch lines in the late 1890s. In 1896 the Carolina Central built a 4.7-mile-long line from Ellenboro to Caroleen, N.C., and the Loganville & Lawrenceville Railroad was built in 1898. The L&L was incorporated that year and built a 10-mile railroad from Loganville, Ga., to a connection with the GC&N at Lawrenceville. The road was leased to the SAL and opened for business on December 1, 1898.

But the most important new construction in the last years of the nineteenth century was the result of a dispute with the Southern Railway System. In 1896 the Norfolk area, which Seaboard regarded as its territory, was invaded by the newly formed Southern. A steamboat affiliate of the Southern began operating between Baltimore and Norfolk in direct competition with Seaboard's Old Bay Line. Moreover, Southern also acquired trackage rights into Norfolk from the south over the Norfolk & Carolina RR, an Atlantic Coast Line subsidiary that had been constructed in 1890. Seaboard regarded the Southern incursion as a violation of a long-standing gentlemen's agreement. In 1877 John Robinson and Thomas Clyde, who then controlled several steamboat companies as well as the Richmond & York River RR, had entered into a covenant by which the Clyde interests consented to stay out of the Norfolk area and the Old Bay Line agreed not to serve Richmond. Such an arrangement would now run afoul of the antitrust laws but it was legal at that time. The 1877 agreement was to be in effect for five years, but both the Clyde and Robinson families continued to honor it until J.P. Morgan formed the Southern Railway from the Clyde railroad holdings in 1894. Seaboard contended that the original agreement was still binding on the Southern as the successor to the Clyde operations. The Old Bay Line sued and started its own retaliatory service between Baltimore and Richmond. In the summer of 1896 Seaboard initiated a serious rate war with the Southern. The lawsuit was unsuccessful and the Old Bay Line's service to Richmond soon ceased, but the rate war was ended only after third parties obtained injunctions restraining the two railroads.

The main consequence of the Southern invasion was that the SAL resolved to build its own rail line to Richmond. As a result, Seaboard soon acquired the Richmond, Petersburg & Carolina Railroad. The RP&C dated back to 1882 when the Virginia & Carolina RR Co. was chartered to build a line from Petersburg, Va., to a connection with the Raleigh & Gaston at Ridgeway Jct. (Norlina), N.C. The V&C acquired some terminal lands in Petersburg and graded some roadbed but never laid any track. The company, in which the city of Petersburg had an interest, failed in 1892 and was reorganized as the Richmond, Petersburg & Carolina RR Co. Construction of the RP&C did not begin until March 1, 1898. By the end of the year the company had completed 20 miles of line from Petersburg south to DeWitt, Va.

In the meantime, the Williams associates, which were already the owners of the Georgia & Alabama Ry., purchased control of the Seaboard Air Line in December 1898. The Williams group was formed by the banking firms of John L. Williams & Sons, of Richmond, and Middendorf, Oliver & Co., of Baltimore. John Skelton Williams, president of the G&A, replaced R.C. Hoffman as president of the Seaboard. Two months later, in February 1899, the Williams syndicate acquired control of the Florida Central & Peninsular Railroad.

At the time the SAL passed into Williams's control, the system consisted primarily of the Seaboard & Roanoke, Raleigh & Gaston, Raleigh & Augusta Air Line, Carolina Central and Georgia, Carolina & Northern Railroads. The system's mainline stretched from Portsmouth to Atlanta, via Raleigh, Hamlet and Monroe, N.C. Principal branch lines extended from Henderson to Durham, N.C., Hamlet to Wilmington, and from Monroe to Rutherfordton, N.C. Seaboard Air Line then operated about 943 miles of track and, of course, the Richmond, Petersburg & Carolina was under construction. The Seaboard system also included the Old Bay Line steamboat operation between Baltimore and Norfolk.

The Williams management continued construction of the Richmond, Petersburg & Carolina and proceeded to bridge the 91-mile gap between the old Seaboard Air Line at Cheraw, S.C., and the Florida Central & Peninsular at Columbia, S.C. The RP&C line from Petersburg to Richmond and from DeWitt to Ridgeway (Norlina) was completed in 1900, and the entire 102-mile line from Richmond to Ridgeway was opened on June 3, 1900. On April 10, 1900, the Seaboard Air Line Railway was organized as the successor to the RP&C. Thus, technically, it was the little RP&C which became the new SAL Railway, although this was only a formality for legal convenience. On July 1, 1900, the whole system, including the original Seaboard Air Line, Florida Central & Peninsular and the Georgia & Alabama, began operation as the new Seaboard Air Line Railway. Most of the component railroads were formally merged into the Seaboard Air Line in November 1901.

CHAPTER TWO

EARLY FLORIDA LINES

The southernmost component of the new Seaboard Air Line Railway was the Florida Central & Peninsular Railroad. It represented the consummation of a bewildering number of mergers, bankruptcies and reorganizations. Included among FC&P's many predecessors were companies which had operated almost all of the railroad mileage existing in Florida before the Civil War.

The first railroad in Florida, and the first segment of the FC&P to be built, was the little Tallahassee Railroad. It operated a 22-mile line from Tallahassee south to Port Leon, a village at Apalachee Bay on the Gulf Coast. Construction began in 1834 and the line was completed in 1836. The track was laid to a width of 5 feet, the gauge of the pioneer South Carolina RR which was to be the standard in much of the South for many years to come. A primitive affair, its resemblance to anything we would now consider to be a railroad was minimal. The track consisted of iron strips laid on longitudinal wooden stringers. The motive power was mules, and the road's passenger coach consisted of a small wagon equipped with two benches holding eight people. In 1838, a European traveler described the line as "the worst railroad in the entire world."

The Tallahassee Railroad evidently did not acquire a locomotive until December 1847. However, the tenure of that machine must have been brief as the railroad appears to have relied exclusively on animal power for several years afterward.

Notwithstanding its crude equipment, the little line was successful, primarily hauling cotton from Middle Florida and Southwest Georgia down to Port Leon for shipment by boat. It transported between 20,000 and 30,000 bales of cotton a year, for which it charged 75 cents a bale. It was proposed to extend the line to Thomasville, Ga., but the idea was defeated as it was feared that Georgia railroads would benefit to the detriment of the Tallahassee line.

Disaster struck in September 1843 when a hurricane hit Port Leon. The town was almost completely destroyed and the railroad's bridge across the St. Marks River, north of the town, was washed away. The bridge was found upriver, still intact but "injudiciously placed." As a result of the storm both the town of Port Leon and the last 1.5 miles of the railroad were abandoned. The railroad's southern terminus was moved to St. Marks. The new terminus was located at the site of the bridge, but across the river and upstream from Port Leon.

In the 1840s the Tallahassee RR joined with a group of other carriers to form the "New Southern Line," a route which transported passengers from New York to New Orleans in one week. The Charleston, S.C.,-Mobile, Ala., segment of the route consisted of a steamboat from Charleston to Brunswick, Ga., a stagecoach from Brunswick to Tallahassee, the Tallahassee RR from Tallahassee to St. Marks, and steamboats from St. Marks to Mobile.

Although the Tallahassee Railroad enjoyed a good business, its management showed little inclination to waste money on trivialities like maintenance and the line was allowed to deteriorate. Its dilapidated state is probably best illustrated by Ernest Melvern, a disgruntled passenger, who recounted his experience in the March 13, 1855, issue of the *Florida Sentinel*:

> I understood that I was to start by railway, and at eight o'clock in the morning. In due time a car about as large as an omnibus was pushed up, and I was asked to get into it. I did so. Two

horses were then attached to it, and we started. The depot is on the border of a kind of a swamp, where there is not a building to be seen. I inquired if so much precaution was necessary in leaving the city, and if locomotives were dangerous to the inhabitants of the forest that stretched away interminably before us. "No," said the man, who performed all of the responsible functions of engineer, conductor and brakeman, "but we go all the way with horses. We have no locomotive. They once had such a thing, but it ran away one day, nobody could stop it. It went straight to St. Marks, and, roaring and hissing, it dashed plumb into the bay; and since that they have never dared to try one."

I soon found that I had little reason to regret the absence of a locomotive. For, on looking down a long line of the road, it appeared as undulating as the sea. The flat "snake head" rails had originally been laid on timbers without any cross ties. As these timbers rested on the sand, they had separated so far that the wheels on one side of the car must run off the track. Now we found a sleeper with no rail, now a rail with no sleeper, and sometimes both were gone. The rails were often fastened by a single bolt in the middle, and both ends were curved in the air, like the ends of a broken hoop. The wags say that a Negro used to go ahead of the car to hold down one end of the rail till the car came to it, then he nailed down the other. A fire in the forest had in one place communicated to the sleepers, and for two miles they were more or less in flames. But on we hurried like salamanders. No effort was made by the driver to save his railroad from destruction! For, he declared, that with all his honors he was not a fireman. I was philosophically cogitating on the numerous advantages of this mode of railway traveling, when suddenly the omnibus trot of our charges was arrested. I was aroused from my reveries when, on looking around, I found that a long freight train was before us, and, what was worse, that it was likely to be so for an indefinite time. It was off the track, and there was no alternative but to help the Negroes get it on again. In spite of a long delay, I worked eagerly, with the hope that we could soon pass them at a switch. But, on inquiry, I learned that there was but one switch on the road, and we had passed that already. So we must patiently follow on as we could. For the benefit of all travelers who shall wish to follow in my footsteps, let me say that such delay as this is of almost daily occurrence here...

My patience diminished quite rapidly, and hearing that we were within three miles of a town called Newport, I resolved to walk there thinking I could make the detour, and reach St. Marks before our train.

The line must have reached its nadir at about the time Mr. Melvern made his journey. The newly organized Pensacola & Georgia RR soon acquired control of the Tallahassee Railroad and the road was reconstructed later in 1855 and in 1856. The wooden stringers were replaced with 56-lb iron T-rails and two 4-4-0 steam locomotives were purchased from the Baldwin Locomotive Works, the *H.L. Rutger* and the *Gen. Bailey*. Finally, the Tallahassee Railroad resembled a real railroad. Although controlled by the P&G, the Tallahassee retained its separate corporate identity for several more years.

Most of the early railroads in Florida were built largely as a result of the Internal Improvement Act of 1854. The act was intended to encourage the construction of a railroad system in the state, primarily lines from Jacksonville to Pensacola and from Fernandina to Cedar Key and Tampa Bay. Companies which built any part of the proposed system were authorized to issue bonds to buy rail and equipment with principal and interest guaranteed by the Florida government. They also received generous grants of lands. Once built, the railroads were to pay one percent per year into the Internal Improvement Fund as a sinking fund to meet the principal when due. A railroad which failed to make the payments could be seized and sold by the trustees of the fund. The father of the act was former U.S. Senator David L. Yulee, of Fernandina. He and several other sponsors of the legislation were involved with companies that later built railroads in response to the act. Three FC&P predecessors can be attributed to the legislation: the Florida, Atlantic & Gulf Central Railroad, the Pensacola & Georgia Railroad, and the Florida Railroad.

The Florida, Atlantic & Gulf Central was built from Jacksonville westward 60 miles to Alligator town, a location which was soon renamed with the more dignified appellation of Lake City. The company had been organized in 1851 but no work had been done due to a lack of funds. Dr. A.S. Baldwin, who was also instrumental in the passage of the Internal Improvement Act, was the first president of the company and he was largely responsible for keeping the project alive during the firm's formative years. Construction finally got under way in the summer of 1857, when grading and track laying began at Jacksonville. Work was delayed several months by a yellow fever epidemic; however, the road reached Baldwin, 19 miles west of Jacksonville, by March 1858. The FA&GC crossed the Florida RR at that point, which was named in honor of Dr. Baldwin. The 5-foot-gauge line was finally completed to Alligator on March 13, 1860. The company had received a federal land grant of almost 30,000 acres and a state land grant of about 165,000 acres. For several years the road apparently owned only one locomotive, the *Jacksonville*.

The Pensacola & Georgia Railroad was chartered in 1852 to build a line from Pensacola, in the extreme western end of the Florida Panhandle, to the Georgia state line. However, it was eventually decided to limit the project to a line from Quincy to Alligator town. The company acquired control of the Tallahassee RR and began building a line eastward from Tallahassee in 1856. By 1860, the road reached Madison, 53 miles from Tallahassee. A 106-mile line was finally completed to Lake City in the fall of 1861, where a connection was effected with the Florida, Atlantic & Gulf Central, creating a rail link between Tallahassee and Jacksonville. The company had also built a 4.5-mile branch line from Drifton to Monticello. The P&G began building a line from the state capital westward to Quincy in 1861. The 24-mile-long Tallahassee-Quincy line was completed in 1863, giving the road a total length of 134 miles.

When the Civil War began there was no railroad between Florida and Georgia. Indeed, the Florida legislature had forbidden any such connection. Thus, as a military measure, the Confederate government ordered the construction of a 49-mile connection between the Pensacola & Georgia's mainline at Live Oak, Fla., and the line of the Atlantic & Gulf RR at Lawton (Dupont), Ga. Each company was to build the portion of the railroad from its respective mainline to the state line. The roadbed was largely completed by the end of 1862, but then progress stopped due to a lack of rail. Construction again got underway in 1864, with the P&G using rail that had been removed from the Florida RR However, the line was not completed until March 1865, too late to do the Confederacy much good. After the war, in 1866, the P&G sold its 23-mile portion of the new line to the Atlantic & Gulf. The line eventually became a part of an important Atlantic Coast Line freight route between ACL's hub at Waycross, Ga., and Florida points.

The most important of the railroads built before the Civil War was probably the Florida Railroad. It was chartered in 1853 to build a line from Fernandina, on Amelia Island in the extreme northeast corner of the state, to Cedar Key on the Gulf of Mexico. The charter was later amended to authorize construction of a line from Fernandina to Tampa Bay, with a branch to Cedar Key. However, it was decided to build the line to Cedar Key first. The railroad was conceived as an alternative or "transit" route to the long hazardous sea voyage around the Florida peninsula. It was anticipated that cargo going from, for example, New York to New Orleans would be carried by ship from New York to Fernandina, by rail from Fernandina to Cedar Key, and then by another vessel from Cedar Key to New Orleans.

The promoter and first president of the Florida RR was David L. Yulee. A native of the West Indies and a Presbyterian of Portuguese Jewish descent, he had long been a power in Florida politics. He had represented the territory of Florida in the U.S. Congress and served as a United States senator from 1845 to 1851 and again from 1855 to 1861. An ardent secessionist and southern fire-eater in 1850, he was much more conservative by 1860. Yulee was burned in effigy by the people of Tampa when it was decided to build the railroad to Cedar Key.

Construction of the Florida RR began at Fernandina in 1855 and the first 10 miles of the line were completed on August 1, 1856. The railroad was laid with 58-lb iron rail imported from England and, like other Florida railroads of the era, built to a gauge of 5 feet. On February 1, 1859, the road reached Gainesville, 99 miles from Fernandina, and the entire 156-mile line was completed to Cedar Key on March 1, 1861. The road ran short of funds during its construction, and the needed capital was raised from a group of New York investors headed by Edward N. Dickerson and Marshall O. Roberts. As a result, control of the line passed to the New York group before the railroad was completed. David Yulee remained actively involved with the company, though, generally serving as vice president

This ornate example of the coach builder's art was constructed for the Florida Transit RR by Jackson & Sharp in 1881. Delaware State Archives

and manager. The company had received federal land grants of 290,000 acres and state grants of 505,000 acres. By the time the railroad was completed it had acquired four 4-4-0 locomotives: the *Abner McGehee*, *Gov. Broome*, *Alachua* and *Marion*.

The Florida RR also began building the proposed line to Tampa Bay, but progress was halted by the Civil War. The only work that had been completed before construction stopped was the grading of a right of way from Waldo south to Ocala.

Unfortunately for the three railroads, they were finished just in time for the Civil War. Florida was mostly wilderness at the time, far from the North and of relatively little military importance. In fact, one Northern newspaper described the state as "the smallest tadpole in the dirty pool of secession." Consequently, little significant action took place within its borders. Nevertheless, the Florida railroads were devastated, in some instances physically and in all cases financially.

The Florida, Atlantic & Gulf Central was unmolested until a Union fleet captured Jacksonville in March 1863. The Yankees eventually mounted an invasion of the Florida interior in February 1864, which began in Jacksonville and proceeded along the FA&GC line. The incursion was subsequently repelled at the only major battle waged in Florida, the Battle of Olustee, on February 20th, which was fought adjacent to the railroad's track. By the end of the war, the FA&GC was described as "two streaks of rust running thru the wilderness."

The Pensacola & Georgia had managed to avoid any damage but it was in a state of disrepair by the end of the conflict. The Tallahassee RR had not been so fortunate, sustaining some damage late in the war after Federal forces landed at St. Marks.

The Florida RR was undoubtedly the hardest hit. Cedar Key was raided by the USS *Hatteras* on January 15, 1862. The railroad station and several freight cars were burned and telegraph lines were destroyed. Fernandina was captured by a Federal fleet a few weeks later, on March 4, 1862. One of the arriving Union ships fired on the last train evacuating the town as it crossed the trestle to the mainland. The rear car was hit, killing two boys. It was detached and the remainder of the train made it to safety. Union forces captured several locomotives and cars when they took Fernandina.

After the evacuation of Fernandina, the Florida RR ceased operating between that point and Baldwin. However, service continued south of Baldwin and the railroad still had access to the Atlantic, at least until the fall of Jacksonville, through its connection with the

FA&GC. The railroad even decided to go into the blockade-running business itself, purchasing the *Silas Henry* in 1862. But that venture came to an end when the *Henry* was captured by the USS *Tahoma* on January 8, 1863.

In 1864, the Confederate army removed the rails north of Baldwin for use on the Pensacola & Georgia RR's Georgia connection which was being built north from Live Oak. David Yulee objected strenuously and the Florida RR even obtained a court order enjoining the removal. But to no avail—the army ignored the injunction and the rail was hauled away.

The Florida RR was also seriously damaged by enemy action in 1864. Baldwin was struck by Federal forces on February 8th. A raiding party landed at Cedar Key on July 29th and advanced 30 miles inland, destroying track and the railroad's bridge across the Waccasassa River. Finally, the town of Starke was raided by the Yankees on August 17th and the railroad station, cars and supplies were burned.

By the end of the war the Florida Railroad was a wreck. The company engineer reported on the state of the line at the time:

> At Cedar Key, the large railroad wharf, the warehouse and depot structures are burned and entirely destroyed; the trestles crossing from the Keys to the mainland, nearly a mile in extent, rotten to such a degree that they will have to be entirely rebuilt before trains can cross again; the structures crossing the water openings west of Bronson entirely rotten, so as to necessitate entire rebuilding; the structures between Bronson and Baldwin in a very inferior condition, so that most of them will need repair, especially the high bridge across Hatchet Creek; the cross ties between the Keys and Baldwin so rotten that much of the iron has bent from lack of support; the iron between the 40th and 10th mileposts, and the three miles on Amelia Island, taken up and carried off to some other road; all of the cross ties of the forty-seven miles east entirely rotten, so as to make it necessary to replace the whole of them before relaying the iron; all the large and costly structures crossing the tide waters and streams on the last thirty miles of the road east rotten or destroyed, among them the two high-truss, Howe bridges over Boggy River and Lofton Creek, the stationary through bridge and the low, Howe truss pivot, over Mills and Plummer swamps; the wharves and warehouses, the depot structure and shops at Fernandina destroyed. The wrecks of three engines standing stripped of everything portable, while a fourth has been stolen entirely. Only two engines are left usable, on the entire line.

As if that wasn't enough, the railroad's founder, David Yulee, was imprisoned after the war. He was arrested in May 1865 and held at Fort Pulaski, near Savannah, allegedly for treason. He remained in custody for almost a year and was released only after obtaining the intervention of General Ulysses S. Grant.

Before long, the Florida RR was rebuilt. Work began at Fernandina and by April 1866 trains were able to run as far as Gainesville. But only the most minimal repairs were undertaken and the track remained in very poor condition for the next decade. The company failed to make the interest and sinking-fund payments on its state-guaranteed bonds and, as a result, the state took possession of the company and sold the road at auction in the fall of 1866. However, Edward Dickerson and his associates remained in control after the company was reorganized in November. The reconstituted company continued to rebuild the line and managed to buy two new locomotives in 1869.

The Florida RR was unprofitable during reconstruction and the company was again reorganized in January 1872, with the same ownership remaining in control. The road was renamed the Atlantic, Gulf & West India Transit Co., but generally just referred to as the Transit Co. At about that time the road owned seven locomotives and 100 cars. Between 1876 and 1881, the dilapidated road was extensively rebuilt.

Finally, the Transit Co. began building the long-proposed line to Tampa Bay. It built the Peninsular RR from Waldo, 14 miles north of Gainesville, south to Ocala. Construction of the 45-mile line, which had been graded before the war, resumed in 1879 and was completed the following year. The Peninsular also built a 2-mile branch from Silver Springs Jct. to Silver Springs. The Peninsular RR was never operated as a separate organization, but rather was leased to the Transit Co.

The Transit Co. also began building the Fernandina & Jacksonville RR in the summer of 1880. The F&J extended from Hart's Road (now Yulee), a point on the Transit Co. line 11 miles west of Fernandina, south to Jacksonville. In April 1881, the 21.5-mile road was completed and leased by the AG&WIT Co.

The Atlantic, Gulf & West India Transit Co. did no better than its predecessor and it defaulted on the interest payments on its bonds and was foreclosed and sold at public auction in 1881. As a result, the road was again renamed and this time actually emerged with a new management. The road became the Florida Transit Railroad and was controlled by a British capitalist, Sir Edward J. Reed, who headed a group of English and Dutch investors. The new Florida Transit RR operated the old Fernandina-Cedar Key line as well as the new F&J and Peninsular lines.

David Yulee's long involvement with the railroad was ended. He moved to Washington to live with his daughter. The old senator finally died in 1886, at the age of 76. He claimed he never made any money from his investment in the Florida Railroad.

The Florida Transit continued to expand the line southward, building the Tropical Florida RR Co. from Ocala, through Wildwood, to Panasoffkee, a distance of 34 miles. Like the Peninsular RR before it, the Tropical Florida was leased and operated by its parent company. Construction of the Tropical line began in 1881 and reached Wildwood the next year. The town would eventually be the site of an important railroad yard but, at that time, the people of Wildwood opposed the new railroad and none would work on its construction. They feared that high winds would blow down the tree-lined right of way in a sort of tunnel effect and destroy their crops. Nevertheless, construction continued. However, the builders encountered considerable difficulty completing the line across the muck of Panasoffkee Swamp. At one point, five pine logs were driven into the mud, one on top of another, without reaching a solid bottom. The last 8 miles from Wildwood to Panasoffkee were finally completed in 1883.

The Florida Transit, Peninsular, and Tropical Florida Railroads were merged into the new Florida Transit & Peninsular Railroad on January 3, 1883. Although leased by the FT&P, the Fernandina & Jacksonville continued as a separate entity in the interim. The Florida Transit & Peninsular only lasted 15 months, until March 1884, when it was merged into the Florida Railway & Navigation Co.

Meanwhile, the other pioneer Florida railroads encountered their share of problems in the years after the Civil War. By the end of the war the Florida, Atlantic & Gulf Central was hopelessly in arrears in its payments to the Internal Improvement Fund. As a result, the trustees of the fund sold it at public auction on March 4, 1868. The purchasers formed a new company known as the Florida Central Railroad Company.

The Pensacola & Georgia also defaulted and the P&G and the Tallahassee RR were both sold at auction on March 20, 1869. After the sale the two lines were consolidated to form the new Tallahassee RR Co. The second Tallahassee RR Co. was sold to the Jacksonville, Pensacola & Mobile RR Co. in May 1870. The JP&M had been chartered by the Florida legislature at the same time as the new Tallahassee RR and given the exclusive right to construct a line from Quincy to Pensacola and on to the Alabama state line. The JP&M also leased the Florida Central in June 1870.

The Jacksonville, Pensacola & Mobile soon ran into new difficulties resulting from an old Civil War claim. When the South seceded, the rails for the Pensacola & Georgia RR's Tallahassee-Quincy extension were in the U.S. Custom House at St. Marks. The Confederates seized the Custom House and subsequently delivered the rails to the P&G. After the war, the U.S. government successfully sued the JP&M, as successor to the P&G, for the amount due the Custom House. Accordingly, the line from Lake City to Quincy, plus the Monticello branch, were sold at auction by the U.S. Marshal on November 1, 1870. The purchaser, J.B. Clark, operated the line for a few months and then sold it back to the JP&M on May 18, 1871.

From its inception, the Jacksonville, Pensacola & Mobile was controlled by a pair of scoundrels, George W. Swepson and Milton S. Littlefield. Swepson, a banker from North Carolina, was a scalawag Confederate veteran who had previously acquired a large position in the Florida, Atlantic & Gulf Central, primarily with the embezzled proceeds of a bond

Photographed at Tallahassee, wood-burning Florida Railway & Navigation Co. 4-4-0 No. 46 was built by the Rogers Locomotive Works of Paterson, N.J., in 1885. Florida State Archives

sale that had been intended for a railroad in his native state. His cohort, Littlefield, was a carpetbagger who had been a general in the Union army. Littlefield finagled an arrangement with the corrupt Florida legislature whereby bonds issued by the JP&M and Florida Central Railroads were exchanged for those of the state. Needless to say, most of the proceeds from the resulting sale of the Florida bonds eventually ended up in their pockets or those of their cronies. About $2,800,000 worth of state bonds were sold at approximately 70 percent of their face value, but only a little over $300,000 of the proceeds were actually used for railroad construction or equipment. Of course the railroads were saddled with liability for the full value of the bonds they had issued to the state.

Although Swepson and Littlefield hardly benefited the railroad, they did manage to extend the JP&M westward from Quincy to River Jct., a town later renamed Chattahoochee, which was located at the confluence of the Chattahoochee, Flint and Apalachicola Rivers. Construction of the 20-mile extension began in April 1870 and was completed in March 1872. But the JP&M never got beyond the Apalachicola River. The long-awaited line from River Jct. to Pensacola was finally built between 1881 and 1883 by the Pensacola & Atlantic RR, a subsidiary of the Louisville & Nashville RR.

The rogues soon lost control of the railroads. The Florida legislature abrogated the state bonds in 1873, and its action was eventually upheld by the U.S. Supreme Court. General Littlefield, who had been president of the JP&M, fell on hard times and soon left the state. His house in Jacksonville was sold by the sheriff. Some time later, the corrupt general, a man of great charm but few scruples, was jailed in New York City for failure to pay a hotel bill.

As a result of Swepson and Littlefield's shenanigans, as well as earlier contretemps, the Jacksonville, Pensacola & Mobile and the Florida Central were both mired in a seemingly endless morass of litigation and receiverships during most the 1870s. Although some effort was made to maintain the railroads, the turmoil was inevitably detrimental to their condition. In 1879, the line between Jacksonville and Tallahassee was still described as "two thin lines of rust," much as it had been just after the war. As if the railroads didn't have enough problems, the car shop at Jacksonville was destroyed by a fire in 1881.

The JP&M's lease of the Florida Central had been short lived, being terminated in October 1871. But the FC continued to be closely associated with the JP&M, at times sharing the same receivers. Finally, both the JP&M and the FC were sold at auction on November 25, 1879, to a firm acting as trustees for the bondholders. The trustees operated the lines until 1882 when they were sold to Sir Edward Reed, the British investor who already controlled the Florida Transit RR. Reed merged the two railroads into a new company, the Florida Central & Western RR Co., on March 4, 1882.

The management of the new Florida Central & Western soon set to work improving the line. Steel rails replaced iron ones. New crossties were installed and the average speed of through trains was increased to 20 miles per hour.

ABOVE:
A low-drivered freight engine, Florida Central & Peninsular 4-6-0 No. 212 was turned out by Rogers in 1893. Pictured here with a neatly painted star decorating her smoke-box front, the 212 became SAL 367, then 543 and finally 1543. She was retired at Jacksonville in 1923 after 30 years of service. Gerald M. Best collection; California State Railroad Museum

FACING PAGE:
Ready to depart for Wannee, "Peggy," the laggardly Atlantic, Suwannee River & Gulf Line local draws a crowd at Starke, Fla., about 1905, sometime after the ASR&G had been absorbed by Seaboard. The locomotive, 4-4-0 No. 324, was originally FR&N 43, built by Rogers in 1885. The Bradford County Telegraph collection

On March 5, 1884, the railroads controlled by Sir Edward Reed were consolidated into a new company, the Florida Railway & Navigation Co. Its principal components were the Florida Transit & Peninsular, Florida Central & Western and Fernandina & Jacksonville Railroads. Also included in the merger was the Leesburg & Indian River RR, which was constructing an 11-mile line from Wildwood eastward to Leesburg. With slightly over 500 miles of track, the FR&N was the first large railroad system in the state. The company's headquarters were at Jacksonville and its principal shops at Fernandina. The FR&N soon began advertising that it operated "Three Great Routes": the Gulf Coast Route between Fernandina and Cedar Key, the Tallahassee Route between Jacksonville and River Jct., and the Golden Fruit Route between Waldo and Panasoffkee.

In September 1884, the FR&N fulfilled the "Navigation" part of its corporate title when it bought the DeBarry-Baya Steamboat Line. The DeBarry Line operated 4 boats between Fernandina and Savannah, Ga., and owned a fleet of 13 vessels operating out of Jacksonville on the St. Johns River. The railroad also owned the Egmont Hotel in Fernandina which was advertised as "one of the most complete hotels in the South," featuring "a bathroom on every floor."

The new railroad continued to expand. The Leesburg branch, which had been completed in June 1884, was extended 10 miles to Tavares in June of the following year, and the line from Waldo 14 miles from Panasoffkee south to Terrell in July 1885.

Considering the doleful history of its predecessors, it is no surprise that the FR&N also soon went bankrupt. In November 1885, only a year and a half after it was formed, the company was placed in receivership for failure to pay the interest on its bonds. H.R. Duval, who had previously managed the Erie Railroad, was appointed receiver.

Nevertheless, the railroad kept growing, even while in receivership. The line was lengthened 39 miles from Terrell southward to Plant City, a point which was reached in 1887. A 2-mile branch was also built from Sumpterville Jct. to Sumpterville. In 1886, the FR&N built and leased the Jacksonville Belt RR Co. The Jacksonville Belt was a 3-mile line which connected the terminal of the former Fernandina & Jacksonville RR, on the east side of Jacksonville, with the terminal of the old Florida Central & Western on the west side of town. In the same year, the railroad also constructed the Fernandina & Amelia Beach Ry. Co. over a 2-mile route between the points in its corporate title. The Amelia Beach Railway eventually became an electric trolley line.

On June 1, 1886, the Florida Railway & Navigation Co., along with a number of other railroads in the Deep South, converted from 5-foot gauge to a gauge of 4 feet 9 inches. The 4-foot 9-inch gauge was close enough to the standard gauge of 4 feet 8 1/2 inches to permit the interchange of equipment. The result of the change was the creation of a nationwide network of more or less standard-gauge railroads. The only remaining exceptions to the national standard were a few scattered narrow-gauge lines, most notably the Denver & Rio Grande RR in Colorado.

Another important event in the 1880s was the eclipse of Cedar Key by Tampa. Cedar Key had been one of the biggest and most important towns in Florida when the Civil War commenced, although, in truth, no town in the state was really very big or very important at that time. It began a long decline once Henry B. Plant's South Florida RR established through service between Tampa and Jacksonville in the late 1880s. Steamship service from Cedar Key to New Orleans was discontinued in 1887 and to Tampa soon afterward. Eventually the railroad to Cedar Key would be abandoned in the Depression of the 1930s.

The receivership of the FR&N was ended when the property was sold at public auction on July 12, 1888, to a group of bondholders headed by W. Bayard Cutting of New York. At the time of the sale the condition of the line was reported as "dilapidated," which seems to have been the usual state of affairs for Florida railroads in the nineteenth century. Cutting organized The Florida Central & Peninsular Railway Co., with "The" in its corporate title. The new company formally took possession on May 1, 1889. H.R. Duval, who had been the receiver of the FR&N, became president of the FC&P.

Soon the FC&P completed the long awaited line to Tampa, opening the 23-mile extension from Plant City to Tampa on May 1, 1890. The FC&P was not, of course, the first railroad to reach the city. The South Florida RR, which would eventually become a part of the Atlantic Coast Line, had opened a line to Tampa from Sanford, on the St. Johns River, in 1884.

The Florida Central & Peninsular also built several other less significant lines. A 29-mile branch from Archer, on the line between Gainesville and Cedar Key, south to Early Bird was completed in December 1891. A 4-mile line from Turkey Creek, near Plant City, was built to Durant in 1892. In 1894, a 7.5-mile branch was constructed from Summerfield to Lake Weir.

The company bought the Tavares, Orlando & Atlantic RR in 1891. The TO&A began building a 32-mile line from Tavares to Orlando in 1882, which was opened on July 1, 1884. In 1890 the road failed to pay the interest on its bonds. As a result, it was foreclosed and ultimately sold at auction to the FC&P. The addition of the TO&A gave the Florida Central & Peninsular a continuous 53-mile line from Wildwood to Orlando. The Orlando branch was extended farther when the FC&P leased the East Florida & Atlantic Railway Co. on January 1, 1892. The EF&A owned a 16-mile line extending from Orlando eastward to Oviedo. The 5-mile segment of the EF&A between Orlando and Winter Park had been built by the Orlando & Winter Park Ry. Co. primarily to carry passengers to the campus of Rollins College in Winter Park, and was opened on February 1, 1889. The remaining 11 miles of the EF&A had been built by the Osceola & Lake Jessup Ry. Co. as an extension of the O&WP and leased to that company upon its completion on October 1, 1890. Both the O&WP and the O&LJ were sold to the East Florida and Atlantic in 1891. In 1894, the FC&P extended the Wildwood-Oviedo line one mile farther to Lake Charm.

For rail connections to the north the FC&P was dependent upon the rival Plant System which owned lines extending from Charleston, S.C. to Tampa. As a result, the Florida Central & Peninsular determined to build its own line north and it incorporated the Florida Northern RR Co., in 1892, to construct a line from Hart's Road (Yulee) to Savannah. The new line, which closely paralleled the Georgia coast, was completed in December 1893. Before the road was finished, the Florida Northern was merged into the FC&P in January 1893 and the name of the merged company was changed to Florida Central & Peninsular Railroad Co. without "The" in its title. Completion of the Florida Northern line gave the FC&P a 138-mile route between Jacksonville and Savannah which was 34 miles shorter than the Plant System route.

In 1892, before the Florida Northern line was even begun, the FC&P had arranged to lease the South Bound RR which operated between Savannah and Columbia, S.C. The lease was to be effective from October 1, 1893. The 135-mile-long South Bound had been completed by Savannah business interests in 1891. The South Bound actually extended from Savannah to Cayce, S.C., just south of Columbia, and operated into the South Carolina capital over the Richmond & Danville RR.

Through passenger service was inaugurated between New York and Florida almost as soon as the line between Savannah and Jacksonville was opened. The trains were handled by the Pennsylvania RR between New York and Washington, the Richmond & Danville between Washington and Columbia, and the FC&P between Columbia and Florida. The most popular train was the *New York & Florida Limited*, which carried through sleeping cars between New York and St. Augustine, Fla.

In February 1899, the Williams and Middendorf group purchased the Florida Central & Peninsular from W. Bayard Cutting and R. Fulton Cutting, and the road was soon advertised as a part of the Seaboard Air Line. To close the gap between the FC&P at Cayce and the original Seaboard Air Line at Cheraw, S.C., construction soon began on a 36-mile extension of the South Bound RR north to Camden, S.C. At that point it was to meet the Chesterfield & Kershaw RR, which had been formed to build a 55-mile line south from Cheraw. Construction of the two lines was completed in April 1900 and through service began on May 10. Operation of the FC&P by the new Seaboard Air Line Railway Co. commenced officially on July 1, 1900, and the line was formally merged into the SAL in 1903.

The through New York-Florida passenger service was discontinued as soon as the Williams group gained control of the FC&P. The Richmond & Danville RR had been succeeded by the Southern Railway in 1894, and a bitter rivalry had rapidly developed between the Southern and the Seaboard Air Line. As a result, John S. Williams, president of the Seaboard, terminated the through train arrangement between the Southern and the FC&P. In retaliation, the Southern soon built a line from Cayce to Hardeeville, S.C., which paralleled the South Bound, and obtained trackage rights over the Atlantic Coast Line to Savannah and Jacksonville.

At the time it was acquired by the Williams syndicate, the Florida Central & Peninsular operated some 944 miles of line and owned about 74 locomotives and over 2,000 passenger and freight cars. The company's traffic and earnings had been considerably enhanced by the Spanish-American War of 1898 and the railroad had been at least marginally profitable throughout most of its history. It was marked improvement over its predecessors' performance, but the FC&P never did pay a dividend.

One final addition was made to the Florida Central & Peninsular system. The FC&P acquired control of the Atlantic, Suwannee River & Gulf Railway in September 1899. The ASR&G had been incorporated in 1893 to build a line from Starke, Fla., to the Suwannee River. By 1896 the company had completed a line from Starke to Buda, a distance of 37 miles. The road, which had been built for the Ambler Lumber Co., also operated several miles of logging spurs. The ASR&G began operation by the SAL on July 1, 1900. Seaboard extended the line 20 miles farther to Wannee, on the Suwannee River, in 1901 and 1902. Natives of the area called the branch the "Peggy line." The name referred to a local expression that an especially lazy man was "too slow to catch Peggy," thus implying that trains on this line almost set a new standard for leisurely travel.

CHAPTER THREE

GEORGIA & ALABAMA RAILWAY

The smallest of the three systems which were consolidated to form the Seaboard Air Line Railway was the Georgia & Alabama Railway. It dated back to 1884 when the Americus, Preston & Lumpkin RR Co. was chartered to build a line from Americus to Lumpkin, Ga. A 3-foot-gauge road, 37 miles in length, was completed between those two points in March 1886. A westward extension to Louvale, Ga., was begun three months later and opened the following year. In 1887 the line was extended eastward to Abbeville, on the Ocmulgee River, and in 1888 the name of the then 105-mile-long narrow gauge road was changed to a more ambitious title: Savannah, Americus & Montgomery Ry. Co. The SA&M began operating a steamboat service on the Ocmulgee and Altamaha Rivers, from Abbeville to the coastal cities of Brunswick and Savannah, in 1889.

On June 1, 1890, the SA&M completed a 65-mile standard-gauge extension eastward from Abbeville to Lyons, Ga., and the original line was soon converted to standard gauge. While the line from Abbeville to Lyons was under construction, the Savannah & Western Railroad, a wholly owned subsidiary of the Central of Georgia was building a connecting railroad to Lyons from Meldrim, Ga., a point on Central's Savannah-Macon mainline. The original intent was for the SA&M and the CofG to operate jointly between Savannah and Americus, with the SA&M granted trackage rights over the Central between Lyons and Savannah and the Central over the SA&M between Lyons and Americus. The joint operating agreement was apparently never consummated but with the completion of the two lines, SA&M did have a direct connection to Savannah. As a result, the riverboat service out of Abbeville was soon discontinued.

The Savannah, Americus & Montgomery next turned west, bridging the Chattahoochee River and entering Alabama. On December 1, 1891, it completed a 95-mile extension from Louvale to Montgomery, Ala. The SA&M thus had a 265-mile mainline between Lyons, Ga., and the Alabama capital. General offices and shops of the company were located at Americus, and the railroad owned some 24 locomotives.

The SA&M also acquired a branch line when it leased the Albany, Florida & Northern Railway in 1892. The AF&N, which was built by the SA&M between 1889 and 1891, owned a 35-mile line extending from a connection with the parent road at Cordele, Ga., southwestward to Albany, Ga.

Like so many other Seaboard predecessors, the SA&M soon ran into financial difficulties. The road entered receivership in 1892 and, in 1895, the line was sold at public auction to a syndicate formed by the banking firms of John L. Williams & Sons, of Richmond, and Middendorf, Oliver & Co., of Baltimore. The purchasers then conveyed the property to a new company, the Georgia & Alabama Railway. John Skelton Williams, the 30-year-old son of the founder of the Richmond banking firm, became president of the new railroad. The old SA&M was thus the first component of the future Seaboard Air Line Railway to be acquired by the Williams associates.

The new Georgia & Alabama Ry. did not include the Albany branch line. The Albany, Florida & Northern was reorganized as a separate company, becoming the Albany & Northern Ry. It was later renamed the Georgia, Southwestern & Gulf RR and finally reverted to the Albany & Northern name. It operated as an independent short line for many years before being acquired by the Southern Railway System in 1964.

TOP:
Photographs of the Savannah, Americus & Montgomery are almost nonexistent. The only known photo is this builder's portrait of SA&M No. 101, Ocmulgee, *a 2-6-0 built by Baldwin in 1889.* Railroad Museum of Pennsylvania

BOTTOM:
The last new locomotive acquired by the "Savannah Short Line" was 4-6-0 No. 139, delivered by Richmond in 1898. Assigned class I-8 by SAL, she went through several renumberings before finally being retired as Seaboard 1574 in 1928. Alco Historic Photos

The Williams regime expanded the Georgia & Alabama and soon turned it into at least a modestly profitable enterprise. In 1896, the G&A leased Central of Georgia's 58-mile-long Meldrim-Lyons branch for a period of 101 years. In addition it acquired temporary trackage rights over Central's mainline for the 17 miles between Meldrim and Savannah, gaining entry into Savannah for the first time. The G&A began developing extensive port facilities on Hutchinson Island at Savannah and started building its own railroad between Meldrim and Savannah in 1899. However, the Meldrim-Savannah line was not completed until after the new Seaboard Air Line Railway began operating the G&A in 1900.

The Georgia & Alabama also added branch lines to its system by acquiring two short lines, the Abbeville & Waycross Railroad Co. and the Columbus Southern Railway. The Abbeville & Waycross was incorporated in 1889. It built a line from Abbeville south to Bowen's Mill, Ga., in 1890 and extended the line to Lulaville in 1891. In 1892 the line went into receivership. In 1896 the A&W reached Fitzgerald, and it was bought by the G&A in that year. The G&A extended the line 8 more miles to Ocilla, Ga., in 1896 and 1897. Total length of the branch line from Abbeville to Ocilla was 30.5 miles.

By far the more important acquisition was the Columbus Southern Ry. It operated a line between Columbus and Albany, Ga., a total distance of 88 miles, which crossed the G&A's mainline at Richland, Ga. The CS was chartered in 1885 as the Columbus & Florida Railway Co., but was soon renamed. It was owned by the Chattahoochee Brick Co., the firm which built the line. Construction began in 1886 and the road was opened for operation on April 12, 1890. Upon completion, the new road was leased by the Georgia, Midland & Gulf RR. GM&G, which eventually became a part of the Southern Railway System, owned a line extending from McDonough, Ga., a point near Atlanta, south to Columbus.

Still at work in home territory, SAL 1523, ex-Georgia & Alabama 128 was photographed at Fitzgerald, Ga., during the twenties. One of three G&A 4-6-0's built by Richmond in 1896 and designated SAL class I-7, No. 1523 remained in service until 1928. In contrast to the builder's photo of sister 129, the former G&A 128 has been modernized with such features as an upgraded cab and new headlight. Also, the blind drivers as seen on the 129 have been re-equipped with standard flanged tires. Railway Negative Exchange

However, the lease was terminated in July 1891 and the Columbus Southern began operating as an independent company. It encountered financial difficulties and was forced into receivership in 1895. After a foreclosure sale the CS was acquired by the Georgia & Alabama in December 1896.

The Georgia & Alabama styled itself as "The Savannah Short Line," and advertised that it possessed the shortest route between Savannah and both Columbus and Montgomery. Its daily passenger train between Savannah and Montgomery featured a buffet parlor car. By 1899 the G&A, along with the Florida Central & Peninsular, was listed as a part of the Seaboard Air Line in the *Official Guide*. It was formally operated as a part of the new Seaboard Air Line from July 1, 1900, and was officially purchased by the SAL on February 20, 1902. At the time it began operation by the Seaboard, the G&A owned 448 miles of track and some 39 locomotives.

Burdened with steep grades in the area around Americus, Ga., the Georgia & Alabama possessed a number of relatively heavy locomotives, including twenty-three 4-6-0's and three 2-8-0's. Freshly outshopped, G&A 129 poses for the builder's photographer at Richmond, Va., in 1896. Attesting to sharp curvatures on the G&A, the 129's center drive wheels are "blind," that is, outfitted with flangeless tires. Harold K. Vollrath collection

Taking in the fresh air, the head-end men on a local job ride the footboards of Baldwin-built H-1 2-8-0 905, easing past the Atlanta depot on July 27, 1933. Bruce R. Meyer collection

CHAPTER FOUR

THE ERA OF EXPANSION 1900–1930

The new Seaboard Air Line Railway's mainlines extended from Richmond to Tampa, a distance of 850 miles, and from Hamlet, N.C., to Atlanta, 325 miles. Major branches included the lines from Norlina, N.C., to Portsmouth, Va.; Hamlet to Wilmington, N.C.; Monroe, N.C., to Rutherfordton, N.C.; Savannah, Ga., to Montgomery, Ala.; and Baldwin, Fla., to River Jct., Fla. The total length of the system was almost exactly 2,600 miles.

To celebrate the completion of the new railroad, two special trains loaded with company officials, reporters and assorted dignitaries were dispatched from Richmond to Tampa on May 30, 1900. Also included was a 32-piece brass band whose red-coated members were all employees from the Portsmouth shops. At towns along the way, proclamations, resolutions and flowers were showered on the railroad's president while crowds cheered and the band tooted. At Tampa, the guests were taken on a steamboat tour of the bay and served a luncheon at which President John Skelton Williams spoke. He proudly noted that the Seaboard was owned in the South and did not owe one cent to a financial institution north of Baltimore. On their return trip north, the trains stopped at principal cities en route: Jacksonville, Savannah, Columbia, Raleigh and Petersburg. The party inspected Seaboard facilities at each point and was entertained lavishly in honor of the occasion.

The trains finally returned to Richmond on the afternoon of Saturday, June 2nd. Upon their arrival, the Richmond Howitzers artillery company fired a 21-gun salute to honor the states served by the Seaboard. The traditional driving of the golden spike was then held at a point just north of the new Main Street Station. The spike was driven with a silver hammer into a predrilled hole by Master John Skelton Williams, Jr., age three, the son of the line's president, perhaps one of the few times on record when a three-year-old was entrusted with a hammer by otherwise rational adults. An older cousin was standing by in case Master Williams was indisposed, but he manfully performed his duties. A telegraph connection transmitted the blows to every station on the line and a flag was raised at each point as the little gandy dancer drove the spike home. The spike was engraved with the Latin inscription *Te Deum Laudemus* (We Praise Thee, God).

That evening 400 guests attended an elaborate 14-course banquet presided over by Governor James H. Tyler of Virginia. Numerous toasts were proposed and no less than ten speeches delivered. It was proclaimed that the Seaboard Air Line was a "Southern system, created by Southern enterprise and Southern money against the machinations of Wall Street, manned by Southern men, devoted to the upbringing of Southern cities, the prosperity of Southern states." The affair lasted past midnight, but someone stopped the clock just before the witching hour so that the Episcopal bishop who was scheduled to pronounce the benediction would not violate the Sabbath.

Through passenger train service between New York and Tampa began the next day, and the Seaboard Air Line Railway began officially operating the Florida, Central & Peninsular and the Georgia & Alabama on July 1st. The new railroad was in business.

The railroad's youthful president, John Skelton Williams, was only 34 years old when the new Seaboard Air Line was formed. Scion of a distinguished old Virginia family, his father's bank was well known in the South as its founder had helped finance the Confederate government during the Civil War. A member of Phi Beta Kappa, John Skelton joined

With her bell tolling, 4-4-0 No. 540 pulls a three-car passenger train into Starke, Fla., around 1910. By this time, the engine, a sister to No. 546 shown on page 41 at Lloyd, has been converted to burn coal. The class G 4-4-0's were built by Richmond in 1895. The Bradford County Telegraph collection

the bank after leaving the University of Virginia. John L. Williams & Sons and its allied firm, Middendorf, Oliver & Co., of Baltimore, got involved in railroad finance in 1893 when they participated in the reorganization of the Savannah, Americus & Montgomery Ry. In 1895, John Skelton submitted a plan to restructure the bankrupt railroad and, when it was adopted, he was elected president of the new Georgia & Alabama Ry., successor to the SA&M. From there, he went on to acquire control of the Florida Central & Peninsular and the original Seaboard Air Line.

Certainly one of the biggest problems which had confronted John Skelton Williams as he assembled the new system was the need for a friendly connection from Richmond to the Northeast. The only railroad running north out of that city was the little Richmond, Fredericksburg & Potomac. It was only 82 miles long, extending from Richmond to Quantico, Va., but it enjoyed a virtual monopoly on traffic moving along the Atlantic seaboard. At Quantico, the RF&P connected with the Washington Southern Ry., a subsidiary of the vast Pennsylvania RR, that ran on into Washington, D.C. The RF&P and the Washington Southern formed the only direct link between Richmond and Washington. At Washington, connections could be effected with the Pennsy or the Baltimore & Ohio for points such as New York, Philadelphia and Pittsburgh. If Seaboard was going to succeed, it was imperative that it have access to the Washington gateway. The Robinson family, which had long controlled both the Seaboard and the RF&P, had sold control of the RF&P to the Atlantic Coast Line in 1885. ACL, which was allied with the Southern Railway System, was not favorably disposed toward the new Seaboard. As a result the RF&P refused to enter into a through traffic arrangement with SAL.

Williams's response to the situation was to propose building his own railroad from Richmond to Washington. Against strong opposition, he obtained a charter from the Virginia General Assembly in March 1900 for the Richmond & Washington Air Line Ry. Co. The proposed line would parallel the RF&P and the Washington Southern and connect with the Baltimore & Ohio in the nation's capital. As Virginia owned a substantial interest in the RF&P, the commonwealth was to be indemnified for any loss on its investment resulting from the construction of the proposed new line. The management of the Pennsylvania RR, envisioning the loss of Seaboard traffic to the B&O, was not pleased by this development and it urged the ACL-RF&P group to relent. Faced with pressure from the Pennsy and the commonwealth as well as the prospect of a parallel competitor, the RF&P finally signed a through traffic agreement with the SAL. As a result, the proposed Richmond & Washington Air Line was dropped and the Virginia General Assembly revoked its charter in February 1901.

Largely at the behest of the Pennsylvania, control of the RF&P was soon neutralized. Operations of the RF&P and the Washington Southern were consolidated in 1901, and a holding company, the Richmond-Washington Co., was formed for the purpose of owning a majority of RF&P stock. Seaboard and the Pennsy, Atlantic Coast Line, Southern, Chesapeake & Ohio and the Baltimore & Ohio each acquired one-sixth of the holding company's stock. Seaboard was thus assured a friendly connection from Richmond to the north. The Commonwealth of Virginia, for its part, retained its two-fifths interest in the RF&P proper.

It is interesting to note that Seaboard's two biggest rivals, the Southern and the Atlantic Coast Line, were created at about the same time and in much the same way as the Seaboard.

TOP:
Seaboard class E 4-4-0 No. 225 pauses at Lloyd, Fla., with a passenger train in 1905. The wood-burning Eight-Wheeler was built by Baldwin in 1888 for the Raleigh & Gaston. CSX Transportation collection

MIDDLE:
Wood-burning 4-4-0 No. 546 is inspected as she simmers in front of the hotel at Lloyd. The village was long a meal stop for trains on the Jacksonville-River Jct. run. Florida State Archives

BOTTOM:
Birmingham Special Freight. When an errant carload of furniture threatened to spoil the June 16, 1914, opening of Birmingham's new Tutwiler Hotel, SAL located the car in Atlanta and dispatched a special move to get the shipment to the Alabama city in time for the event. Handled by Ten-Wheeler 686, the extra set a long-standing record for freights on the Atlanta-Birmingham run. Cooling its wheels, the 686 pauses beside the roundhouse with PRR 49261 (the urgently sought furniture load) and side-door caboose SAL 49880 after the special's arrival at Birmingham on June 15, 1914. CSX Transportation collection

TOP:
Its smoke-box door ajar, 0-6-0 No. 1007 reposes at North Charleston, S.C., in May 1924. The begrimed F-3 class yard engine was built by Pittsburgh in 1900.

BOTTOM:
Charlotte Harbor & Northern's sole 4-4-0, No. 8, heads the line's daily passenger run at Arcadia, Fla., in September 1924. Built by Baldwin in 1913, the Eight-Wheeler became SAL 103. She was sold to Dowling-Camp Lumber Co. in 1933.
Both photos, Harold K. Vollrath collection

timore & Ohio in the nation's capital. As Virginia owned a substantial interest in the RF&P, the commonwealth was to be indemnified for any loss on its investment resulting from the construction of the proposed new line. The management of the Pennsylvania RR, envisioning the loss of Seaboard traffic to the B&O, was not pleased by this development and it urged the ACL-RF&P group to relent. Faced with pressure from the Pennsy and the commonwealth as well as the prospect of a parallel competitor, the RF&P finally signed a through traffic agreement with the SAL. As a result, the proposed Richmond & Washington Air Line was dropped and the Virginia General Assembly revoked its charter in February 1901.

Largely at the behest of the Pennsylvania, control of the RF&P was soon neutralized. Operations of the RF&P and the Washington Southern were consolidated in 1901, and a holding company, the Richmond-Washington Co., was formed for the purpose of owning a majority of RF&P stock. Seaboard and the Pennsy, Atlantic Coast Line, Southern, Chesapeake & Ohio and the Baltimore & Ohio each acquired one-sixth of the holding company's stock. Seaboard was thus assured a friendly connection from Richmond to the north. The Commonwealth of Virginia, for its part, retained its two-fifths interest in the RF&P proper.

It is interesting to note that Seaboard's two biggest rivals, the Southern and the Atlantic Coast Line, were created at about the same time and in much the same way as the Seaboard.

TOP:
Seaboard class E 4-4-0 No. 225 pauses at Lloyd, Fla., with a passenger train in 1905. The wood-burning Eight-Wheeler was built by Baldwin in 1888 for the Raleigh & Gaston. CSX Transportation collection

MIDDLE:
Wood-burning 4-4-0 No. 546 is inspected as she simmers in front of the hotel at Lloyd. The village was long a meal stop for trains on the Jacksonville-River Jct. run. Florida State Archives

BOTTOM:
Birmingham Special Freight. When an errant carload of furniture threatened to spoil the June 16, 1914, opening of Birmingham's new Tutwiler Hotel, SAL located the car in Atlanta and dispatched a special move to get the shipment to the Alabama city in time for the event. Handled by Ten-Wheeler 686, the extra set a long-standing record for freights on the Atlanta-Birmingham run. Cooling its wheels, the 686 pauses beside the roundhouse with PRR 49261 (the urgently sought furniture load) and side-door caboose SAL 49880 after the special's arrival at Birmingham on June 15,

In a rare view circa 1910, the junction depot at Archer, Fla., is flanked by a pair of local trains. On the right, a wood-burning Mogul heads an eastbound train from Cedar Key; on the left, a 4-4-0 pauses with its train on the branch line to the Early Bird Mine.
H.J. Doherty collection

The Southern Railway System was formed in 1894 when the Richmond & Danville RR System, which extended from Washington, D.C., and West Point, Va., to Greenville, Miss., was merged with the East Tennessee, Virginia & Georgia Ry., which operated a network of lines from Bristol, Va., to Memphis, Tenn., and from Chattanooga, Tenn., to Brunswick, Ga., and Mobile, Ala. The formation of the Atlantic Coast Line had an especially striking resemblance to the consolidation of the SAL. It reached its basic form in 1902 when the ACL, which owned a network of lines between Richmond and Charleston, S.C., acquired the Plant System which extended from Charleston to Tampa. Coast Line thus owned a competing line from Richmond to Savannah, Jacksonville and Tampa. Both the Southern and the Coast Line were under the influence of J. Pierpont Morgan, the banking tycoon who practically ruled American finance at the time.

The new system created in 1900 was far from complete. Over the course of the next 30 years it would almost double in size, adding another 1,900 miles of line through both new construction and the acquisition of smaller railroads. The first new line to be added was a 51-mile extension down the West Coast of Florida from Durant south to Sarasota. Construction of the line began in August 1901 by the grandiosely named United States & West Indies Railroad and Steamship Co. The US&WI Co. was soon succeeded by the more modestly titled Florida West Shore Ry. The West Shore line was finished in 1903 and operated by SAL from its completion. The line was extended 4 miles farther south, to Fruitville, in 1905.

Another early addition to the Seaboard Air Line was a 4.5-mile-long branch from Dickerson, a point on the Henderson-Durham line, to Oxford, N.C. The little line was built in 1902 by the Oxford & Coast Line RR Co., an SAL subsidiary, and operated by Seaboard from its completion.

The first really major addition to the newly consolidated Seaboard Air Line was the extension of the line from Atlanta to Birmingham, Ala. At the time, Seaboard was allied with the St. Louis-San Francisco RR (Frisco) which owned a line from Birmingham to Kansas City. It was anticipated that entry into Birmingham would give Seaboard a direct connection with the Frisco as well as access to the coal fields of northern Alabama. The Birmingham extension was accomplished by purchasing the generically named East & West RR, which stretched 120 miles from Cartersville, Ga., to Pell City, Ala., and building new lines connecting the E&W to Atlanta and Birmingham.

Dating back to 1870, the East & West RR included the first segment of the future Seaboard Air Line to be constructed in Georgia. The oldest portion of the line was originally chartered in 1866 as the Cartersville & Van Wert RR Co. to build a line from a connection with the Western & Atlantic RR at Cartersville westward to Cedartown, Ga. The promoter of the Cartersville & Van Wert was Hannibal I. Kimball, a carpetbagger who was closely associated with Rufus Bullock, Georgia's Republican governor. In 1869, the State of Georgia agreed to endorse the road's bonds at the rate of $12,500 per mile. The name of the road was changed to the Cherokee RR in 1870 and 14 miles of 3-foot-gauge line was built from Cartersville to Taylorsville, Ga., in that year. The company received state endorsements to the tune of $575,000, although how much actually reached the railroad is conjectural. In any event, only five percent of the line's capital was ever paid in and it never completed more than the 14 miles of line to Taylorsville. The Cherokee RR defaulted on its bonds in 1871 and a receiver was appointed. The line was finally sold under foreclosure to the Cherokee Iron Co. in 1879. The price was a mere $22,500, considerably less than $575,000 endorsed by the state.

The Cherokee Iron Co. was also known as the Cherokee Iron & RR Co. It built a 3-foot-gauge line from Taylorsville, westward 22 miles to Cedartown, Ga., which was completed in October 1879, and in October of 1882 completed a 10-mile extension from Cedartown to the Georgia-Alabama state line at Esom Hill, Ga. One month later the railroad properties of the Cherokee Iron Co. were leased to the East & West RR Co. of Alabama, and the line was sold outright to the E&W in 1886.

The East & West RR of Alabama was chartered in 1882 and in that year constructed a 64-mile-long narrow-gauge line from the Georgia-Alabama state line, at Esom Hill, westward to Broken Arrow, Ala. (Broken Arrow was later known as Coal City and is currently called Wattsville.) In 1885, it was proposed to extend the line all the way from Birmingham to Gainesville, Ga., a total distance of about 200 miles, and in 1887 the company completed a 6-mile extension from Broken Arrow to Pell City. At Pell City the E&W connected with the Georgia Pacific Ry. (Southern) line to Birmingham. The road was converted to standard gauge in 1888, but unfortunately also entered receivership in that same year. In 1892, the E&WofA leased the little Tredegar Mineral Ry., which built a 3-mile line from a connection with the East & West at Tredegar, Ala., to Jacksonville, Ala. On May 29, 1893, the entire East & West of Alabama was sold at a foreclosure sale to Eugene Kelly of New York, and the company was reorganized as the East & West RR Co. the following year. However, the new company never built any additional lines, although Kelly intended to extend the line to Birmingham.

Seaboard purchased all of the capital stock of the East & West RR Co. on April 23, 1902, and merged it into a new subsidiary, the Atlanta & Birmingham Air Line Ry., the following year. The A&BAL proceeded to build a 43-mile line from Howells (Atlanta) to a connection with the E&W line at Rockmart plus a 37-mile line from Coal City to Birmingham. It also rebuilt the meandering line between Rockmart and Coal City, eliminating some 6.5 miles of circuitous trackage. In Birmingham, the Seaboard line connected with the Birmingham Belt Ry., a subsidiary of the Kansas City, Memphis & Birmingham RR Co. (later incorporated into the Frisco) and obtained trackage rights over the KCM&B from Birmingham to Bessemer, Ala., a distance of 18 miles. When the project was completed, Seaboard had a 165-mile line from Atlanta to Birmingham plus branches from Rockmart to Cedartown, Tredegar to Jacksonville, Ala., and Coal City to Pell City, and trackage rights to Bessemer. The line to Birmingham was opened for freight traffic on December 5, 1904, and for passenger traffic on July 2, 1905.

... led to the end of John Skelton Williams's

middle name of Fortune. Ryan had been a thorn in the side of former Seaboard president R.C. Hoffman. As a large stockholder in the Seaboard & Roanoke, he had stoutly opposed the merger of the old Seaboard Air Line with the Georgia & Alabama and the Florida Central & Peninsular, obtaining some 16 injunctions in an attempt to block the consolidation. Given the history of the G&A and the FC&P, Ryan's position was not totally unreasonable. Nevertheless, he finally withdrew his opposition in February 1900 and sold his Seaboard holdings to the Williams syndicate in February 1901. But SAL ran short of funds as a result of obligations it incurred in connection with building the Atlanta-Birmingham line. Williams had intended to issue first mortgage bonds in the summer of 1903, but the market was so weak that the bonds could not be sold. To obtain the needed funds, he thus borrowed $2,500,000 from Ryan. As a consequence of the loan a seven-man voting trust was formed to control the Seaboard. Its members included Ryan and two of his allies, three Seaboard directors who were also associated with the Frisco and Rock Island Railroads, and John S. Williams. Under this arrangement, Ryan and his allies soon gained control of the railroad and Williams was ousted in something of a coup. The insurrection was actually engineered by S. Davies Warfield, a large Seaboard stock holder and occasional business associate of Ryan, who would later play a prominent role as president of the Seaboard during the twenties.

Williams was replaced as president by James M. Barr, who had previously served as first vice president and general manager of the railroad. Barr had only a public school education and had started his railroad career as a messenger boy in the office of a Pennsylvania RR division superintendent.

The new baron of the Seaboard, Thomas Ryan, was born in Virginia in 1851. His family was left impoverished by the Civil War, and he was penniless when he went to Baltimore at the age of 17. But he eventually became one of the richest men in the world, with a fortune estimated to be between $50 million and $100 million. He was considered one of the most daring plungers in New York and was described as "the most adroit, suave and noiseless man that American finance had ever known." He had previously been involved in the reorganization of several railroads and, at one time, was the czar of the New York subway system, which he was accused of milking. He was instrumental in forming the American Tobacco Co. and would later be credited with saving the Equitable Life Assurance Society when he bought control of the company in 1905.

Although embittered by his defeat, John Skelton Williams remained on the railroad's board of directors and he and his allies fought to regain control of the Seaboard. He complained vociferously, contending that the railroad had been stolen from Southerners by a group of New York capitalists. Williams ignored the fact the T.F. Ryan was also a native Virginian and overlooked that he, himself, had agreed to the loan from Ryan which enabled the tycoon to gain control of the company. Nevertheless, his complaints gained considerable sympathy from Southerners. But the Williams group were unsuccessful. They sold their Seaboard stock to Ryan in August 1904 and John S. Williams resigned from the board. By the end of the year Ryan and his associates controlled almost two thirds of Seaboard's capital stock. But even though he disposed of this stock, the garrulous Williams continued to harshly criticize the railroad's management for several years to come, accusing it of corruption and incompetence. The taciturn Ryan didn't bother to reply to Williams's charges, although Barr and some of his other associates did try to defend themselves.

Williams soon attempted to form another railroad system between the Upper South and the Gulf. Between 1906 and 1910 he consolidated several short lines into the Georgia & Florida Ry. and, in 1906, also acquired the bankrupt Carolina Northern RR which he reorganized as the Raleigh & Charleston RR. The Georgia & Florida eventually extended from Augusta, Ga., to Madison, Fla., but it proved unsuccessful. The line entered receivership in 1915, where it languished for many years. The destitute road was finally acquired by the Southern Railway System in 1963. The Raleigh & Charleston extended only 41 miles from Lumberton, N.C., to Marion, S.C. It was sold to the Seaboard in 1911 and operated as an SAL subsidiary for many years afterward.

A Seaboard engineer poses with his handsome 4-4-0 on a passenger train at Hamlet, N.C., about 1915. Class G-1 No. 182 was outshopped by Rhode Island in May 1900 carrying road number 603. CSX Transportation collection

Thomas Ryan established a holding company, The Seaboard Co., to exercise dominion over the Seaboard Air Line RR. It acquired most of the railroad's securities in 1905 and remained in control of the railroad until Ryan terminated his interest. Ryan, of course, controlled the holding company.

Disaster struck the Seaboard in 1906 when the general office building in Portsmouth was destroyed by fire in March. Even worse, a passenger train collided with an extra freight train between Hamlet and Rockingham, N.C., on July 22nd. Twenty-two people were killed and 35 injured. Several other lesser accidents occurred in 1906 and 1907. John S. Williams naturally pointed to the mishaps as evidence of mismanagement.

James Barr resigned as president of the SAL in April 1906 and was succeeded by Alfred Walter who had previously been president of the Lehigh Valley RR. Walter died after less than a year in office and was replaced by William A. Garrett who was elected president in February 1907. Garrett was a former general manager of the Queen & Crescent Route. He had been with the Seaboard for only about three months when he became president of the company.

Seaboard continued to grow during the early years of the twentieth century, adding several small lines. Among these was a 13-mile line extending from Plant City south to Welcome, Fla., which would eventually give Seaboard access to the vast "Bone Valley" phosphate beds. The Plant City-Welcome line had been opened in 1898 as a tram log road by the Wornell Lumber & Veneer Co. An SAL subsidiary, the Plant City, Arcadia & Gulf Ry., rebuilt the line in 1905 and 1906 and it was opened as a common carrier in the latter year. Seaboard operated it from the time it opened. A 5-mile spur from Keysville Jct., near Welcome, to Nichols was added in 1907 and a 1.5-mile spur to Coronet in 1909. A 12-mile ... from Edison Jct. to Agricola, was constructed in 1909 and 1910.

... Tallahassee Southeastern Ry.,

ever, it managed to build only 6 miles of line extending from Tallahassee southeastward, which was constructed in 1891. The FG&W was foreclosed in 1895 and reorganized as the Tallahassee Southeastern, which intended to build a line from Tallahassee to Gainesville. In 1899 the line was extended to Wacissa, 21 miles from Tallahassee. Twelve more miles were graded from Wacissa across the Aucilla River. Seaboard organized the Tallahassee, Perry & Southeastern Ry. in 1905 to acquire the Tallahassee Southeastern. The TP&S extended the line 11 miles from Wacissa to Covington in 1906, and 8 more miles from Covington to Waylonzo in 1907. A roadbed was graded all the way to Perry, but track was never laid. SAL operated the line from 1906 until it was formally merged into the parent company in 1909. The portion of the line from Covington to Waylonzo was apparently used only as a logging line and never actually operated by TP&S or Seaboard.

In South Carolina, the 22-mile-long Catawba Valley Ry. was added to the SAL in 1907. It extended from a connection with the Hamlet-Atlanta mainline, near Catawba, south to Great Falls. The southernmost 10 miles of the road, from Fort Lawn to Great Falls, were built by the Southern Power Co. in 1906 and the remainder of the line was constructed by the CV Ry. the following year. Seaboard operated the line from its completion.

Seaboard also acquired control of several short-line railroads which were operated as separate subsidiaries. Among these was the Charlotte, Monroe & Columbia RR, a 17-mile road extending from McBee to Jefferson, S.C., which was constructed between 1901 and 1903. It had been chartered to build from McBee, on the Hamlet-Columbia line, to a connection with SAL's Hamlet-Atlanta line at Monroe, N.C. If completed, it would have provided Seaboard with a short route between Charlotte, N.C., and Columbia, S.C., bypassing Hamlet. However, the CM&C was never extended to Monroe and was to remain just another insignificant short line.

In 1903, SAL established a close relationship with the little Savannah & Statesboro Ry. Co., guaranteeing, among other things, the short line's bonds. The S&S extended 32 miles from Cuyler, Ga., on Seaboard's Savannah-Montgomery line, to Statesboro, Ga. In addition, the Statesboro line operated over Seaboard tracks from Cuyler to Savannah, a distance of 20 miles.

SAL acquired its most important subsidiary in 1907 when it purchased control of the Macon, Dublin & Savannah RR. The MD&S operated a 92-mile-long line from Macon, Ga., to a connection with the Seaboard at Vidalia, Ga. Control of the MD&S created a through route between Macon and Savannah. The Macon line was to operate as a separate SAL subsidiary until 1958, when it was finally merged into the parent company.

The McBee-Monroe line was not the only SAL project which failed to reach fruition. One major proposal during the early 1900s was the construction of a line from Charleston, S.C., westward via Augusta and Athens, Ga., to Chattanooga, Tenn. The proposed line would have crossed the Columbia-Savannah mainline at Hammond, S.C., and connected with the Hamlet-Atlanta mainline at Athens. To construct the line, Seaboard formed a subsidiary, the Chattanooga, Augusta & Charleston Air Line Ry. Co. It was announced in 1901 that a contract had been let for construction of the Charleston-Augusta segment, but no actual construction appears to have ever been undertaken.

Seaboard did eventually reach Charleston, albeit from the north, not the west, but the railroad never made it to Augusta or Chattanooga. It was proposed at one time or another for Seaboard to enter Augusta from three different directions: from the north by the old Raleigh & Augusta Air Line and from both the east and the west by the Chattanooga, Augusta & Charleston line. But although Seaboard eventually managed to reach almost every other place of consequence in Georgia, Augusta eluded its grasp. Ironically, the Augusta Union Station was built on land that had once been owned by Seaboard.

SAL was never very prosperous during the early 1900s and the company was placed in receivership on January 2, 1908. The railroad had reported modest net earnings in 1905 and 1906, but posted a loss in 1907. The receivership was attributed to a number of factors including competition with the Southern and the Atlantic Coast Line, low traffic density in the Southeast, inadequate and dilapidated equipment, a loss of investor confidence in Seaboard securities due to the Ryan-Williams feud, the drain on the road caused by the Birmingham extension, and the financial panic of October 1907. S. Davies Warfield and R.

Its tender heaped high with coal, L-4 class Ten-Wheeler 749 eases up to the turntable at Hamlet, N.C. In the background of this pre-World War I view, the roundhouse leads are crowded with aging road engines and at least one slope-tanked yard goat. North Carolina Division of Archives and History

Lancaster Williams, brother of John S., were appointed co-receivers. John Skelton Williams, long highly critical of SAL's management and who had predicted financial disaster, was almost elated by the receivership.

The receivership proved relatively brief, however. The railroad's finances were reorganized without the necessity for a foreclosure sale or the establishment of a new company. The railroad was discharged by the court and returned to its stockholders on November 11, 1909. The receivership was unusual in that the company's stock was not disturbed and its funded debt was actually increased, although its fixed charges were decreased by about nine percent. New mortgages were executed during the receivership and the proceeds used for much needed new equipment and other improvements, or "betterments" in railroad accounting jargon. Among these was the installation of an early telephone train-dispatching system between Raleigh and Monroe, N.C. Although the plan was criticized in some quarters for failure to reduce the company's capitalization thus leaving it in a weak condition, Seaboard's stock rose to new highs after the reorganization. Interestingly, John Skelton Williams and his ally, J. William Middendorf, were elected to the board of the reorganized company. M.S. Meldrum became its president.

In May 1908, during the course of the receivership, another Ryan-owned holding company, the Cumberland Corp., acquired control of The Seaboard Co. Thomas Ryan thus directed the railroad through a pyramid arrangement. He controlled the Cumberland Corp., which controlled The Seaboard Co., which in turn controlled the SAL Ry. The Cumberland Corp. also controlled the predecessors of the Clinchfield RR which were building a line from Spartanburg, S.C., northward to the coal fields of Tennessee and West Virginia. The new railroad connected with the Seaboard at Bostic, a point near Rutherfordton, N.C.

Thomas Fortune Ryan retired from business in December 1908. At that time, he resigned as director of 34 companies, one of which was, of course, the Seaboard Air Line. But the Cumberland Corp. and The Seaboard Co. remained in control of the railroad. Finally, in June 1912, a syndicate headed by S. Davies Warfield bought the Cumberland Corporation's shares in Seaboard. The Seaboard Co. was dissolved and T.F. Ryan's control of the railroad was ended. John S. Williams's tenure as a director was also terminated for the last time. Warfield became chairman of the board and William J. Harahan president of the railway company. Harahan resigned as vice president of the Erie RR in order to assume the

TOP:
Its smoke-box door ajar, 0-6-0 No. 1007 reposes at North Charleston, S.C., in May 1924. The begrimed F-3 class yard engine was built by Pittsburgh in 1900.

BOTTOM:
Charlotte Harbor & Northern's sole 4-4-0, No. 8, heads the line's daily passenger run at Arcadia, Fla., in September 1924. Built by Baldwin in 1913, the Eight-Wheeler became SAL 103. She was sold to Dowling-Camp Lumber Co. in 1933.
Both photos, Harold K. Vollrath collection

presidency of the Seaboard. One consequence of the change in ownership was that SAL's ties to the Clinchfield RR were dissolved.

Thomas Ryan lived in luxurious retirement until his death in 1928. John Williams soon entered government service. In March 1913, he was appointed Assistant Secretary of the Treasury by President Woodrow Wilson. He was named Comptroller of the Currency in January of the following year, a position he held until the end of the Wilson administration in 1921. As Comptroller he helped organize the Federal Reserve system and he was highly critical of the banking industry, attacking the concentration of banking control "in the hands of a dozen men." He advocated Federal insurance of bank deposits, a system not adopted until after the failure of numerous banks during the Depression of the thirties. While retaining the post as comptroller, he also served as director of finances and purchases for the U.S. Railway Administration when the federal government took over the railroads during World War I.

After leaving the government, Williams again resumed his banking career. He died suddenly in 1926 at the age of 61. At the time of his death, John Williams was chairman of the board of directors of the Richmond Trust Co., as well as receiver of the Georgia & Florida Ry. A somewhat old-fashioned Southern gentleman, Williams was categorized by a banking trade journal that had frequently opposed him in the government as "highly efficient but unnecessarily harsh."

In 1908 Seaboard began the development of a network of new lines in eastern South Carolina which culminated in the completion of an alternative route between Hamlet and Savannah, via Charleston. The railroad's management reasoned that the extensions would give Seaboard access to the seaports of Charleston and Georgetown, S.C., as well as considerable on-line business hauling cotton, tobacco and vegetables. Moreover, the proposed Hamlet-Savannah route would have much easier grades than the existing line via Columbia and would obviate the need to double-track the Columbia line.

To build the new Carolina lines, a group of supposedly independent railroads was formed, the first of which was the North & South Carolina Ry. Chartered in 1908, the new company promptly leased the Seaboard branch line from Hamlet to Gibson, N.C. It extended that line south from Gibson to Dillon, S.C., in 1909, reached Mullins the next year and the Peedee River, 78 miles from Hamlet, in 1911. The N&SC and another Seaboard affiliate, the Georgetown & Western RR, built a bridge across the Peedee, completing the structure on December 1, 1911.

The Georgetown & Western RR dated back to 1881 when its predecessor, the Georgetown & Lanes RR, was chartered. In 1882 and 1883 the G&L built a 5-foot-gauge line from the port town of Georgetown westward 36 miles, through Andrews, to a connection with the Northeastern RR of South Carolina (later Atlantic Coast Line) at Lane's Depot. The new line went into receivership in 1885 and was succeeded by the Georgetown & Western in 1887. The road converted to standard gauge the following year. The Atlantic Coast Lumber Co. acquired control of the G&W in about 1900, but the line again entered receivership in 1902, not emerging until 1912. Nonetheless, some 40 miles of logging spurs were constructed between 1901 and 1911. Chief among them was a line extending from Andrews northward for 28 miles. In 1911, that line was rebuilt to mainline standards under Seaboard supervision, and extended 5 miles farther north to a connection with the North & South Carolina Ry. at the Peedee River. Upon completion of the Peedee River bridge, the G&W was granted trackage rights over the N&SC for about 2 miles into the town of Gresham. The nature of the relationship between the G&W and the SAL during this period is not exactly clear. All of the little road's stock was owned by the Atlantic Coast Lumber Co. until 1915, but the G&W was obviously under Seaboard influence when the line to the Peedee was constructed. In any event, the Georgetown & Western's mainlines were sold to the Carolina, Atlantic & Western Ry., another SAL subsidiary, on May 1, 1915. The short line's logging spurs and equipment were retained by the parent lumber company.

The Carolina, Atlantic & Western had been formed in 1914 by the merger of four SAL subsidiaries which either were building or had already completed lines in South Carolina: the North & South Carolina Ry., the South Carolina Western Ry. Co., the South Carolina

TOP:
Ready for installation, bridge timbers and pilings lie in shallow water at the river's edge, while crews on the floating pile driver outfit continue work on the bridge over the Kissimmee River on December 16th, 1924. The entire line was completed only one month later. R&LHS collection; California State Railroad Museum

MIDDLE:
Hard at work on the day after Christmas, laborers lay track north of the Kissimmee River in 1924. R&LHS collection; California State Railroad Museum

BOTTOM:
Marking Seaboard's extension to the Florida Gold Coast, the President's Special arrives for the opening of the Miami Line. Richmond-built P-2 class Pacific 836 is emblazoned with the herald of the fabled Orange Blossom Special *and sports a rabbit, presumably for luck.* CSX Transportation collection

Western Extension Ry. and the Charleston Northern Ry. The South Carolina Western Ry. had been chartered in 1910 and completed a 38-mile line from McBee, S.C., on SAL's Hamlet-Columbia mainline, eastward to Florence in the following year. In 1912, the Western built branch lines from Hartsville to Sumpter and from Lydia to Timmonsville. The South Carolina Western Extension Ry. had been incorporated in 1913 and, at the time it was merged into the CA&W, was building a 32-mile extension of the South Carolina Western from Florence eastward to a connection with the Georgetown & Western's Andrews-Peedee River line at Poston, S.C. The Charleston Northern Ry. had also been incorporated in 1913 and was building a 57-mile line from Andrews south to Charleston when it was absorbed by the CA&W. The new CA&W completed the Florence-Poston line in 1914 and the Andrews-Charleston line in 1915.

After absorbing the Georgetown & Western in May, the Carolina, Atlantic & Western was itself merged with the SAL in November 1915. Actually, the Carolina line was used as a vehicle to rearrange the corporate structure of the Seaboard, and technically it was the surviving corporation. The CA&W was renamed Seaboard Air Line Railway Company and the old Seaboard Air Line Ry. was merged into the renamed firm. Seaboard thus acquired the official designation "Company" for the first time.

At the time of the merger, the CA&W operated some 328 miles of track, comprising the Hamlet-Charleston mainline, the Georgetown-Lanes line of the old G&W, the McBee-Poston line and the

Seaboard at Savannah in 1916. Proudly sporting an eagle atop her sand dome and with decorations adorning her headlight, well-polished class K 4-6-0 No. 38 simmers in the midday sun at Savannah Union Station. Gerald M. Best collection; California State Railroad Museum

Sumpter and Timmonsville branches. The line from Charleston to Savannah was under construction and, in addition, the CA&W owned all of the stock of the Charlotte, Monroe & Columbia RR, the short line from McBee to Jefferson, S.C.

The Charleston-Savannah line, 90 miles long, was placed in operation on December 31, 1917, and several spur tracks off the line were built the next year. A new bridge was built over the Savannah River, at Savannah, and construction of numerous fills was required over the low country of coastal South Carolina. The new route between Hamlet and Savannah was approximately 16 miles longer than the old route via Columbia, but it had considerably easier grades. A steam locomotive could handle about 127 percent more tonnage on the Charleston line than it could over the Columbia line. As a result, Seaboard began routing all of its through freight trains over the Charleston line. However, through passenger trains continued to operate via Columbia.

Seaboard also continued to expand in Florida during the years before World War I. A 10-mile branch of the Starke-Wannee line, from Buda to Norwills, was completed in 1909. The Archer-Early Bird branch was extended 32 miles from Early Bird south through Dunnellon and Hernando to Inverness in 1910 and 1911 and the Sarasota branch 16 miles from Fruitville south to Venice in 1912. The Plant City-Welcome line was slowly extended eastward: from Nichols to Mulberry, a distance of 3 miles in 1911; Mulberry to Bartow, 8 miles in 1913; Bartow to Lake Wales and Baynard, 19 miles in 1915; and from Baynard to Walinwa, 10 miles in 1916. The last 7 miles of the line, from Walinwa to Nalaca, were completed by the Kissimmee River Ry. in 1917. SAL also built a branch line from Bartow to Pembroke in 1914.

In 1912, the company purchased all of the stock of the Tampa Northern RR Co. The Tampa Northern operated a 49-mile line from Tampa northward to Brooksville, Fla., plus a 14-mile-long branch line from Tooke Lake Jct. to Tooke Lake. The TN had been incorporated in 1906, as a subsidiary of the Atlanta, Birmingham & Atlantic RR, to build a line from Tampa to Thomasville, Ga., where it was to connect with the AB&A to form a through line from Atlanta to Tampa. The AB&A was controlled by H.M. Atkinson, an Atlanta financier who was instrumental in the firm that was ultimately to become the Georgia Power Co. By October 1907, the TN had completed 30 miles of line from Tampa to Fivay Jct. It then purchased a logging line from the Aripeka Saw Mill Co. which extended from Fivay Jct. to Brooksville. TN reconstructed about 9 miles of the logging line, from Fivay Jct. to Enville Jct., and abandoned the remainder, building a new 10-mile line from Enville Jct. to Brooksville. The entire line from Fivay to Brooksville was opened on January 1, 1908.

Unfortunately, H.M. Atkinson's railroad empire proved to be a financial failure and the AB&A was forced into receivership in 1909. It was eventually reorganized as the Atlanta, Birmingham & Coast RR and ultimately absorbed by the Atlantic Coast Line after World War II. As a result of AB&A's collapse, the TN never got any farther north than Brooksville, although it did purchase the Aripeka Saw Mill Co.'s line from Tooke Lake Jct. to Tooke Lake in 1911.

SAL operated the Tampa Northern as a separate subsidiary for several years. In 1925, Seaboard leased the Tampa Northern and extended SAL's Archer-Inverness branch southward to connect with the TN line at Brooksville. The result was the creation of an alternative route between Waldo and Tampa, via Gainesville, Archer and Brooksville.

In 1913, Seaboard organized the East & West Coast Ry. to build a line from Manatee, Fla., on the Plant City-Venice branch, eastward to Arcadia, Fla. Construction of the 48-mile line commenced that year and was completed in 1915. The E&WC was operated as a separate subsidiary, using Seaboard rolling stock until 1925 when it was leased by SAL. Seaboard had little need for the line after 1928 when it acquired the Charlotte Harbor & Northern Ry., which also served Arcadia. As a result, the E&WC line was abandoned during the Depression.

A more important acquisition in 1913 was the Tampa & Gulf Coast Ry., which Seaboard used to build a line from Tampa to St. Petersburg, Fla. The T&GC Ry. was established in 1909 and purchased a 10-mile logging line from the Gulf Pine Co. extending from Lutz, Fla., a point on the Tampa Northern RR 15 miles north of Tampa, westward through Lake Fern to Gulf Pine. In 1909 and 1910, the T&GC extended the line 11 miles westward to Tarpon Springs and in 1912 it purchased a 7-mile-long lumber line from J.M. Weeks & Co. extending from Lake Villa to Port Richey. The next year the T&GC lines west of Lake Fern were sold to a new Seaboard subsidiary, the Tampa & Gulf Coast RR Co. The portion of the line from Lutz to Lake Fern was not acquired. In June 1913, the new Seaboard subsidiary began constructing a 47-mile line to St. Petersburg from a connection with the Tampa Northern at Gulf Coast Jct., 7 miles north of Tampa, plus an 8-mile connecting line from the Tampa-St. Petersburg line at Tarpon Springs Jct. to the original T&GC line at Lake Fern. Both lines were completed in 1914, and the road also built a 3-mile branch line from Indian Rocks Jct. to Indian Rocks Beach, which was finished in 1915. The T&GC, of course, operated into Tampa over the Tampa Northern. When completed, the Tampa & Gulf Coast RR had a main line from Tampa to St. Petersburg plus branch lines to Tarpon Springs, Elfers (Port Richey) and Indian Rocks Beach. Styled as the Orange Belt Route, the T&GC, like the Tampa Northern and the East & West Coast, was operated as a separate Seaboard subsidiary for several years. It was finally leased by the Seaboard in 1927.

SAL did dispose of one small Florida branch line before World War I. In 1915, it leased the Silver Springs branch to the Ocklawaha Valley RR, an independent short line that was building a line from Palatka to Ocala, Fla.

Seaboard added another short line subsidiary in 1916 when it organized the Florida Central & Gulf Ry. to acquire the Standard & Hernando RR Co. The S&H extended 28 miles from Hernando to Port Inglis, Fla., and connected with the SAL at Dunnellon. The FC&G functioned as a separate Seaboard subsidiary until it was abandoned in 1930.

America entered World War I in April 1917. The national railroad system soon became snarled by the demands of wartime traffic. Railroad employees rushed off to join the military, and yards and ports on the East Coast were choked by traffic awaiting shipment to the battlefields of Europe. Freight cars ended up sitting on sidings for weeks, serving as *de facto* warehouses. In an effort to remedy the chaos the Federal Government took over the railroads, Seaboard included, on December 26, 1917, forming the United States Railroad Administration for the purpose of operating the lines. Since it was owned by the Seaboard, even the

Seaboard began buying gas-electric motor cars for branch-line passenger service in 1917. One of the road's first two "doodlebugs," GE-Wason car 2001, pauses at Archer, Fla., about 1920. H.J. Doherty collection

Old Bay Line was commandeered by the USRA. In theory the government rented the railroads for the war's duration. The conflict ended on November 11, 1918, and the railroads were returned to private operation on March 1, 1920.

S. Davies Warfield was elected president of the Seaboard in July 1918, but he was, of course, prevented from actually exercising authority over the road until the USRA relinquished its dominion in 1920. Solomon Davies Warfield was a man of varied interests. Born in 1859 of an old Maryland family, his father was prominent in Baltimore business and political affairs. After completing his education, young Davies served a clerkship with two Baltimore investment firms. While recuperating from a bout of illness at his grandmother's country home, he invented a number of agricultural gadgets, including corn cutters and corn silkers, and he established a firm for their manufacture.

A Democrat, he became active in politics and was narrowly defeated when he ran for mayor of Baltimore in 1891. In 1894, he was appointed postmaster of the city, a position he held until 1905. In 1898, while still postmaster, he organized the Continental Trust Co., the instrument of most of his later financial dealings. He had been associated with John S. Williams in the consolidation of the Seaboard and he had served variously as a trustee, director, receiver and chairman of the board of the company. He was also heavily involved with cotton mills and public utilities in his native state. In 1910, he retired as chairman of the Consolidated Gas, Electric Light & Power Co. in order to devote more of his time to the Seaboard. A man of sterling character, he had great nervous energy and drove both himself and his associates. He was described as dominating and self-centered, but not lacking in social charm.

Warfield was president of the National Association of Owners of Railroad Securities, a group which he organized during the war, and he was highly critical of the federal government's operation of the Seaboard. Among other things he contended that while only about 7 percent of the rolling stock SAL had turned over to the USRA was "bad order," i.e., in need of repair, 40 percent of the equipment the railroad received back from the government was in that unsatisfactory condition.

Seaboard was undoubtedly in bad shape at the end of the war. The railroad had been under-maintained during the conflict, the company had bought no new freight or passenger cars since 1914 and some 5,000 of its freight cars were indeed bad order. To rehabilitate the line the company borrowed almost $20 million from the U.S. government between 1920 and 1923. Moreover, Warfield vigorously pressed Seaboard's case for compensation for the period of federal operation, finally obtaining a fee of $7,800,000 per annum from the USRA interim, versus $6,500,000 the government had originally offered.

S. Davies Warfield believed strongly in the future of the South, especially Florida, and he proposed an enormous expansion program which would enlarge Seaboard from 3,500 to more than 5,000 miles of line. Not all of his plans were realized. Among others, he proposed to build a line from Atlanta to Jacksonville, via Macon, which was never constructed. But SAL did acquire two important small railroads, the Charlotte Harbor & Northern and the Georgia, Florida & Alabama, and the railroad built 451 miles of new line during the twenties, all of which were in Florida.

Seaboard leased the Charlotte Harbor & Northern Ry. in early 1925. Known as the Boca Grande Route, or irreverently as the "Cold, Hungry & Naked," the CH&N was an important phosphate road extending 97 miles from the Bone Valley beds at Mulberry, Fla., down to the port of South Boca Grande on Gasparilla Island. A subsidiary of the American Agricultural Chemical Co., which had built the road, the CH&N connected with SAL at Bradley Jct. and with the East & West Coast Ry. at Arcadia. The line was originally chartered in 1897 as the Alafia, Manatee & Gulf Coast RR Co. to build a road from Plant City to Charlotte Harbor but its name was changed to Charlotte Harbor & Northern when construction finally commenced in 1906. The portion of the line from Boca Grande north to Arcadia was completed in 1907, and the section from Arcadia to Bradley Jct. was built in 1909 and 1910. The road was extended farther north to South Mulberry in 1911. In addition, the CH&N built a nine-mile branch line from Cottman to Tiger Bay in 1911, and a four-mile branch from Achan to Ridgewood in 1913. The Tiger Bay branch was abandoned in 1922. There were some 90 trestles on the CH&N, totaling over three miles of track. The most important bridges were over the Myakka River and Gasparilla Pass.

The Charlotte Harbor & Northern operated extensive port facilities at South Boca Grande for the loading of lumber and phosphate. The phosphate terminal was to be used by the Seaboard for many years to come. In addition, a subsidiary of the little road operated a creosoting plant at Hull, Fla., which was inherited by SAL. Prior to the Seaboard lease, CH&N operated a through Pullman sleeping car from Boca Grande to Jacksonville which was handled by the Atlantic Coast Line north of Mulberry. Afterward, CH&N passenger service was switched to a connection with SAL via Bradley Jct. and Plant City. The original SAL lease had been for only three years. When it expired, Seaboard bought all of the Boca Grande Line's capital stock and extended the lease for 999 years. The little road was eventually merged into Seaboard in 1946. The CH&N owned ten locomotives when SAL first leased the line: eight 2-8-0's, one 4-6-0, and a single 4-4-0.

The biggest and most important new construction project was the extension to Miami. It was one of the last major railroad lines to be built in the United States. The new line extended from Coleman, a point near Wildwood, in a southeasterly direction across the Plant City-Nalaca branch at West Lake Wales, to West Palm Beach. At West Palm Beach the line turned almost due south following the coast line to Miami. A branch line extended from Hialeah farther south to Homestead, Fla., the southernmost point ever reached by Seaboard.

To build the Coleman-West Palm Beach segment, Seaboard formed a subsidiary, the Florida Western & Northern RR Co. Construction began in 1924. Hundreds of workmen and the latest equipment were used on the project. Roadbed gangs each averaged building a mile of roadbed a week and one track-laying gang put down 8,317 feet of track in one day. The 204-mile line to West Palm Beach was completed in a mere nine months, on January 21, 1925, a considerable engineering feat at the time. A few days later, four special trains from New York arrived in West Palm Beach with 500 guests of the railroad who had been invited to participate in the celebrations marking the completion of the new line. Shortly afterward, Seaboard inaugurated the posh *Orange Blossom Special* on the New York-West Palm Beach run.

The line south of West Palm Beach was built by another SAL subsidiary, the Seaboard-All Florida Ry. Construction of the 66-mile West Palm Beach-Miami line began in February 1926 and was completed on December 19th. Operation commenced on January 8, 1927. The West Palm Beach-Miami line ran parallel to the Florida East Coast Ry. and generally lay about two miles west of the existing line. Seaboard built a yard at Hialeah, just outside Miami, and finished the 28-mile branch to Homestead later in 1927.

Seaboard's Miami extension introduced the first rail competition to Florida's Gold Coast. Prior to the arrival of the Seaboard, the entire Atlantic coast of Florida south of Jacksonville had been the exclusive domain of the Florida East Coast Ry. Henry Flagler's pioneer FEC had opened South Florida to development, reaching the then minuscule village of Miami in 1896. Since the FEC didn't reach the Gulf Coast and the Atlantic Coast line never extended to Miami, Seaboard made much ado over the fact that it was the only railroad serving both coasts of South Florida.

In addition to the West Palm Beach line, the Florida Western & Northern constructed two other small but important lines elsewhere in Florida, both of which were built in 1925. The Valrico Cut-off extended from Valrico, a point near Tampa, 12 miles east to a connection with the Plant City-Nalaca line at Welcome Jct. Its construction not only resulted in a shorter route between Tampa and the phosphate beds around Mulberry and Bartow, but also created a reasonably direct rail route between Tampa and Miami. In addition, it reduced the mileage between Tampa and Sarasota and Venice.

Perhaps even more important was the 13-mile-long Gross Cut-off. It extended from Gross, a point in extreme North Florida on the Savannah-Jacksonville mainline, southwest to Callahan, a town on the original Florida RR line between Fernandina and Cedar Key. It shortened the mileage between Savannah and Baldwin, Fla., and enabled Seaboard to bypass the congested Jacksonville gateway. As the rival Florida East Coast and Atlantic Coast Line were compelled to interchange traffic at Jacksonville, Seaboard was able to beat their best time on perishable traffic moving from the Miami area to Potomac Yard at Washington.

SAL also extended its lines down the West Coast of Florida in 1926 and 1927, building a 69-mile line from Hull, on the Charlotte Harbor & Northern, south through Fort Myers to Naples. Service to Fort Myers was inaugurated on January 7, 1927, with the first trains bringing Florida Governor John Martin and President Warfield as well as some 600 guests of the railroad. In addition to the mainline, two branch lines were constructed, a 31-mile branch from Fort Myers east to LaBelle and a 9-mile line from Punta Rassa Jct. to Punta Rassa, where Seaboard planned to develop an extensive deep-water port. The portion of the new lines north of the Estero River was built by the Seaboard All-Florida Ry.; the 21-mile segment from the Estero to Naples was constructed by another SAL subsidiary, the Naples, Seaboard & Gulf Ry.

Farther north, the 19-mile gap between Brooksville and Inverness, Fla., was closed in 1926 when the Brooksville & Inverness Ry. was completed. None of the companies that built the various Florida extensions in the twenties appear to have ever existed as actual operating railroads. All were leased by Seaboard as their lines were completed.

The biggest "foreign" railroad acquired by Seaboard during the 1920s was the Georgia, Florida & Alabama Ry. Seaboard leased the GF&A for 99 years, effective January 1, 1928. The mainline of the GF&A extended 183 miles from Richland, Ga., south through Tallahassee, to the Gulf Coast at Carrabelle, Fla. The road's importance to the SAL was mainly that it served to bridge the gap between Seaboard's Jacksonville-River Jct. line at Tallahassee and its Savannah-Montgomery and Columbus-Albany lines at Richland. Acquisition of the GF&A gave Seaboard a reasonably direct route between Florida points and the important gateways of Columbus, Ga., and Montgomery, Ala. At those two cities connections could be effected with other railroads, most notably the Central of Georgia at Columbus, and the Louisville & Nashville and the Mobile & Ohio at Montgomery, for the movement of traffic to and from the West and Midwest.

In 1895, the Georgia, Florida & Alabama had been organized as the Georgia Pine Ry. Co. The Georgia Pine Ry. had completed 40 miles of line from Bainbridge, Ga., north to Arlington, Ga., by 1898, and it changed its name to Georgia, Florida & Alabama Ry. in 1901. During the following year the line was extended south 40 miles from Bainbridge to Tallahassee and north 26 miles from Arlington to Cuthbert, Ga. In 1906 the GF&A built an 11-mile branch from Havana to Quincy, Fla., and it absorbed the Carrabelle, Tallahassee & Georgia RR which owned a line extending from Tallahassee to Carrabelle. It was eventually proposed to extend the GF&A north to Columbus and, as a result, 27 miles of line were added from Cuthbert north to Richland in 1910. But Seaboard already had a line from Richland to Columbus and Richland was to remain the northern terminus of the GF&A.

The Carrabelle, Tallahassee & Georgia RR actually antedated the GF&A. It was begun in 1888 when the Augusta, Tallahassee and Gulf RR Co. built a 12-mile line from Carrabelle north to the Ocklocknee River. The AT&G was succeeded by the CT&G RR in 1891 and it extended the line to Tallahassee in 1893, giving the line a total length of 50 miles. For many years the CT&G and, later, the GF&A operated the steamboat *Crescent City* in a connecting service between Carrabelle and Apalachicola, Fla. The GF&A discontinued the steamboat service in 1923, but the vessel was sold to the Wing Boat Line which continued its operation for several more years. At one time it had been proposed to extend the CT&G farther north from Tallahassee to Thomasville, Ga., a project that also had been considered years earlier by the owners of the pioneer Tallahassee RR. But nothing ever came of the idea and no railroad ever was built between Tallahassee and Thomasville.

The GF&A's general office and shops were located at Bainbridge and the road's most impressive structure was a long drawbridge over the Flint River at that point. Load restrictions on the bridge would later limit the types of locomotives Seaboard could run over the GF&A line. During the twenties, the GF&A's daily local passenger train carried a Pullman on a leisurely schedule between Atlanta and Tallahassee. The sleeper was handled by the Central of Georgia north of Cuthbert. At the time it was leased by Seaboard, the GF&A owned twenty-two steam locomotives: eight 2-10-0 Decapods; five 2-8-0 Consolidations, five 4-6-0 Ten-Wheelers, three 4-4-0's and a single 0-6-0 switch engine.

Seaboard also acquired control of two smaller Florida short lines, which continued to be operated as separate companies. It bought the Tavares & Gulf RR in 1926. The short line connected with SAL's Orlando branch at Tavares and extended from that point to Winter Garden and Ocoee, with a branch to Clermont. The big road acquired control of the Tampa & Jacksonville Ry. in the following year. The T&J extended from Sampson City to Emathla, crossing the Seaboard at Gainesville. Seaboard formed a new subsidiary, the Jacksonville, Gainesville & Gulf Ry., to operate the Sampson City-Emathla line.

In addition to building new lines, Seaboard made a number of other major capital improvements during the 1920s. Heavier rail and rock ballast were laid on the mainline. Automatic block signals were installed between Richmond, Hamlet and Monroe, N.C., and between Savannah and Jacksonville. The line was double tracked between Baldwin and Starke, Fla., and block signals were also installed between Starke and Wildwood. And the company moved most of its general offices from Portsmouth to a new building in Norfolk.

The railroad's president, S. Davies Warfield, died October 24, 1927, leaving a fortune estimated to be worth $5,500,000. Unmarried, he directed that the bulk of his estate be used to establish a home for elderly women. A man of numerous achievements, the Old Bay Line named a new steamboat in his honor. But his renown was to be vastly overshadowed by that of his niece, the twice-divorced Wallace Warfield Simpson. She set the British Empire on its ear in 1936 when Edward VIII renounced the throne in order to obtain her hand in marriage.

Warfield was succeeded as president by 43-year-old Legh R. Powell, Jr., a Seaboard employee since 1902 when he had begun working in the controller's office in Portsmouth.

The new chairman of the board was Robert L. Nutt, former vice president of the company, who had been with the railroad for 35 years. Both praised Warfield and pledged to continue his policies.

Powell and Nutt had their work cut out for them. By the end of the twenties Seaboard was in trouble. The railroad was overextended. It had incurred high fixed charges in order to finance its recent expansion and its revenues were declining precipitously. Railway operating revenues fell from a peak of $67,025,000 in 1926, to $61,790,000 in 1927 and $57,245,000 in 1928.

Much of the problem was attributable to the fact that Seaboard's new lines had been built at the height of the Florida real estate boom, a period of frenzied speculation when parcels of choice—and sometimes not so choice—swamp land changed hands, sight unseen, several times a day. Like all such speculative binges, it was fueled by the "greater fool theory"—the sucker's notion that an even greater fool would come along to pay an even greater price for his newly acquired stock or bonds or tulip bulbs or Florida mud flat. Of course the supply of greater fools soon ran out and the boom collapsed. In Florida's case, the bubble burst in the fall of 1926, with a little help from a hurricane that reminded potential real estate tycoons that some of Florida was more suitable for bass than bungalows. The boom's impact on Seaboard had been twofold: high prices during the boom had added to the costs of the railroad's new construction, and the real estate market collapse took Seaboard's revenues with it.

Indicative of the railroad's situation was a decision the Interstate Commerce Commission rendered in May 1928. Seaboard was attempting to acquire yet another short line, the South Georgia Ry. It was an 83-mile-long line, of little import, which stretched from Adel, Ga., to Perry and Hampton Springs, Fla., and crossed Seaboard's Jacksonville-Tallahassee line at Greenville, Fla. Seaboard was probably eying the SG as a link in a possible line from Atlanta to Tampa. However, the ICC denied SAL's application to acquire the little line on the reasonable grounds that Seaboard couldn't afford it.

Seaboard's management tried hard to save the day. In an effort to increase passenger business, the company dabbled in other forms of transportation. In 1928 it launched a highway subsidiary, the Motor Transportation Co. of the South, providing bus service between Jacksonville and Tallahassee and in the area around Tampa, which was coordinated with train schedules. In 1930, it inaugurated a short-lived rail-air service between New York and Latin America. Seaboard's aviation partner was the New York, Rio and Buenos Aires Line, a pioneer airline that was soon absorbed by Pan American. Passengers rode Seaboard trains from New York to Miami and NYR&BA "air yachts," i.e., flying boats, from Miami to Havana or South America. Service was provided weekly to Buenos Aires and three times a week to Havana. Elapsed time between New York and Havana was 39 hours and 24 minutes. The flying boats were advertised as "capable of landing upon and riding any Sea, insuring perfect safety"—a highly questionable claim to anyone familiar with either aviation or the sea.

More importantly, the railroad's finances were restructured and additional capital was raised. The company floated a new stock issue in early 1930, receiving over $20 million in cash. But it wasn't enough. The stock market had crashed on October 29, 1929, marking the onset of the Great Depression of the 1930s. Highway and water competition intensified and railway operating revenues fell even further, from $58,000,000 in 1929 to $49,600,000 in 1930. It became clear that the railroad was going to fall far short of earning its fixed charges in 1930. Finally, on December 23, 1930, pursuant to a suit filed by a creditor, the Bethlehem Steel Co., Seaboard was forced into receivership. It was the first major railroad to go bankrupt during the Depression. The heady expansion of the Roaring Twenties was over.

CHAPTER FIVE

RECEIVERSHIP AND RESURRECTION 1930–1967

Seaboard's bankruptcy petition was filed in the United States District Court for the Eastern District of Virginia at Norfolk. As co-receivers, the court appointed the road's president, Legh R. Powell, Jr., and a vice president of the Pennsylvania RR, Ethelbert W. Smith. It was to be a long receivership. The Depression, the most dismal era in America's economic history, was to last throughout most of the thirties and Seaboard would remain in bankruptcy for over 15 years, until after the end of World War II.

Seaboard may have been the first railroad to go bankrupt during the Depression, but it was hardly the last. Before the Depression had run its course, almost one-third of the railroad mileage in the country would be in the hands of receivers. Casualties of the hard times included such major lines as the Missouri Pacific, Frisco, Chicago & Northwestern, Rock Island and New Haven. In the Southeast, Seaboard was joined in bankruptcy by the Central of Georgia, Florida East Coast and the Norfolk Southern (the original Norfolk Southern, stretching between Norfolk and Charlotte, not the current industry giant of the same name). Significantly, Seaboard's main rivals, the Southern and the Atlantic Coast Line, both managed to survive the Depression without resorting to the bankruptcy courts.

At the end of 1929, Seaboard stood at a peak of 4,490 miles of line. One more branch was added in 1930, a 15-mile line constructed from Bellwood, Va., near Richmond, to the industrial town of Hopewell, Va. As with most SAL extensions, the new line was built by a subsidiary, in this instance the Prince George & Chesterfield Ry., and then leased to the parent company. Except for a few spur tracks, the Hopewell branch was to be the last Seaboard line ever constructed.

But the Depression was a period of retrenchment, and some 200 miles of branch line were abandoned in the early 1930s. The Tooke Lake branch in Florida was abandoned in 1930. Fifteen miles of line from Hesperides to Nalaca, Fla., were also trimmed off in 1930, and the Loganville branch, in Georgia, was another early victim of the Depression. The line between Andrews and Lanes, S.C., formerly a part of the Georgetown & Western RR, was abandoned in 1932. The line between Tallahassee and Waylonzo, Fla. was scrapped in 1933, as were the last 5 miles of the Wannee branch, between Bell and Wannee, Fla. The Manatee-Arcadia, Fla., line, which had been built by the East & West Coast Ry., was torn up in 1934. The most historic line to be abandoned was the western end of the old Florida RR from Archer to Cedar Key, a distance of 45 miles, ripped up in 1932.

Several Seaboard subsidiaries also sustained abandonments in the early thirties. The Florida, Central & Gulf was abandoned in its entirety in 1930, as was the Savannah & Statesboro in 1933. A portion of the Jacksonville, Gainesville & Gulf was scrapped in 1930, and a segment of the Raleigh & Charleston in 1933. The remainder of both roads would finally be abandoned a few years later.

Seaboard even filed for permission to abandon the newly acquired Georgia, Florida & Alabama RR in

New pulp mills contributed to the railroad's revival in the late thirties and remained a staple of local traffic for years to come. Headed by a former GF&A 2-8-0, SAL Extra 922 West, a westbound Alabama Division local freight has two loaded wood racks on the head end as it gets under way out of Pitts, Ga., at 3:30 P.M. on December 27, 1947.
David W. Salter

TOP:
The newsreel cameras are rolling and photographers are lined up to shoot the newest thing on rails as brand-new E4A 3006 arrives in Hollywood, Fla., with what is believed to be the inaugural run of the streamlined Silver Meteor. *Introduced as a seven-car all-coach speedster, the New York-Miami streamliner began operation in February 1939.* H.J. Doherty collection

BOTTOM LEFT:
Seaboard's last new steam locomotives were ten 2-6-6-4's purchased from Baldwin in 1935 and 1937. Still new, an R-2 class Twin Pacific gets a freight under way at an unknown location, circa 1938. M.B. Cooke; David W. Salter collection

BOTTOM RIGHT:
Trailing an 11-car heavyweight consist, Seaboard class M 4-8-2 No. 206 storms out of Atlanta, Ga., with No. 6, the Robert E. Lee, *in 1939. The Richmond-built Mountain, one of ten delivered to SAL in 1914, will serve its employer for another decade before being bumped by diesels.* Railway Negative Exchange

1933. But the application was really just a negotiating ploy to obtain more favorable terms on its lease of the GF&A. Unamused, the Interstate Commerce Commission denied the application. It was just as well; the line between Tallahassee and Richland eventually became a very important link in Seaboard's freight operations.

E.W. Smith served as a co-receiver for only two years. He was replaced on January 1, 1933, by Col. Henry W. Anderson. Anderson was a Richmond lawyer who had long been involved with various railroads and had previously served as counsel to SAL's receivers. During World War I, he had been president of the Virginia War Relief Association, Virginia director of the American Red Cross, and chairman of the Roumanian Commission for the American Red Cross. He had been decorated by several foreign governments for his relief work in the Balkans.

Seaboard's and the nation's fortunes reached their nadir in 1932, the depths of the Depression. The railroad's freight tonnage had fallen from a high of 20,966,030 tons in 1926 to a low of 8,772,640 tons in 1932, and gross revenues had shrunk from $58,151,908 in 1929 to $30,740,335 in 1932. The next year was only barely better than 1932. The company then slowly started to recover but the railroad did not finally return to profitability until 1941.

One factor which contributed to Seaboard's recovery was the development of the pulp and paper industry in the Southeast. During the late 1930s several big pulp mills were built in Seaboard territory. The mills consumed prodigious quantities of pulpwood and shipped vast amounts of pulp and paperboard, most of it by rail. The arrival of the plants resurrected moribund little fishing villages: Georgetown, S.C., Fernandina, Fla., and St. Marys, Ga. (The last named was served solely by the the St. Marys RR, a short line whose only outlet to the world was via a connection with Seaboard at Kingsland, Ga. Before the mill arrived, it was joked that St. Marys' populace ate so much sea food that their stomachs rose and fell with the tide.) Bigger towns as well, such as Savannah and Jacksonville, also received an economic shot in the arm from new pulp mills. The mills may have belched sulfurous fumes and they didn't do the local water quality a lot of good, but they meant jobs for their communities and traffic for the Seaboard.

Despite tight finances, Seaboard launched a series of capital improvements during the thirties, adding air conditioning to existing passenger cars and ordering new streamlined passenger equipment and diesels for its premier passenger trains. Pullman delivered the first of ten lightweight streamlined cars to the railroad in late 1936. Featuring air conditioning and reclining seats, the six coaches and four combines offered new comfort to passengers on the *Orange Blossom Special*, but Seaboard had even bigger things in store for its New York-Florida flagship.

In October and November 1938, Seaboard received nine Electro-Motive E4's, the first "production" 567-engined locomotives built. Delivered in three A-B-A sets and assigned to the *Orange Blossom Special*, the slant-nosed, twin-engined carbody units debuted the strikingly handsome green, orange and yellow "citrus" scheme that would be worn by Seaboard passenger units for nearly two decades.

Several months later, a seventh E4A arrived on the property, and on February 3, 1939, SAL 3006 departed Miami with a seven-car train of brand-new, stainless-steel Budd passenger cars, inaugurating Seaboard's newest Florida-New York name train, the *Silver Meteor*. Boasting a smartly appointed chair-tavern car, a 48-seat diner and punctuated by a round-end chair-observation car, the all-coach, all-stainless steel *Meteor* was "America's newest and smartest coach train...on the FASTEST schedules ever offered coach passengers between Eastern cities and Florida." "Seaboard," noted Col. Anderson, "was too poor to have anything but the best."

The dieselization of the *Orange Blossom Special* and the advent of the *Silver Meteor* not only ushered Seaboard passengers into a new age, it marked the end of an era for the railroad itself. After delivery of the E4's, SAL never bought another new steam locomotive. The road's first diesel switcher, EMC SW1 1200, arrived in March 1939, followed by E4A's 3007-3013 and E4B's 3103-3104 in October and November.

Prior to delivery to the Seaboard, the final unit of the order, E4A 3014, was exhibited at the 1939 New York World's Fair as General Motors 1939. Following its display, the unit

TOP:
Standing on the cab steps, the brakeman aboard Q-3 Mike 358 pulls orders from the hoop as the pump-faced Baldwin slams past the depot at Emory, Ga., with a northbound freight in 1940. Hugh M. Comer

BOTTOM:
Swollen to 14 cars by wartime traffic, No. 192, the northbound Palmland, *pauses at Columbia, S.C., in June 1942. In charge of the heavy New York-bound name train is M-2 class Mountain 244, one of 36 Baldwin-built 4-8-2's purchased by Seaboard during the mid-twenties Florida boom. Like many of her class, the 244 has been improved with the addition of a feedwater heater, automatic stoker and high-capacity 12-wheel tender.* George E. Votava

was returned to La Grange, reconditioned, upgraded and outshopped as SAL 3014. Mechanical refinements applied during this procedure warranted a new model description and SAL 3014 was delivered to the railroad in January 1940 as the first E6.

World War II turned Seaboard's fortunes around. The war began in Europe in September 1939, but of course the United States did not get directly involved until the Japanese bombed Pearl Harbor on December 7, 1941. Even before America was attacked, the war spurred the U.S. economy. Seaboard freight tonnage increased from 15.6 million tons in 1939, to 19 million in 1940, to 24.6 million in 1941, the highest up to that time in the company's history and the first occasion it had exceeded the previous highs of 1926 and 1927. Business really boomed once the U.S. was at war. American industry cranked up to full throttle. New shipyards and war plants were constructed in the South, and military bases proliferated in Seaboard's territory. Competition from coastal shipping virtually disappeared as the vessels were either sunk by Hitler's U-boats or reassigned to transporting troops and supplies to the war zones. Highway traffic was stringently curtailed. As a result, SAL freight traffic doubled from 1939 to 1943, reaching a peak of over 33 million tons in the latter year. The surge in passenger traffic was even more spectacular, patronage increasing fourfold during the conflict.

To cope with burgeoning wartime traffic, Seaboard purchased new locomotives, acquiring 44 FT's (22 A-B sets), 19 diesel switchers (8 Baldwins, 7 EMD's and 4 Alcos) and 4 E-units during the war. The railroad was sold on the superiority of diesels over steam, but restrictions imposed by the War Production Board limited the builders' production and put new diesel

Mikes, five rather decrepit Elgin, Joliet & Eastern 0-8-0's and five hand-me-down Consolidations. Still desperate for power, the railroad leased a group of Chicago & North Western class J Mikados, as well as additional steam locomotives from the Norfolk & Western.

Another important innovation which helped Seaboard sustain the wartime demand was Centralized Traffic Control. CTC is a system whereby a dispatcher can command a section of railroad by remote control. Sitting at a control board, he can monitor and direct the progress of trains hundreds of miles away, remotely operating the switches and signals on his portion of track. The system transforms a railroad into something akin to a giant model-train layout. With the flick of a few levers, the dispatcher can direct a train into a siding or command it to stop, start or maintain its progress. Train orders are virtually eliminated and it is no longer necessary to stop for a crewman to throw a switch leading a train into a passing track. The system vastly increases the capacity of a rail line. A single-track line equipped with CTC and sufficient passing tracks can handle almost as many trains as a double-track railroad equipped with conventional block signals.

The first CTC installation on the Seaboard, 64 miles from Richmond to Cochran (Alberta), Va., was completed in December 1941, just in time for the war. It was the first CTC installation in the Southeast. The system was subsequently extended southward to

TOP LEFT:
Seaboard's first diesel freight locomotives were 6 semi-permanently coupled A-B sets of FT's delivered from Electro-Motive in June 1942. Before the end of World War II, SAL purchased a total of 22 two-unit, drawbar-connected FT sets. Already six years old, class engines 4000 and 4100 lead an eastbound freight out of Atlanta, approaching Emory University, in July 1948. David W. Salter

TOP RIGHT:
Leaning from the cab of their Q-3 Mike, the crew of SAL Extra 370 South exchange greetings with a trainman on the caboose of a northbound at Brown Street Yard in Richmond, Va., on June 15, 1945. CSX Transportation collection

MIDDLE LEFT:
In 1947, Seaboard re-equipped the Silver Meteor *with new Budd-built stainless-steel equipment, but matching streamlined Pullmans were not immediately available. Prior to the introduction of stainless-steel sleepers on the* Meteor, *E7's 3023 and 3026 approach Opa-locka, Fla., with northbound No. 58 on September 15, 1947. Along with seven new Budd-built cars, No. 58's 11-car consist includes three heavyweight Pullman sleepers and a single Budd coach from the original 1939* Silver Meteor *equipment.* David W. Salter

MIDDLE RIGHT:
Seaboard E7's 3035 and 3040 kick up the dust as they pass 41st Street in Birmingham, Ala., with No. 33, the Silver Comet, *on May 23, 1948. The crack streamliner debuted on its New York-Birmingham run on May 18, 1947, but with delivery of stainless-steel sleepers still more than a year away, No. 33's consist includes three heavyweight Pullmans.* Frank E. Ardrey, Jr.

BOTTOM LEFT:
Substituting for regularly assigned EMC-St. Louis power car 2027, SAL P-4 Pacific 878, an RPO, baggage car and coach cross a wooden trestle just east of Seville, Ga., in September 1950. Formerly Western Maryland 151, the 878 was one of ten WM Pacifics purchased by SAL in 1943, and one of the last steam locomotives to operate on the Richland-Vidalia section of the Alabama Division. David W. Salter

BOTTOM RIGHT:
Her once-proud dress of olive drab, yellow and orange is faded and dirty, and E7A 3029 is far from the glamor of her normal Silver Fleet duties as she brings No. 26 into Savannah, Ga., on July 4, 1948. Nicknamed the "Boll Weevil," and usually operated with a gas-electric motor-car train, Nos. 25 and 26 provided the only passenger service over the East Carolina line between Hamlet, Charleston and Savannah. Not surprisingly, the "Boll Weevil" was one of many local passenger trains abolished in the 1950s. R.D. Sharpless; F.E. Ardrey, Jr., collection

---

Raleigh. The CTC enabled the Richmond-Raleigh mainline to handle as many as 50 trains a day during the war years. Another section of Centralized Traffic Control was placed in operation between Savannah and Thalmann, Ga., in 1943. It was estimated that the CTC saved the average freight train one hour on the 65-mile run between those points.

Seaboard could have used a lot more CTC for reasons of safety as well as efficiency. Almost all of the railroad was single track and several important lines were devoid of block signals. As a result, some serious accidents occurred during the forties. Two passenger trains, the southbound *Orange Blossom Special* and the northbound *Sun Queen*, collided at Hypoluxo, Fla., on February 19, 1942. On May 6 of the same year, two freights collided head-on near Roanoke Rapids, N.C., causing an estimated $750,000 damage. It was the worst accident on the Portsmouth line since 1837.

Wartime prosperity notwithstanding, several more branch lines were abandoned during the early forties. The line between Coal City and Pell City, Ala., was scrapped in 1942, and the short branch from Tredegar to Jacksonville, Ala., was ripped up in 1945. Two segments of the Fort Myers extension were also abandoned in 1942: the lines from Punta Rossa Jct. to Naples and from Alva to La Belle. In addition, two former branches of the old Georgia, Florida & Alabama were torn up during the period: from Tallahassee to Carrabelle and from Havana to Quincy, Fla. Finally, the 17-mile-long line between Lydia and Timmonsville, S.C., was scrapped around 1945.

The decade also witnessed the demise of several Seaboard subsidiaries. The Charlotte, Monroe & Columbia RR was abandoned in 1940 and the Chesterfield & Lancaster RR in the following year. The Jacksonville, Gainesville & Gulf met its end in 1943 and the Raleigh & Charleston was scrapped in 1946.

TOP:
Slogging through the backwoods of Georgia, class B-1 2-10-2 No. 2498 works westbound tonnage between Rockmart and Cedartown, Ga., on March 20, 1948. R.D. Sharpless; F.E. Ardrey, Jr., collection

BOTTOM LEFT:
Flying white flags, Seaboard DR-12-8-3000 "Centipede" 4503 approaches Atlanta, Ga., with an Extra East on June 27, 1947. Geared for 93 mph, the steam generator-equipped Baldwin was purchased for high-speed passenger and perishable service, but along with its trouble-prone sisters (SAL 4500-4513), spent most of its career working lesser trains. Among the first Seaboard Centipedes to be removed from service, 4503 was retired in 1957 and scrapped. R.D. Sharpless; F.E. Ardrey, Jr., collection

BOTTOM RIGHT:
Long after the mighty Mikes and Mountains were gone, Seaboard 1001—appropriately assigned class ODD—remained. Used for switching on street trackage and industrial spurs in Columbus, Ga., the little 0-4-0T was the only steam locomotive on the Seaboard roster from 1953 until she was finally retired in 1959. With better than a decade of service still ahead, the diminutive Baldwin is hard at work in streets of Columbus in 1948. Sam Appleby; David W. Salter collection

TOP:
Continuing am ambitious Centralized Traffic Control program begun in 1941, Seaboard signalmen install a CTC signal at Greenwood, S.C., in December 1960. By 1965, the railroad had 1,754 miles of main line controlled by CTC. CSX Transportation collection

BOTTOM LEFT:
Sparks and the acrid smell of acetylene and hot metal fill the air as workers tend to the somber business of reducing M-2 Mountain 247 and B-1 2-10-2's 2487 and 2482 to piles of scrap at Portsmouth, Va., in October 1953. Several more 2-10-2's quietly await their fate amid the dismembered part of previous victims. CSX Transportation collection

BOTTOM RIGHT:
Certainly one of Seaboard's most important post-war capital improvements was the construction of a sprawling hump yard at Hamlet. In this 1954 view, the hump track and retarders have been installed, but the yard office and hump tower are still under construction. CSX Transportation collection

TOP: *Cresting the steep grade just south of Gainesville, Ga., Gainesville Midland 2-10-2's 209 and 208 doublehead heavy southbound tonnage destined for Athens on a Sunday afternoon in March 1959. One of steam's last stands, Gainesville Midland was not dieselized until Seaboard acquired control of the line in 1959 and brought in Alco RSC2's and RSC3's to replace the road's celebrated Decapods. Both of the former Seaboard Decapods have been preserved: 208 at Winder, Ga., and 209 Gainesville.* David W. Salter

BOTTOM LEFT: *Savannah-bound with No. 82, the* Alaga, *GP9 1954 and a trio of modified RSC2's rumble over a low wooden trestle near Pitts, Ga., in April 1963. Among Seaboard's earliest hood units, the RSC2's were modified from A1A-A1A to B-B configuration in 1954-55.* David W. Salter

BOTTOM RIGHT: *Handling the hottest train on the road, SDP35's 1105, 1106 and GP30 509 blast through Ridgeway, N.C., with 52-car TT-23 in November 1966. In 1965, TT-23 ranked as the fastest freight in the land, posting scheduled running times averaging 60.8 mph over the 135-mile Savannah-West Jacksonville portion of its New York-Florida run.* Curt Tillotson, Jr.

Line was the surviving company, but Seaboard's ownership interest was reduced from 100 to 50 percent as a result of the consolidation.

Seaboard even took the "Air Line" portion of its name seriously in the early forties and formed an aviation subsidiary, Seaboard Airways, Inc. The airways company proposed to operate an airline from Boston and New York to Miami and New Orleans which would generally follow the railroad's routes. However, the Civil Aeronautics Board frowned on railroad-owned airlines and it denied Seaboard's applications for operating authority in 1944. Seaboard Airways never got off the ground, literally or figuratively.

Seaboard finally emerged from receivership, effective August 1, 1946. The assets of the company had been sold at an auction held on the passenger platform at the Portsmouth station on May 31, 1945, and a new company was formed to take over the railroad. The new corporation was named Seaboard Air Line Railroad Co., using the term "railroad" to distinguish it from the old SAL Railway Co. Legh R. Powell once again became president and his co-receiver, Henry W. Anderson, became chairman of the board.

The South boomed after World War II. For generations following the devastation of the Civil War, the region had been an economic backwater, somnolent and impoverished. Now, after decades of anticipation, a "New South" was emerging at last. Population grew rapidly and new industry poured in. Expansion in South Florida and around Atlanta was especially phenomenal.

As the South prospered so did the Seaboard. In 1947, revenue freight tonnage reached 35,261,000 tons, higher than the wartime peak established in 1943. And it continued to grow, reaching 43,000,000 tons in 1951 and 51,000,000 in 1959. Seaboard had managed to lose money in 1945, the final year of the war, but it was the last year the railroad would ever sustain a loss. Net income increased from slightly over $6 million in 1947 to almost $21 million in 1953.

In the halcyon postwar years, the new Seaboard Railroad renovated its passenger service. The *Silver Meteor* was re-equipped and the *Orange Blossom Special* was refurbished. New streamliners were introduced: the *Silver Star* on the New York-Florida run and the *Silver Comet* between New York, Atlanta and Birmingham. The *Gulf Wind* commenced operating between Jacksonville and New Orleans.

Unfortunately, Seaboard's passenger business did not hold up as well as freight traffic after the war. Patronage dropped steadily once peace returned. Seaboard eventually discontinued the *Orange Blossom Special* in 1953, and almost all of its branch-line passenger trains were dropped during the 1950s as potential passengers took to the automobile. Nevertheless, Seaboard continued to enjoy a considerable passenger patronage, far better than most railroads, and the road maintained an extensive high-quality service until well after the merger with Atlantic Coast Line.

Seaboard rapidly dieselized its locomotive fleet after the war. The railroad, which bought its last new steam locomotives in 1937, sold its biggest and newest steamers, the ten R class 2-6-6-4's, to B&O in 1947. By 1949, more than 75 percent of its passenger-train miles and 65 percent of its gross freight-train miles were performed by diesels. In the following year, the road was totally dieselized—almost. There was one exception: Baldwin 0-4-0T No. 1001, used for switching on former trolley tracks in the streets of Columbus, Ga., remained on the roster until 1959. Seaboard's steam roster, which had numbered 542 locomotives in 1938, had yielded to a fleet of 490 diesel units.

Seaboard also made a number of capital improvements. A big new phosphate elevator for shipboard loading was built at Seddon Island, Tampa, in 1947. New conventional flat yards were built at Tampa in 1950, Savannah in 1953 and Tallahassee in 1955. A vast new hump-retarder yard, containing 58 classification tracks, was completed at Seaboard's hub, Hamlet, N.C., in November 1954. Shop facilities to maintain the new diesel locomotives were constructed, the largest of which were at Jacksonville and Hamlet. Track was improved with heavier rail, treated ties and rock ballast. Centralized Traffic Control was gradually extended until it covered most of the major lines on the system. By 1965, over 1,700 miles of road was under CTC, and the railroad was indeed in first-rate condi-

After leading Seaboard through thick and thin for almost 25 years, Legh Powell retired as president in 1952. He was succeeded by John W. "Jess" Smith. Born in Baltimore in 1900, Jess Smith graduated from the University of Maryland with a degree in engineering. While at the University he had been a member of the football, track and baseball teams and president of the Student Assembly. He had taken time out from his studies to serve as a lieutenant during World War I. He joined Seaboard in 1924 as an engineering inspector of new construction projects and worked his way up through the Maintenance of Way, Engineering and Operating Departments until he became administrative vice president in 1950.

Only one significant abandonment occurred during the years after World War II. In 1952, the Fort Myers extension was abandoned from Hull southward, a total distance of 65 miles. The line which had been built during the height of the Florida boom of the twenties had never been much of a success. It largely paralleled the existing Atlantic Coast Line route to Fort Myers and traffic had been limited mostly to a little timber. By 1952, the timber traffic had pretty well dried up and the bridge over the Caloosahatchee River, more than one mile long, needed to be replaced. The scant traffic didn't justify rebuilding the bridge so Seaboard scrapped the line.

One final abandonment occurred a couple of years later, in 1954, when a 13-mile segment of the old Florida RR between Yulee and Nassau (Callahan), Fla., was ripped up. However, that abandonment had little impact on anything except perhaps skunks and 'possums. There was nothing between Yulee and Callahan but piney woods anyway. The "Fanny," the daily local freight between Baldwin yard and Fernandina, was merely rerouted over the Gross Cut-off between Callahan and Gross and the mainline between Gross and Yulee.

The Macon, Dublin & Savannah RR, Seaboard's long time subsidiary, was finally merged into the parent road on March 1, 1958. The short line, extending between Vidalia and Macon, Ga., had been controlled by SAL since 1905; however Seaboard had not acquired all of the line's stock until 1945. The MD&S was the last addition to the Seaboard proper. The merger with the 92-mile-long line gave Seaboard a total length of 4,146 miles. The MD&S became the Macon Sub-Division.

In August 1958, the company relocated its general offices from Norfolk and Portsmouth to Richmond, a move that had been proposed by John Skelton Williams at the turn of the century. To house the railroad's offices, a new eight-story building was erected on West Broad Street. Prophetically, the new general office building overlooked the Atlantic Coast Line mainline.

One last addition was made to the Seaboard system in 1959, when the railroad acquired all of the stock in the Gainesville Midland RR. However, GM remained as a separate SAL subsidiary and was never merged into the big road. The Midland extended 42 miles from a connection with SAL, at Athens, Ga., northward to Gainesville, Ga. One of the last railroads in America to use steam locomotives, it was still using them exclusively when Seaboard took over. Seaboard, of course, immediately replaced the coal burners with diesels.

On a sadder note, the Baltimore Steam Packet Co. (the Old Bay Line) terminated its passenger service between Baltimore and Norfolk in 1961. The company continued freight operations for a little while longer, but finally wound up its affairs in 1962. The Old Bay Line had been in operation for well over a century and was providing the last overnight steamboat service in America when it went out of business.

The beginning of the end for SAL came in 1958 when Seaboard and Atlantic Coast Line first considered a merger. After studying the matter, the two railroads filed a formal application with the Interstate Commerce Commission for permission to merge on July 20, 1960. It was to be a marriage of competing parallel lines. Coast Line, like Seaboard, extended from Richmond to Florida and both served the same six states. Indeed, SAL and ACL reached no less than 75 points in common and, with but a few exceptions, every major town served by one of the roads was also served by the other.

The principal advantage of the proposed consolidation was that it would lead to the elimination of myriad duplicate facilities, resulting in a stronger, more efficient company. The disadvantage was that it would end competition between the long-time rivals. In fact, the merger would result in only one railroad serving such important cities as Tampa, St.

Still going strong after 23 years and several million miles of service, venerable E4 3002 pauses in Raleigh with First 33, the southbound Silver Comet, *in June 1962. The green flags carried by the 3002 indicate that the* Sunland, *normally combined with the* Comet *from Richmond to Hamlet, is running as a separate section.*

J. Parker Lamb

Petersburg, Orlando and Wilmington. But the contention was that by 1960 there really wasn't any meaningful competition between railroads anymore. The real rivalry was between railroads and other modes of transportation, especially trucks.

Seaboard and Coast Line were comparable in size, although ACL was somewhat the larger. Coast Line operated 5,700 miles of line versus Seaboard's 4,100 miles and, in 1965, ACL's railway operating revenues were $201 million as compared to $181 million for SAL. Both lines were profitable; Seaboard had a net income of $16 million in 1965, and Coast Line had $18 million. But ACL overshadowed SAL by virtue of its ownership of one-third of the capital stock of the Louisville & Nashville RR. A 6,000-mile system extending from the Ohio River to the Gulf of Mexico, L&N was the dominant railroad in much of Kentucky, Tennessee and Alabama. Not only did Coast Line control the L&N, but ACL and L&N jointly controlled several other important smaller railroads: Clinchfield, the Georgia RR and the West Point Route (Atlanta & West Point and the Western Ry. of Alabama). Altogether ACL controlled some 12,000 miles of rail line throughout the Southeast.

The proposed merger was opposed mainly by other railroads. Florida East Coast was less than enthralled by the impending marriage of its principal connection, ACL, with its only rail competitor, Seaboard. Central of Georgia contended that it would be surrounded by a combined Seaboard Coast Line. Gulf, Mobile & Ohio, Illinois Central and Southern objected to the consolidated railroad controlling the L&N, and IC and Southern each argued that it should be enabled to acquire ACL's interest in the Louisville & Nashville. In addition, Southern contended that for it to remain competitive the ICC should, as a con-

By a nine-to-two vote, the Interstate Commerce Commission approved the merger on December 2, 1963. A majority of the commissioners found that, while the merger partners were both profitable, they were not making a fair return on their investment. They agreed with the applicants' argument that competition between railroads was not a very important factor. The two dissenting commissioners questioned whether permitting the merger of two strong, prosperous competing lines would be in the public interest. The Commission's decision was appealed to the Federal Courts, and the U.S. District Court for the Middle District of Florida set aside the ICC decision and remanded the case back to the Commission. But on December 22, 1965, the U.S. Supreme Court vacated the District Court decision, in essence approving the merger. The union was finally consummated, July 1, 1967. The redundantly named Seaboard Coast Line Railroad Co. was born.

The Seaboard Air Line, as we knew it, passed into history. But it went out with a flourish. The company's revenue freight tonnage in 1966, its last full year of operation, was almost 62 million tons, the highest in the railroad's history and the first time it had ever topped 60 million. Moreover, Seaboard carried more passengers that year than in any year since 1958.

Technically, ACL was merged into SAL and the surviving corporation was then renamed Seaboard Coast Line, but that was a mere formality for legal convenience. The new railroad was predominantly under the influence of former Coast Line people. Even though it was officially headquartered in Richmond, most of its general offices remained in Jacksonville, the location of ACL's main offices. Coast Line's president, W. Thomas Rice, became president of the SCL. The Air Line's John Smith became the chairman of the board. The new railroad adopted ACL's uninspired black color scheme for its locomotives. Even its cabooses were painted Coast Line orange instead of Seaboard's traditional red.

Seaboard remained largely intact during the years immediately following the merger. However, some lines were soon abandoned in favor of alternative former ACL lines. The most notable were the line between Charleston and Savannah and most of the line from the Chattahoochee River to Montgomery, Ala. Subsequently, all or part of several other major Seaboard mainlines have been scrapped, including the lines between Richmond and Raleigh, Atlanta and Birmingham, and Savannah and Jacksonville. In addition, the line between West Palm Beach and Miami was sold in 1988, to be used for local passenger commuter service. Thus, while some former Seaboard lines are still heavily used for freight traffic, only a shadow of the old SAL remains.

Since 1967, Seaboard Coast Line has gone through several incarnations. It established a holding company in 1969, Seaboard Coast Line Industries, to control the railroad. In the mid-seventies SCL RR began referring to itself and its affiliates as the "Family Lines." Other members of the "Family" included Louisville & Nashville, Clinchfield, the Georgia RR and the West Point Route, but each railroad continued to maintain its separate corporate identity. More importantly, on November 1, 1980, SCL Industries and Chessie System, Inc., merged to form CSX Corp. Chessie was a holding company which controlled two famed old railroads: Chesapeake & Ohio and the Baltimore & Ohio. In December 1982, Seaboard Coast Line RR and the L&N were finally merged to form the Seaboard System Railroad, which, of course, remained a subsidiary of CSX Corp. The Clinchfield and the Georgia RR were also included in the new Seaboard System RR. Seaboard System changed its name to CSX Transportation Inc. on July 1, 1986, and on August 31, 1987, Chesapeake & Ohio was merged into CSX Transportation. The Baltimore & Ohio had already been incorporated into the C&O by that time.

What remains of the Seaboard Air Line is now but a small part of CSX Transportation. CSX is a truly massive amalgamation of rail lines. It extends from Philadelphia to New Orleans and from Chicago to South Florida. As of this writing, it has some 19,000 miles of line. Of course, CSX Transportation itself is a mere component of an even bigger conglomerate, CSX Corp. CSX Corp. owns ships, barge lines and vast real estate interests, as well as railroads. Seaboard's name has disappeared and it may now just be a drop in the conglomerate bucket, but at least it accounts for the "S" in CSX. That's more than Coast Line, B&O or L&N could say.

CHAPTER SIX

THE RAILROAD

Seaboard's lines were located in the piedmont plateau and the coastal plain. From Richmond to Columbia its main stem closely followed the fall line, the geographic demarcation line between the two regions. Between the fall line and the sea, the coastal plain tends to be flat and, near the coast, frequently swampy. North and west of the line, in the piedmont, the country is more rolling. The fall line itself marks the first rapids, upstream from the sea, in rivers flowing into the Atlantic or the Gulf. Since the falls represented the limits of navigation and provided a source of power for early mills, they were inevitable sites for town development. Richmond, Petersburg, Columbia, Augusta, Macon, Columbus and Montgomery were all located on the fall line. In addition to following the fall line, Seaboard's mainline crossed the Carolina sandhills in the area between Raleigh and Columbia so that the road was hilly and circuitous. There were some 298 curves on the Virginia Division mainline between Richmond and Hamlet, N.C., a distance of 253 miles. Seaboard was anything but an "air line" along that portion of its road.

East and south of Columbia, on the coastal plain, it was another matter, however. The plain extends all the way south into Florida and that state is, of course, resoundingly flat. There are some hills in the center of the Sunshine State and in the area around Tallahassee. But the highest point in all of Florida has an elevation of only 345 feet, hardly enough to give even the most dedicated hypochondriac a nosebleed. Naturally, Seaboard lines traversing the coastal plain were generally straight and level. In the coastal region Seaboard could claim the longest stretch of straight track in America, on the Wilmington branch, plus another long section of tangent line in South Florida on the edge of the Everglades. Thus, at least in the coastal plain, the "air line" designation was not such a misnomer.

Seaboard did have one mountain line, the Birmingham Sub-Division between Atlanta and Birmingham. That line crossed the southern fringes of the Appalachian Mountains and bored through the only tunnels on the railroad. Fortunately for the Seaboard, however, its grades were relatively modest.

LEFT:
Hamlet-bound, GP9's 1922 and 1969, FT's 4016 and 4116 and GP7's 1802 and 1702 roll 123-car hotshot No. 75 through the North Carolina hills near Norlina on Thanksgiving Day 1962. J. Parker Lamb

RIGHT:
At better than a mile a minute, the Merchandiser *hits her stride on the "Ridgeway Race Track," as GP30 524, GP18 400, GP30 520, F3A 4029 and GP7 1777 slam through Manson, N.C., with 126 cars in October 1965.*
Curt Tillotson, Jr.

Crossing the southern fringe of the Appalachians, the Birmingham Sub-Division was the nearest thing Seaboard had to a mountain line. Heading up No. 16, E6 3001 pilots the five-car local through a deep cut east of Rockmart, Ga., in the summer of 1948. True to the mountainous nature of the terrain, the railroad later installed slide fences at this location. Dick Sharpless; David W. Salter collection

COMPETITION

Seaboard was squeezed between its two bigger and stronger rivals, the Southern Railway to the west and the Atlantic Coast Line to the east. It was at something of a competitive disadvantage as its rivals had generally superior lines to Seaboard's. Moreover, Southern and ACL had both been under the influence of J.P. Morgan during the late nineteenth and early twentieth centuries and they tended to cooperate with each other. Thus, Southern possessed trackage rights over ACL lines into Portsmouth and Jacksonville and the two roads jointly owned the Chesapeake Steamship Co., which long competed with SAL's Old Bay Line on Chesapeake Bay.

Southern had a well-maintained double-track mainline from Washington to Atlanta, with major branch lines to Richmond, Portsmouth and Raleigh. Its Washington-Atlanta line was 59 miles shorter than the joint SAL-RF&P route between the two cities. Southern was thus a formidable competitor for traffic from Washington, Richmond or Raleigh to Atlanta or Birmingham. Thanks to its trackage rights over the Atlantic Coast Line, Southern also had a competitive route from Washington to Jacksonville via Charlotte, Columbia and Savannah. But fortunately Seaboard didn't have to compete with Southern in most of Florida. The little town of Palatka, 55 miles south of Jacksonville, marked the limit of Southern's penetration into the state.

ACL's mainline from Richmond to Jacksonville was also double tracked and, as it was located on the flat coastal plain, generally straighter than SAL's line and with easier grades. However, there wasn't much difference in their overall mileage between the Virginia and Florida gateways as ACL had the longer route from Savannah to Jacksonville. In Florida, ACL competed with SAL at just about every significant point. Coast Line had a line from Jacksonville, via Orlando, to Tampa plus another line from Jacksonville to St. Petersburg. About the only major Florida area ACL didn't serve was the east coast.

For Miami traffic, Seaboard competed with the Florida East Coast which had a double-track line from Jacksonville to Miami. FEC's route to Miami was significantly shorter than

TOP:
Led by GP9 1922, a quartet of Geeps wheel Georgia Division freight No. 28, the Iron Master, *east of Floyd, Ga., on May 15, 1965.* David W. Salter

BOTTOM:
Heading for Fernandina with the daily local freight known as the "Fanny," RS3's 1680 and 1655 tread carefully through the swamps near Yulee, Fla., on April 22, 1961. After abandonment of the Yulee-Callahan section of the former Florida Railroad, the Baldwin-Fernandina local was routed north to Gross, then south over the main line to Yulee, then east to Fernandina. Bruce R. Meyer

SAL's, which swung through the center of the state. FEC collaborated closely with the Southern, and especially ACL, at Jacksonville. But unlike Southern and Coast Line, FEC was financially weak, being enmeshed in bankruptcy from 1931 to 1960.

Between Florida and the Midwest, SAL confronted the same two competitors: ACL and Southern. Again, Seaboard's routes were generally longer than its rivals'. From Florida to the Midwest, SAL used two routes: one from Jacksonville or Baldwin north to Savannah, then west via the Macon, Dublin & Savannah RR to a connection with the Central of Georgia at Macon; the other from Jacksonville west to Tallahassee, then north over the old GF&A line to a connection with the CofG at Columbus, or either the Louisville & Nashville or the Gulf, Mobile & Ohio at Montgomery. Southern had a direct route from Jacksonville to Atlanta and ACL, after it absorbed the Atlanta, Birmingham & Coast RR in 1945, had a direct route to both Atlanta and Birmingham. Moreover, Coast Line had a cut-off from Albany, Ga., to Tampa which bypassed Jacksonville. SAL's route to Atlanta, via Macon and the CofG, was some 75 miles longer than its rivals', thus placing Seaboard at a serious competitive disadvantage. However, its route between Jacksonville and Montgomery was only 8 miles longer than the Coast Line route between the Florida gateway and the Alabama capital.

Seaboard was, at least, the only railroad to serve both coasts of South Florida and it possessed the only direct line from Florida to the west, thanks to its connection with the Louisville & Nashville at River Jct., Fla. While the River Jct. route was used for passenger trains from Jacksonville to New Orleans, it was not very important for freight traffic. Seaboard usually routed freight from Florida to the west via a connection with the L&N at Montgomery.

Seaboard also had plenty of competition from other modes of transportation. Before World War II, several steamship lines offered freight and passenger service along the South Atlantic coast. Clyde-Mallory Lines operated ships from New York to Charleston, Jacksonville and Miami, as well as from New York to Tampa. The Merchant & Miners Line sailed between Philadelphia, Baltimore, Savannah, Jacksonville and Miami. Pan-Atlantic Line pro-

TOP LEFT: *Seaboard's post-war prosperity rode largely on the revenues of redball freights such as No. 27, the* Capital. *Putting away the miles at better than one per minute, the Washington-Birmingham hotshot roars through Greystone, N.C., with GP30's 520 and 525, GP18 407, GP9 1810 and 120 cars in February 1966.* Curt Tillotson, Jr.

TOP RIGHT: *On the Carolina Division, E7 3018 and an E8 roll No. 10, the* Palmland, *through Kingsland, Ga., on April 23, 1966.* J.H. Wade; F.E. Ardrey, Jr., collection

BOTTOM LEFT: *Headquartered at Tampa, the South Florida Division comprised Seaboard's lines in the southwest portion of the Sunshine State. Racing over the Tampa Sub-Division at 75 mph, E7 3040 slices through Turkey Creek, Fla., with No. 158, the St. Petersburg-Wildwood section of the* Silver Meteor, *in March 1961.* David W. Salter

BOTTOM RIGHT: *Westbound in Seaboard's most bucolic territory, former GF&A 2-8-0 920 works an Alabama Division local freight near Seville, Ga., on April 24, 1948.* David W. Salter

Georgia RR, operated from Savannah to New York and Boston. Most of the steamship operations were terminated by World War II and never resumed. But after the war, Refrigerated Steamship Line provided an express service for citrus fruit from Florida to New York, which lasted several years, and Seatrain Lines ferried freight cars between Savannah and New York.

In the air, Seaboard's primary competition was from Eastern and National Airlines between New York and Florida, and Eastern and Delta from New York to Atlanta and Birmingham. The airline competition became more intense with every stride in aviation. The airlines progressed from Douglas DC-3's and Lockheed Lodestars before the war, to DC-6's and Constellations during the fifties, to jets in the sixties. Each succeeding generation of aircraft was bigger, faster, more comfortable, and more appealing to passengers. Air transportation advanced from an expensive novelty for the adventurous to widespread public acceptance. With the advent of the jets, airplanes supplanted trains as the first choice for long-distance transportation.

Seaboard's principal intermodal competition came from the highways, however. For passengers, the competition was not nearly so much from the Lockheed Constellation, nor even the Greyhound bus, as it was from the prosaic family Chevy. The convenience of the automobile was difficult to combat. Similarly, the main competition for freight came from trucks. And of course there were plenty of trucking outfits vying for Seaboard's business, especially the more lucrative perishable and general merchandise traffic. Moreover, the motor carriers had an artificial advantage over the railroads, at least with regard to farm products. In addition to whatever inherent advantages the trucks had, primarily speed and flexibility, they also had the benefit of government policies. While railroad freight rates were tightly regulated by the federal and state governments, highway transportation of agricultural commodities was unregulated. The truckers were free to undercut railroad rates on perishables and there was little Seaboard could do to respond. It is hardly surprising that the railroads lost much of their perishable traffic in the years after World War II. The situation didn't begin to redress itself until the inauguration of "piggyback," trailer-on-flatcar service, in the early sixties.

OFFICES AND ORGANIZATION

Like most railroads, Seaboard's general offices were located in the city from which it originated. In Seaboard's case, it was Portsmouth, Va. However, completion of the line to Richmond in 1900 shifted the company's mainline to the Virginia capital and the line to Portsmouth was reduced to the status of a branch line. Accordingly, John Skelton Williams intended to move the company's headquarters to Richmond when he consolidated the SAL in that year. Nevertheless, Seaboard's general offices remained in the Tidewater area for many more years. They were long located in a large building which also housed the Portsmouth passenger station. In the late twenties, the offices were moved across the Elizabeth River to a new building on West Butte Street in Norfolk. A number of offices remained in Portsmouth, however. Finally, in 1958, Seaboard moved its headquarters to Richmond, to a new building located at 3600 West Board Street.

During the thirties, Seaboard was organized into six operating divisions. The Virginia Division, headquartered at Raleigh, comprised all the lines north of that city. The North Carolina Division, with offices located at Hamlet, N.C., consisted of the lines radiating from Hamlet north to Raleigh, east to Wilmington, south to Columbia, and west to Monroe, Charlotte and Rutherfordton, N.C. The Georgia Division, with headquarters in Atlanta, covered the line from Monroe to Birmingham. The South Carolina Division comprised the "East Carolina" line from Hamlet to Savannah via Charleston, and the line from Columbia through Savannah to Jacksonville and Baldwin, Fla., as well as the line from Savannah west to Montgomery. Its offices were in Savannah. The North Florida Division, headquartered in Jacksonville, consisted of the lines from Jacksonville west to River Junction, Fla., and from Baldwin south to Miami. The South Florida Division, with offices in Tampa, covered the lines generally south and west of Waldo, Wildwood and West Lake Wales, Fla. The divisions were divided into sub-divisions which were each named after a principal town on the line.

Prior to World War II, the divisions were restructured. The North Carolina Division was abolished and its lines were divided among other divisions. The mainline from Hamlet to Raleigh was reassigned to the Virginia Division, and the old Carolina Central line from Wilmington to Rutherfordton went to the Georgia Division. The South Carolina Division absorbed the line from Hamlet to Columbia and was renamed the Carolina Division. At the same time a new division was created, the Alabama Division, with headquarters at Americus, Ga. It comprised the lines from Savannah to Montgomery and from Bainbridge to Columbus, Ga. The Alabama Division lasted only until 1956, when it was again combined with the Carolina Division and the number of operating divisions was reduced to five. In addition, the line from Hamlet to Wilmington was eventually transferred from the Georgia

TOP:
Left-hand running on the double-track North Florida Division main, Q-3 class 2-8-2 No. 378 passes the center siding at Maxville, Fla., with a northbound freight on March 26, 1949. David W. Salter

BOTTOM:
Seaboard's steepest grades were on the Alabama Division around Americus, Ga. On May 11, 1947, Decapods 524 and 518 doublehead Alabama Division time freight No. 82, the Alaga, east of Pitts, Ga. At Vidalia, "Russian" Decapod 518 will cut off and return light to Americus, while the 524 will handle the train to Savannah unassisted. David W. Salter

ROADWAY

Seaboard was almost entirely a single-track railroad. During the sixties only a little less than 100 miles of the system's lines were double track. Short stretches were strategically located on the Virginia Division mainline between Richmond and Hamlet. There were 6 miles of double track just south of Richmond, 5 miles between Norlina and Middleburg, N.C., and another 6 miles just north of Raleigh. The largest stretch on the division was 23 miles between South Aberdeen and Hamlet, N.C. In addition, SAL enjoyed the use of 10 miles of double track from Raleigh south to Fetner, N.C., thanks to a paired-track arrangement with the Southern Ry. Most of the line between Aberdeen and Hamlet was reduced to single track after Centralized Traffic Control was installed on that section in 1962. In Florida, the railroad had 27 miles of double track between Baldwin and Starke plus 5 more miles between Wildwood and Coleman. Although the tracks were signaled in both directions, trains on the Baldwin-Starke double track normally ran on the left.

Seaboard was burdened with relatively few steep grades. As might be expected, the longest sustained grade, six miles, was on the mountainous Birmingham line. But the ruling grade on the Birmingham Sub-Division was kept to a relatively modest one percent. Probably the most important grade from an operational standpoint was Southern Pines Hill on the busy Virginia Division mainline: four miles of 1.1 percent grade northbound from Aberdeen to Southern Pines, N.C. During the steam era, a class Q-3 2-8-2 was stationed at Aberdeen as a helper for the hill. Other one percent grades on the Virginia Division main stem included one in Richmond northbound from Brown Street to Hermitage Yard. A steeper grade on the Virginia Division was on the Portsmouth line, a 1.2 percent grade southbound for three miles from Thelma to Summit, N.C. Surprisingly, the steepest grades on the railroad were on the Savannah-Montgomery line in the area around Americus, Ga.: 1.8 percent between Helena and Americus and another grade of 1.8 percent between Richland and Americus. A single GP7 was rated at only 1,450 tons from Americus to Richland, its lowest rating on the SAL. In contrast, it was rated for 3,500 tons on the flat line between Andrews, S.C., and Jacksonville, Fla.

There were only three tunnels on the entire Seaboard, all located on the Birmingham line: Divide Tunnel east of Rockmart, Ga., Hardwick Tunnel between Wattsville and Odenville, Ala., and Roper Tunnel located between Parsons and Irondale, Ala. The three bores were all concrete lined and totaled 2,964 feet in length.

Seaboard may have had few tunnels, but the road did not lack for bridges. Its largest were the structures over the James River at Richmond and the Roanoke River at Weldon, N.C.; and the drawbridges over the Broad River on the Charleston-Savannah line near Hanks, S.C., the Chattahoochee River where it forms the Georgia-Alabama boundary on the Montgomery Sub-Division, and two structures over the Savannah River, one near Clyo, Ga., on the Columbia Sub-Division and the other on the so-called East Carolina line at the city of Savannah. The railroad owned a large number of drawbridges, especially along the South Carolina and Georgia coast. There were eleven such bridges on the Charleston Sub-Division between Andrews and Savannah and four more on the Jacksonville Sub-Division between Savannah and Jacksonville. Important drawbridges, or at least those over the busiest streams,

TOP:
Led by "Babyface" Baldwin DR6-4-1500 2700, Tampa-Venice train 257 crosses the mile-wide Manatee River at Bradenton, Fla., in March 1955. Bringing up the markers of the four-car local is a Pennsylvania Pullman, a through sleeper from New York. Jim Scribbins

MIDDLE:
There's little doubt who owns this bridge. Working the northbound Hamlet-Raleigh local, GP9 1971 and F3 4031 ease across the Haw River near Moncure, N.C., in March 1962. J. Parker Lamb

BOTTOM:
One of the biggest bridges on the Virginia Division mainline was the 500-foot-long, 70-foot-high deck-girder structure across the Tar River south of Kittrell, N.C. Crossing the Tar in June 1966, GP9 1977, F3's 4032, 4027, 4028 and two more Geeps head north with 120-car fast freight 280. Curt Tillotson, Jr.

included the structures crossing the North East and Cape Fear rivers near Wilmington, and over the Cooper and Ashley rivers. In addition, two bridges spanned the Stono River on the Andrews Sub-Division; others crossed the Satilla and Trout rivers on the Jacksonville Sub-Division; the St. Lucie Canal and the South Fork of the New River on the Miami line; the Big Manatee River at Bradenton, Fla., on the South Florida Division; and the Gasparilla Pass near Boca Grande, Fla. With the exception of the structures on the Wilmington and Boca Grande lines, the bridges were all interlocked. Trains were usually limited to 45 mph over the drawbridges.

Before World War II only limited portions of the Seaboard were equipped with signals. Automatic block signals existed only on the mainline between Richmond and Hamlet, and the lines between Hamlet and Monroe, N.C.; Savannah and Jacksonville; and Starke and Wildwood, Fla. Major segments of the railroad were "dark," i.e., operated solely by timetable and train order. Just before the war, Seaboard began installing Centralized Traffic Control on its busiest lines. The first installation went into service in December 1941 between Richmond and Alberta, Va. Eventually CTC was in effect almost all the way between Richmond and Miami, including both lines between Hamlet and Savannah and the Gross Cut-off. The only exceptions were a few short segments of double track. The CTC was controlled

CHESAPEAKE & OHIO
2327
SEABOARD
3048
S E A B O A R D
SOUTHERN
2106
SOUTHERN
21397

DILLON SUPPLY CO
MILL SUPPLIES and
DILLON SU
STEEL AND PIPE
1917
1795
SEABOARD
P

FACING PAGE, TOP:
Posed for company photographers in 1949, C&O K-3a 2-8-2 2327, an A-B-A of Seaboard E7's and Southern RS2 2106 stage a three-way meet at the famed triple crossing in Richmond, Virginia. CSX Transportation collection

FACING PAGE, BOTTOM:
Easing past the Hamlet wreckers with southbound No. 75, GP9 1917 and an A-B-B-A of FT's grind through downtown Raleigh, N.C., as steam cranes 71978 and 71979 prepare to rerail E7A 3027 at 4 P.M. on April 8, 1961. Just hours earlier, excessive speed caused the E7 and five cars of Hamlet-Richmond local No. 4 to derail on the ten-degree curve approaching the Raleigh station. Eight crew members and four passengers were injured in the incident, which proved fatal to the 16-year-old E7.
J. Parker Lamb

THIS PAGE, TOP:
Amid the clatter of selectors, chattering train phones and barking radios of the Jacksonville dispatching office, a Seaboard dispatcher works the CTC panel controlling the main line to Wildwood.
CSX Transportation collection

MIDDLE:
Heading up an Extra North, GP9 1914, a trio of F's and another Geep wait in the clear as GP7's 1715 and 1724 advance into Raleigh Yard with No. 85 at dusk in August 1962.
J. Parker Lamb

BOTTOM:
Prior to the installation of CTC, the operator at Kingsland, Ga., hoops train orders to the conductor on No. 280 in the summer of 1952.
Fraser Hale

trolled a switch at Hialeah, 407 miles away. At the time it was installed, it was the most remote facility controlled from a CTC board in the United States. CTC was also installed on the lines between Baldwin and Tallahassee, Fla., Coleman and Sulphur Springs, Fla., Atlanta and Birmingham, and Clinton and Greenwood, S.C. Automatic block signals were installed on the rest of the line between Hamlet and Atlanta. By 1965, some 2,010 miles of mainline were equipped with signals, of which 1,754 miles were under CTC.

One noteworthy feature of the SAL was the greatest length of straight track in the United States. Located on the Wilmington Sub-Division, the curveless stretch was 78.86 miles long. It extended from milepost 261.99 near Laurel Hill eastward to milepost 340.85 near East Arcadia, N.C. The tangent track might have been built even longer. The curve at the east end of the line was a barely perceptible half of a degree and there was no apparent reason for a curve at that point. The railroad then extended for another distinction belonged to an 85.3-mile stretch of the Canadian Pacific in Saskatchewan. And it was a mere trifle compared to the longest straight track in the world, 297 no doubt boring miles across Australia's Nullarbor Plain. Seaboard also owned the eighth-largest stretch of straight track in America, 57.4 miles on the Miami Sub-Division between Okeechobee and West Palm Beach, Fla.

Undoubtedly the most renowned physical feature on the Seaboard was the famous three-level railroad crossing in Richmond. Located just south of Main Street Station, the crossing was created in 1901 when the Chesapeake & Ohio built a long bridge spanning the downtown riverfront. C&O's James River Division was on the uppermost level. Seaboard's elevated mainline was in the middle, and the Southern Railway's line to West Point, Va., was at ground level. The triple crossing was believed to be one of only two such rail crossings in the world, the other being located at Peterborough, England. The Chessie overpass had a clearance of 17 feet 3 inches, the lowest on the Seaboard between Richmond and Hamlet and almost 5 feet lower than the standard clearance of 22 feet.

The Seaboard was in excellent physical shape when it merged with Coast Line. At the end of 1965, almost 500 miles of track were laid with heavy rail weighing 152 lb per linear yard. Another 1,200 miles were laid with 112-lb or 115-lb rail and 1,600 miles with 100 lb-rail. Some 400 miles of track were of continuous welded rail. Company-owned radio stations permitted dispatcher-to-train radio communication over much of the system. And the railroad was equipped with some 73 automatic hot-box detectors. The infrared devices could detect overheated wheel bearings on passing trains and transmit information on the location of defects to monitoring devices in the dispatching office.

Indicative of the Seaboard's condition during the sixties were the speed limits. In general, passenger trains were permitted a maximum speed of 79 mph over the entire mainline from Richmond to Miami. The only exception was the Hamlet Sub-Division between Hamlet and Columbia where they were confined to 70. Freight trains operating via the low line through Charleston were authorized a maximum speed of 60 mph all the way between Richmond and Miami. Of course there were numerous locations where the speeds were more restricted, but the prevailing limits give an idea of the condition of the track in general. Between Hamlet and Monroe, N.C., the top passenger and freight speeds were also 79 and 60, respectively. From Monroe to Atlanta they were 75 and 50, while on the Birmingham Sub-Division the passenger limit dropped to 60. In Florida, the passenger and freight limits between Coleman and Tampa were 75 and 60. The maximums were lower on the Portsmouth and Tallahassee Sub-Divisions. On both lines passenger trains were restricted to 59 and freights to 49 mph. Freights were also limited to 49 mph on the Savannah-Montgomery and Tallahassee-Richland lines, and 40 mph was the speed limit on the line between Monroe and Rutherfordton, N.C.

FREIGHT YARDS

Seaboard maintained freight yards, of course, in or near all of the larger cities it served. In Richmond, the main terminal was Hermitage Yard, about four miles north of Main Street Station, and a mile south of RF&P's Acca Yard. There was also a smaller facility, Brown Street Yard, located between Main Street Station and Hermitage, which served as an interchange point with the Chesapeake & Ohio Ry. At Raleigh, the yard was located a couple of miles northwest of downtown. In Atlanta, Seaboard's facilities were located at Howells Yard, northwest of the city. The Georgia Division headquarters, as well as extensive shops, were also located at Howells. The Birmingham yard was a relatively small facility, one mile east of Terminal Station. In Jacksonville, the yard and shops were located at West Jax, about four miles west of downtown.

Seaboard's yard at Tampa had originally been at Gary, two miles east of Tampa's Union Station. But the railroad built a new facility to serve Tampa in 1950, Yeoman Yard, two miles farther east. Yeoman had 28 tracks with a capacity for 1,700 freight cars. By 1953, it was handling some 1,500 cars every 24 hours and keeping 25 switching crews busy. At that time, 59 diesel units were maintained at Tampa, more than anywhere else on the system.

In the Miami area, Seaboard's yard was located in the town of Hialeah, which was also the home of the famous race track. The yard was about seven miles from SAL's stub-end Miami passenger station and featured an enormous loop track where passenger trains could be turned.

Certainly one of the most important points on the Seaboard was the old city of Savannah and probably the most modern conventional yard on the system was the terminal at that city. Built in 1953 at a cost of $3.75 million, it was constructed at a time when most new railroad yards were of the hump-retarder type. However, SAL management opted for a conventional flat yard because it felt that large blocks of perishable cars would be moved more expeditiously through that type of terminal. At the time, large movements of fruits and vegetables were arriving at Savannah in blocks of cars. It was not unusual for the perishable blocks to be departing within 35 minutes of their arrival, a feat which could not be duplicated if the cars had to be humped.

The yard was located west of the city, near Telfair Jct. With a capacity for 2,400 cars, it consisted of a 41-track classification yard with two switching leads at each end. The classification tracks varied in capacity from 23 to 150 cars. Three could accommodate 150 cars and four could handle 100 cars. Seven of the longer tracks were used for both arriving and departing trains. The yard included a running track, an "island" icing platform capable of icing 20 refrigerator cars on each side, car repair facilities and a diesel locomotive shop. When the yard was new, 55 diesel locomotives were assigned to its shop for maintenance and repair. To save switch-engine time, separate service facilities for yard engines were located at the north end of the terminal near the yard office.

Some of the Seaboard's most important yards were at small towns that were prominent on the railroad's map if no one else's. One was Baldwin, Fla., the little town 18 miles west of Jacksonville at the junction of the Jacksonville-Chattahoochee line, the Gross Sub-Division to Savannah and the mainline to South Florida. Several through freight trains, as well as certain crack passenger trains, operated over the Gross Cut-off, bypassing Jacksonville. In addition, freight moving between South Florida and SAL's western gateways at Columbus and Montgomery was switched at Baldwin, and the little town was an important re-icing point for refrigerator cars.

An even more important small town yard in Florida was at Wildwood. Located in the center of the state, it marked the junction of the lines from Miami, Tampa and Orlando with the mainline north to Baldwin and Jacksonville. The yard there was a relatively small facility with a capacity of 800 cars. But it was busy; as many as 80,000 cars a month moved through the town. Wildwood yard had the second biggest icing plant on the system, with two tracks capable of handling 15 reefers each and a daily icing capacity of 300 tons. It was used mostly to pre-ice empty cars before they were loaded.

Other significant small town yards included Mulberry Yard, in the heart of Florida's

LEFT:
A lone Geep, a pair of F3's, three Baldwin switchers and a quartet of RSC2's occupy the shop tracks, while a Baldwin yard engine shuffles cabooses and two GP7's wait on the head end of a southbound freight in this bird's-eye view of SAL's new Savannah yard, not long after the facility opened in 1953. CSX Transportation collection

RIGHT:
Ready to work the consist of a southbound freight, Baldwin DS4-4-1000 No. 1459 waits in the wings as GP9's 1962, 1979, 1970 and a pair of F3's cut off their train in the receiving yard at Hamlet, N.C., in August 1961. J. Parker Lamb

LEFT:
The West Jacksonville shops, as seen from the air, in February 1949. The new five-bay diesel shop is behind and to the right of the roundhouse. The older steam locomotive shops are in the center of the picture behind the diesel shop, and the car shop is to the left of the steam shop. Kalmbach Publishing Co.

RIGHT:
Cradled by the 160-ton overhead crane, class M 4-8-2 No. 208 undergoes heavy repairs at Howells Shop in Atlanta, Ga., in January 1947. CSX Transportation collection

FACING PAGE:
Inside the West Jacksonville shop, FT 4015 looks on as the overhead crane hoists a freshly reconditioned EMD 567 engine. Seaboard Air Line

Charlotte and Rutherfordton diverged from the mainline to Atlanta; Bainbridge, Ga., on the old GF&A where the North Florida and the Alabama Divisions converged; and Americus, Ga., the location of Alabama Division headquarters. A once-busy yard was located at Norlina, N.C., the junction point of the Portsmouth line with the Richmond-Raleigh mainline. But the southern terminus for Portsmouth trains was transferred southward to Raleigh in the 1950s and Norlina languished.

The most important yard of all was located at Hamlet, N.C., the little town near the South Carolina state line that was at the heart of the Seaboard. Five major lines converged at that point: the mainline north to Richmond, the old Carolina Central line east to Wilmington, the Georgia Division line west to Atlanta and Birmingham, and the two lines south to Savannah—the old line via Columbia and the East Carolina line via Charleston. The quintessential railroad town, the village was named not by an admirer of Shakespeare, but because it was, indeed, a hamlet. A railroad first reached the town just before the Civil War when the Wilmington, Charlotte & Rutherford built its line west from Wilmington. It became a junction point in 1877 when the Raleigh & Augusta Air Line completed its line south from Raleigh.

Seaboard built a new automated hump-retarder yard at Hamlet, which opened on November 29, 1954. Beginning three miles north of the town depot, the yard stretched for a like distance along the east side of the mainline to Raleigh. Claimed to be the most modern rail yard in the world when it was new, the vast facility had a total capacity of 5,000 cars. It replaced a cramped and outmoded rider-hump facility which was located one mile north of town. The yard and its diesel shop cost about $8.5 million, more than twice the cost of the new Savannah yard opened in the previous year.

The heart of the terminal was the hump and the 58-track classification yard. The hump, located at the north end of the classification yard, was 20 feet higher than the lowest level of the tracks. Ranging in capacity from 22 to 57 cars, the classification tracks were divided into groups of 8 or 9. The terminal also included a 10-track receiving yard, located north of the hump, and an 11-track departure yard to the hump's east. In addition, there was a shorter 6-track local yard which was considered part of the departure yard. Altogether there were 113 tracks totaling 70 miles in the terminal.

There were eleven retarders: one master retarder, three intermediate retarders and seven group retarders. Cars to be classified were pushed over the hump at a constant speed, either the normal rate of four mph or a slow speed of two mph. Upon being released at the crest, each car would pass over three retarders: the master, one intermediate and one group retarder, and a maximum of eight switches before entering its designated track. A car or group of cars would be automatically directed to the proper track at the touch of a button by the hump conductor. The cars were retarded automatically by the master and intermediate retarders. The final machine, the group retarder, was controlled by an operator who could adjust the speed of the car leaving the retarder, considering its rolling resistance, the number of cars already in its designated classification track and the distance it would have to roll. The equipment was designed so that a car would couple to the other cars in the track

4015
SEABOARD
AIR
LINE
RAILROAD
THROUGH THE HEART OF THE SOUTH

TOP:
Two years after Seaboard passenger trains stopped calling on C&O's Main Street Station, SAL GP9 1927, two F3's and a trio of GP7's rumble past the Richmond, Va., landmark with northbound freight No. 280 in October 1961. J. Parker Lamb

MIDDLE:
In Atlanta, SAL used Terminal Station which it reached over Southern tracks. The busy terminal was also used by Central of Georgia and the Atlanta & West Point. Robert Niesz collection

BOTTOM:
In November 1958, Seaboard purchased a one-third interest in the Richmond Terminal Company, owner of the Broad Street Station in Richmond, Va. Accordingly, SAL trains vacated C&O's Main Street Station in Richmond, Va., in favor of the Broad Street Station, used by RF&P and ACL trains. CSX Transportation collection

at no more than four mph. A cut of up to five cars would normally be operated over the hump at one time.

Cars approaching the hump passed car-inspection booths located on each side of the hump lead track and over a drag detector, which automatically detected anything amiss beneath the car. Each car could be weighed, as needed, by electronic scales as it moved over the hump. At the south end of the classification yard were two trimmer leads designed so that two switch engines could work in the area simultaneously, performing such functions as switching cars that could not be humped and transferring cars from the classification yard to the departure tracks.

The Hamlet yard also had a large diesel shop, a wheel shop and a freight-car running-repair facility. The terminal had two cleaning tracks with a capacity of 50 cars each, a caboose track with a capacity for 23 cabs, and a stock-pen track which could hold 15 cattle cars. Four cars could be spotted at the unloading chutes at the stock pen. An icing platform at the south end of the yard could accommodate 50 cars on each side. Perishable trains sometimes departed from the icing platform without being humped.

When the new Hamlet yard was built, the standard freight car was only 40 feet long and anything much over 50 feet was a rarity. But the advent of trailers on flatcars (TOFC) a few years later introduced the 85-foot piggyback rack. The long cars caused problems on the hump. At times a track switch would be thrown under one of the TOFC cars, resulting in each truck ending up on a separate track. As a consequence, SAL began letting the piggyback cars coast into an open classification track and be switched by one of the trimmer engines.

Hamlet was, of course, the busiest point on the system. In 1965 it was dispatching 13 through freight trains a day in addition to locals and extras.

SHOPS

For much of the steam era Seaboard's most important locomotive repair facility was at Portsmouth. The shop consisted of a large concrete building constructed in 1916. It contained 15 tracks in the erecting bay, plus machine and blacksmith shops, and was equipped with a 250-ton overhead traveling crane. However, in 1936, the locomotive work was moved to Jacksonville and the West Jax shop became the most important steam-repair facility on the railroad. The West Jax facility consisted of an 18-track 117-foot x 380-foot back shop erected in 1910. Its roof was not high enough for an overhead crane so a Whiting hoist was used to wheel and unwheel locomotives. Other steam locomotive shops were at Savannah and Howells. The Savannah shop had a four-track back shop built in 1908, which contained a 200-ton overhead crane. The Howells shop was bigger, having six tracks. It was equipped with a 160-ton overhead traveling crane. Most locomotive repairs were performed at West Jax, Savannah or Howells in the later years of steam. The heaviest steam power, R class 2-6-6-4's and B class 2-10-2's, were assigned to Howells. However, a considerable amount of heavy steam repairs was performed at roundhouses, especially at Hamlet. The Hamlet roundhouse was capable of performing Class Three repairs on 2-6-6-4's, work which involved removal and repair of all the boiler flues.

Dieselization inevitably involved changes in the locomotive repair facilities. Seaboard constructed a diesel shop at West Jax in 1947. The new facility featured a 300-ton transfer table which moved locomotives to each of the shop's five bays. Another major diesel shop was erected at Hamlet when the new yard was built at that point in 1954 and enlarged in 1962. Smaller diesel shops were built at Savannah and Hialeah. Eventually most of Seaboard's diesel road locomotives were assigned to pools operating out of either Hamlet or Jacksonville.

Major car-repair work was done at Portsmouth, Jacksonville and Tampa. The Tampa car shop, located near the Florida phosphate beds, concentrated on hopper cars. Passenger-car repairs were performed in the old locomotive shop at Portsmouth. But Portsmouth wasn't restricted to passenger-car repairs. The shop there also did freight work. During the fifties, it converted hundreds of gondola cars into wood racks. Portsmouth was also the site of the railroad's major scrap dock where many SAL steam locomotives and cars met their end. West Jax did heavy repairs on boxcars and other types of freight rolling stock. Light repairs could be done at other points such as Savannah and Hamlet, and a wheel shop was also located at the North Carolina town.

MARINE TERMINALS

As befitted its name, SAL served a number of seaports and the company operated several marine terminals of its own. In Portsmouth, the railroad owned a terminal near the mouth of the Southern Branch of the Elizabeth River. Seaboard's Portsmouth piers were used at various times for ocean-going vessels and as the local terminal of the Old Bay Line. The railroad owned several pieces of floating equipment which it used in the Hampton Roads area, notably the tugboat *Seaboard* and a small fleet of covered lighters.

Seaboard's most important general-purpose marine terminal was located at Savannah, on Hutchinson Island, just across the Savannah River from the heart of the city. Construction of the Hutchinson Island terminal was begun in 1899 for the Georgia & Alabama Terminal Co., a subsidiary of John Skelton Williams's old Georgia & Alabama RR. As originally built, the terminal consisted of four piers, served by three slips, their lengths varying from 1,300 feet to 1,900 feet. Pier No. 1 was used for naval stores, No. 2 for lumber, No. 3 for cot-

ABOVE:
When completed in 1919, Florida's Jacksonville Terminal—modeled after Pennsylvania Station in New York City—was the largest station in the South. Seaboard, Atlantic Coast Line and Florida East Coast each held a 25 percent interest in the terminal, while the remaining quarter was divided between Southern and its subsidiary Georgia Southern & Florida. Jacksonville Convention Center collection

BELOW:
Dressed in new light-green and coral colors, E8 3051 prepares to depart Birmingham, Ala., with the northbound Silver Comet *on July 3, 1959.* J. Parker Lamb

included more than three miles of waterfront facilities. The island was connected to the city by a steel railroad bridge and at one time was served by some 16 miles of track. Seaboard records indicate that extensive fire-protection facilities were installed before 1918. Nevertheless, Piers 3 and 4 were seriously damaged in a fire on February 14, 1919. Over the years Seaboard discontinued use of some of the facilities and substantial portions of the complex were leased to various industries. Seaboard long operated a little passenger ferry, the *Island Girl*, between Hutchinson Island and downtown Savannah.

In Florida, Seaboard operated specialized terminals for loading phosphate rock aboard ships at Tampa and Port Boca Grande. At one time there had also been a phosphate pier at Fernandina. The facilities at Tampa had originally been developed by the Florida Central & Peninsular Ry. The terminal at Port Boca Grande had been constructed for the Charlotte Harbor & Northern Ry. in 1907 and was acquired by SAL when it absorbed the CH&N in 1925. The Boca Grande terminal also included facilities for loading lumber.

In 1947, Seaboard built a large new phosphate elevator at Seddon Island, near downtown Tampa. It included a motor driven loading tower which could be moved along the dock over special elevated tracks until it was opposite the hold of the waiting ship. The tower supported a boom conveyor which emptied into a loading spout from which the phosphate was discharged into the ship. The tower was fed by a series of conveyor belts which moved the phosphate from eight track hoppers into which railroad covered hopper cars had dumped the rock. The hopper house from which the cars were unloaded was built 12 feet above normal track level. Cars would be pulled up the incline to the hopper house by a cable attached to an electric car-haul engine. The holding tracks for the loaded cars were built on a descending grade so the cars could be fed by gravity to the base of the incline. Once unloaded, the cars would be released and roll on a descending grade through a spring switch and up a gravity kickback, then back through the switch to a storage yard for empties. Through this means some 90 cars could be unloaded without the need for a locomotive. The whole operation could proceed without interruption and a ship could be loaded at a rate of 1,500 tons an hour, about twice the rate of the previous elevator. The loading spout was equipped with an automatic trimmer which eliminated the need to adjust the load aboard ship by hand.

The Seddon Island terminal was a highly modern facility for its day, but neither it nor a similar ACL terminal at Tampa was provided with storage sheds. They were almost overwhelmed by the boom in phosphate loading in the sixties. As a result Seaboard Coast Line replaced both in 1969 with a new facility at Rockport, a few miles south of Tampa.

PASSENGER STATIONS

Seaboard shared union stations with other railroads in several of the larger cities it served, notably Richmond, Savannah, Atlanta, Birmingham, Tampa and Jacksonville. It also occupied Raleigh's Union Station until 1942, when it moved to a new station of its own. In addition, it used the union station in Montgomery, Ala., until 1951, when it discontinued its local passenger-train service to that city.

For many years SAL used Main Street Station in Richmond. The structure, which marked Seaboard's zero milepost, was owned by the Chesapeake & Ohio. It was completed in 1901, soon after Seaboard first reached the Virginia capital. The station was supposedly styled after a Rhineland castle, although Victorian eclectic might be a more apt description of its architecture. The tracks were elevated which, of necessity, limited the amount of trackage in the station. As a result, Seaboard-RF&P RR through trains were required to make an extra stop at Hermitage Yard for locomotive and engine-crew changes, train inspections and any needed switching operations. Main Street Station itself was used only to pick up and discharge passengers and change train crews.

Seaboard eventually moved from Main Street Station to Broad Street Station on April 26, 1959. Broad Street, which was about three miles north of the C&O station, had more track space available plus the advantage of being located adjacent to Hermitage Yard. As a result, the need for an extra stop in Richmond was eliminated. Broad Street Station was also newer than Main Street Station, having been opened in 1919, and more attractive, being constructed in the classic revival style. Prior to Seaboard's move, it had been jointly owned by the Atlantic Coast Line and the RF&P and used for their through trains as well as all RF&P local trains. In addition, the building housed RF&P's general offices. When it moved, SAL acquired a one-third interest in Richmond Terminal Co., the corporation which operated

ABOVE:
On the point of a southbound freight, FT 4010 idles by the Raleigh, N.C., passenger station on a warm August evening in 1962. J. Parker Lamb

BELOW:
The pink stucco Miami Station was built in something of a Spanish style. The stub-end station could accommodate trains of up to 18 cars. Anything longer had to be doubled to avoid blocking Tenth Avenue. Passengers who didn't want to patronize the dining car could obtain provisions from the grocery store conveniently located in the corner of the depot. David W. Salter

TOP: *Doubleheaded on a wartime edition of the* Palmland, *M-2 class Mountains 240 and 248 pause at Columbia, S.C., with No. 192 on May 3, 1942.* George E. Votava

BOTTOM: *Virginia Division locals meet at Bellwood, Va., as Q-3 Mike 371 backs the First Hopewell Switcher past sister 360 in charge of the Second Hopewell Switcher on July 2, 1950.* D. Wallace Johnson

At the time it vacated Main Street, Seaboard passengers accounted for about two-thirds of the station's customers. Even after the move SAL trains continued to rattle Main Street Station as Seaboard's mainline ran right beside the structure. In addition to Broad Street and Main Street, Richmond had a third railroad station, Hull Street Station, a small facility that was used by the Southern Ry.

Seaboard shared the Savannah Union Station with Atlantic Coast Line and Southern. It was a stub-end affair which required that through SAL trains back into the station. As a result, some of Seaboard's better trains bypassed Savannah, making only a brief stop at a small facility at West Savannah. The Union Station, which was located on West Broad Street, had an octagonal waiting room and a large train shed. Central of Georgia, the first railroad to serve Savannah, did not share the Union Station but rather operated its own depot, a historic structure built in 1861, that was just down the street. Savannah Union Station was vacated in 1963 to make way for a new highway, and Seaboard and Coast Line built a new through station on the western outskirts of the city. Southern did not participate in the new station as it had ceased passenger service to Savannah by that time.

In Atlanta, SAL used the Atlanta Terminal Station. When it first entered the city in 1892, Seaboard used Union Station, but it moved to Terminal Station in 1916. To reach the station, SAL had trackage rights over the Southern for about 2.5 miles from W&A Jct. southward to the terminal, and Seaboard passenger trains operating through Atlanta were required to back into the station. Terminal Station was completed in 1905 in something of a Spanish style. It originally had a large train shed, but the shed was removed in 1925. The station was jointly owned by the Atlanta & West Point, Central of Georgia and Southern Railroads. Seaboard was only a tenant, without an ownership interest in the station. The smaller Union Station, which was only about two blocks from Terminal Station, was used by the Louisville & Nashville, Georgia RR and Atlantic Coast Line. It had also been used by the Nashville, Chattanooga & St. Louis RR, until it was merged into the L&N in 1957, and the Atlanta, Birmingham & Coast until it was absorbed by the ACL in 1945.

In Alabama's largest city, SAL shared Birmingham Terminal Station with Central of Georgia, Illinois Central, St. Louis-San Francisco and the Southern Railway System. It jointly owned the terminal with the other railroads. The large Spanish-style station was built about 1906. Louisville & Nashville, the other major railroad serving Birmingham, maintained its own passenger station.

Seaboard and the Atlantic Coast Line occupied Tampa Union Station. It had been built in 1910 and was a relatively small station with eight stub-end tracks. When new, the Tampa

Union Station had also been used by the Tampa & Gulf Coast and Tampa Northern Railroads, both of which were later absorbed by the Seaboard.

The biggest union station used by Seaboard was the Jacksonville Terminal, which it shared with the other railroads entering the city: ACL, Southern and Florida East Coast. It was by far the busiest railroad station in the South. The station was operated by the Jacksonville Terminal Co., a jointly owned subsidiary of the four tenant railroads.

During the railroad era, Jacksonville billed itself as the "Gateway to Florida," and that wasn't much of an exaggeration. Jax Terminal was to Florida railroad passengers then much as the Atlanta airport is to southeastern airline passengers now. It was almost impossible to go to or from the Florida peninsula by train without going through Jacksonville. Only a handful of trains destined for South Florida bypassed the city.

The station building itself was a large classic revival structure, fronted by 14 Doric columns, that had been opened in 1919. It was served by 15 stub-end tracks and 11 through passenger tracks. The terminal was oriented so as to funnel trains to the Florida East Coast which approached the station from the southeast. Seaboard's mainline to Baldwin and the south approached the station from the west, and its northbound mainline to Savannah was northwest of the station. It was thus, in effect, a stub-end station as far as Seaboard was concerned and SAL trains going through Jacksonville were required to back into the station.

The Jacksonville Terminal was a vast facility. Three interlocking towers were required to control traffic in the terminal. It had a coach yard with a capacity for 115 cars. Its railway express plant was one of the largest in the country, capable of handling 250 cars. To service both its own and tenant railroads' locomotives, the Terminal Company had an 11-stall roundhouse and a 100-foot turntable as well as a coaling tower and refueling facilities for both diesels and oil-burning steamers. Seaboard, however, normally serviced its passenger locomotives at West Jax Yard, four miles west of the station. Jax Terminal Co. operated a fleet of fourteen 0-6-0's, ten coal burners and four oil burners. They were later replaced by ten EMD diesel switchers.

During the war year of 1944, the terminal handled an average of 105 trains a day. In its heyday Jax Terminal Co. employed as many as 2,000 people during the winter season, making it the second largest employer in the city. But most of its customers were just passing through. An estimated 80 to 85 percent of the station's patrons were neither departing from nor arriving at Jacksonville.

In addition to the large union stations, Seaboard also shared several small-town stations with other railroads. Among these were the stations in Weldon, N.C., Pembroke, N.C., Ocala, Fla., and Plant City, Fla., all of which were used jointly with the Atlantic Coast Line. The station and small freight yard at River Jct. (Chattahoochee), Fla., the junction point for SAL-L&N trains between Jacksonville and New Orleans, was of course shared with the Louisville & Nashville. ACL and the little Apalachicola Northern RR also utilized the yard and they too used the station until they discontinued passenger service to the town. Interestingly, even though River Jct. was only the terminal of a short ACL branch line, Coast Line performed the switching for all the railroads in town.

Seaboard did not share union stations in all of the larger cities it served. It used its own facilities in Portsmouth, Charlotte, Wilmington, Columbia, St. Petersburg, West Palm Beach and Miami. The biggest of these was at Portsmouth, where the passenger station was included in a large building that housed a number of the company's offices before its general headquarters were moved from Norfolk to Richmond.

The railroad's smaller stations varied in style, reflecting the many different companies that had built portions of the Seaboard and the varying eras in which they had been constructed. A few on the north end of the system, such as those in Raleigh and Petersburg, were Georgian structures. The stations on the West Beach-Miami line were erected in the Spanish fashion, which was in vogue when the line was built in the 1920s and also reflected Florida's history. But most of Seaboard's depots were wooden frame structures typical of small-town railroad stations across the country, except that the SAL stations, being in the South, had segregated waiting rooms.

buff with brown trim. However, the railroad changed its color scheme to solid white in the 1950s.

One small-town Seaboard station attained a modicum of renown years after the departure of its last passenger train. The station in Plains, Ga., on the Savannah-Montgomery line, became famous when local hero Jimmy Carter used it as his official campaign headquarters in his successful bid for the presidency in 1976.

STEAM LOCOMOTIVES

Seaboard's steam locomotive fleet was a rather undistinguished lot. The road owned only ten really modern steam locomotives, the R-1 and 2 class 2-6-6-4's delivered by Baldwin in 1935 and 1937. Few of its engines had the benefit of the best of steam technology. None had roller bearings or cast-steel frames, and few were equipped with feedwater heaters. Nevertheless, Seaboard did manage to wring outstanding performances from its class M-2 4-8-2's, and its class F-7 0-6-0's were among the best steam switch engines ever constructed.

A common characteristic of many of Seaboard's steamers was Vanderbilt tenders. SAL first adopted the cylindrical Vanderbilt-style tenders in 1914 and most of its subsequent road locomotives were so equipped. The road was also partial to the Baker valve gear, and the majority of its later steam engines featured that valve motion. Like virtually all railroads in the East, Seaboard fed its iron horses on a diet of coal. However, SAL did convert a half-dozen M-2 Mountains, five Pacifics and three Mikes to oil burners after World War II.

Seaboard's main passenger locomotives were sixty-one 4-8-2 Mountains, classes M, M-1 and M-2, built by Alco between 1914 and 1926. The Mountains handled almost all of the road's principal passenger trains. Fifteen of the most modern M-2 class were re-equipped with large tenders in the thirties and used for some extraordinarily long runs, operating all the way between Richmond and Jacksonville without change. Branch line and local passenger trains were usually assigned 4-6-2 Pacifics.

The backbone of Seaboard's freight locomotive roster was its 2-8-2 Mikados. The road owned a total of 170 locomotives of the type in five different classes. They were operated over all of the railroad's principal lines except the Alabama Division lines west of Vidalia, Ga., and north of Bainbridge, Ga., where they were precluded by weight restrictions on the bridges over the Chattahoochee and Flint Rivers. By far the most numerous class of steam engine on the railroad was the Q-3 2-8-2's. Seaboard acquired 117, Nos. 334-450, between 1923 and 1926. Basically they were a modified version of the USRA light Mikado, a standardized design developed by the United States Railroad Administration during World War I.

Another important type of freight locomotive on the Seaboard was the light 2-10-0, or Decapod. The railroad owned a total of fifty-one of these engines, most of which were the so-called Russian Decapods. They had originally been ordered from American builders by the Russian Czarist government. But when they couldn't be delivered due to the Bolshevik Revolution of 1917, some 200 of the machines were assigned to various U.S. railroads by the federal government. With their light axle loading, the Decapods proved ideal for many parts of the Seaboard, especially the Alabama Division lines which couldn't accommodate Mikados.

For heavy freight service, Seaboard owned twenty-five 2-10-2, Santa Fes, which had been acquired in the World War I era. The first 10, class B, were built to the railroad's specifications by the Baldwin Locomotive Works in 1918. The remaining engines, class B-1, were built to the USRA "light" design in the following year. Both classes were poorly counterbalanced and hard on track, especially the USRA machines. As a result, the B-1's were initially restricted to 25 mph and the B's to 30 mph. To ameliorate the problem, all of the USRA locomotives and five of the class B engines were eventually re-equipped with disc-type main drivers. The new drivers improved their riding qualities sufficiently to permit operation at 40 mph.

The road's biggest and newest steam locomotives were ten simple articulated 2-6-6-4's built by Baldwin in 1935 and 1937. Prior to development of the 2-6-6-4's, articulateds had generally been slow, plodding machines suitable only for drag freight or helper service. But not only were Seaboard's articulateds used in high-speed freight service, they were also reg-

ularly assigned to passenger trains. Although the 2-6-6-4's were successful, their tenure on the Seaboard was relatively brief as they were rendered superfluous by diesels. As a result all ten were sold to the Baltimore & Ohio in 1947.

Seaboard owned some ninety-two switch engines in the late thirties, all but two of which were 0-6-0's. The road's best steam switch engines were fifty Baldwin-built class F-7's, Nos. 1101-1150, built in 1927 and 1928. The largest 0-6-0's ever built, SAL's F-7's were also generally considered to be the most efficient locomotives of that wheel arrangement.

Rounding out Seaboard's steam roster was an assortment of older 2-8-0's, 4-6-0's and light 4-6-2's that were used for switching and branch-line and local freight chores. Many of the 2-8-0's had been inherited by SAL when it absorbed smaller roads such as the Georgia, Florida & Alabama and the Charlotte Harbor & Northern.

On an October 1962 night, veteran E4 3008 idles in the company of RSC3 1540 and GP7 1710. J. Parker Lamb

DIESEL LOCOMOTIVES

Seaboard's diesel locomotive fleet could perhaps best be described as eclectic. It included some thirty-eight different models from Alco, Baldwin, Electro-Motive and General Electric. As on most railroads, Electro-Motive products predominated, but only barely. Alco supplied a large minority of SAL's diesels, and the railroad was also a good Baldwin customer. In the final years of its existence, Seaboard added GE to its list of builders, with the acquisition of fifteen U30B's in 1966–67. SAL stabled some rare models such as the Baldwin "Centipede," Alco RSC-2, Electro-Motive SDP35 and Baldwin DR-6-4-1500, possessed by few other railroads.

The company was something of a diesel pioneer. It was the first railroad to acquire

TOP:
Just weeks old, GP30 503 rests at the Raleigh, N.C., engine terminal along with older Geeps in December 1962. J. Parker Lamb

BOTTOM:
Battle-scarred and bedecked with icicles, Seaboard FT's 4017 and 4117 stand ready to depart Raleigh, N.C., with an Extra South on a cold night in January 1963. The veteran freighters are on their last legs and within weeks they will be traded in to EMD on GP30's already a-building at La Grange. J. Parker Lamb

1503 in 1947, and purchased its last freight-cab units, eleven F3's, three FA1's and three FB1's the following year. Yet, in other respects, the railroad was conservative. Some of its first diesels were equipped with friction bearings and it was slow to adopt dynamic brakes, not ordering them until 1960.

Seaboard's principal passenger diesels were a fleet of Electro-Motive E units, twenty E4's, three E6's, thirty-five E7's, eleven E8's and a single E9. The railroad's first true diesel locomotives were the E4's purchased in 1938 and 1939.

Almost alone among major railroads SAL regularly used its E units in high-speed freight service during the 1950s and 1960s. The railroad was well served by its first diesels. No. 3000, the first E4, had run an astounding 4.5 million miles by the time it was retired in 1964. To replace its oldest passenger diesels, SAL acquired twenty dual-service Electro-Motive SDP35's in 1964, Nos. 1100-1119.

Seaboard's first freight diesels were forty-four of Electro-Motive's famous FT model acquired during World War II. The FT's were built as 2,700-hp semi-permanently connected cab and booster sets, two of which could be combined in mutiple-unit operation to create a single 5,400-hp A-B-B-A locomotive. As the first successful freight diesel locomotive, the FT is undoubtedly the most significant single diesel model ever built. More than any other diesel it spelled doom for the steam locomotive.

After World War II, Seaboard bought its last freight cabs, F3A's 4022-4031, FA1's 4200-4202 and FB1's 4300-4302. Its most noteworthy acquisitions, however, were Baldwin DR-12-8-3000's 4500-4513, purchased from 1945 to 1948. Commonly called Centipedes because of their multifarious 2-D+D-2 wheel arrangement, these huge machines developed 3,000 hp. They were the biggest and most powerful diesel locomotives of their era, but they suffered from numerous mechanical problems and had relatively short careers, being scrapped in 1957 and 1961.

The bulk of SAL's first-generation diesel freight fleet consisted of Electro-Motive and Alco road switchers. The road owned forty-four Alco model RSC-2 and RSC-3 units which rode on six-wheel A1A trucks for light axle loading. More conventional Alco road switchers included some ninety-two 1500- and 1600-hp model RS-2 and RS-3 units which were equipped with four-wheel B-type trucks. The most common diesel type on Seaboard's roster was EMD's ubiquitous model GP7. Seaboard acquired 123 of these 1500-hp road switchers between 1950 and 1952. In addition, the road purchased fifty-six EMD GP9's, the model which succeeded the GP7, when it began replacing its oldest diesels in the late fifties. The railroad eventually concentrated its Alco units in Florida and its Electro-Motive units at the north end of the system. The only Baldwin road switchers on the Seaboard roster were RS12's 1466-1475 delivered in 1952–53.

Surrounded by the tools of his trade, the yardmaster oversees his domain from his office in the tower at the crest of the Hamlet Yard hump. Lewis P. Watson; CSX Transportation collection

SAL purchased its first dynamic brake-equipped diesels in 1960: Alco RS-11's 100-109 and EMD GP18's 400-409. True second-generation diesels, categorized by higher horsepower and sealed car bodies with centralized filtered-air intake systems, were added later in the sixties. These comprised thirty-five Electro-Motive GP30's, ten EMD GP35's and fifty-one GP40's, twenty-six Alco C-420's and fifteen of General Electric's model U30B.

After sampling single units from Alco, Baldwin and EMC in 1941, Seaboard gave the lion's share of its switcher orders to the Eddystone builder, acquiring a total of fifty-three BLW yard engines. Following the delivery of VO660 1202 in February 1941, SAL purchased seven VO1000's, thirty-five DS4-4-1000's and ten S12's. Alco placed a distant second, providing a single S1, thirteen S2's and ten S4's, while Electro-Motive's contribution to the SAL switcher fleet was limited to eight units, SW1 1200 and NW2's 1406-1412.

Seaboard's passenger diesels were long painted in the Electro-Motive designed green, yellow and orange "citrus" color scheme introduced on the first E4's. The early locomotives in this scheme had silver underbodies and trucks but these components were painted black on later units. The railroad adopted a simpler scheme for its passenger diesels in 1955, pale-green car bodies with red striping and lettering, and dark green roofs and ends.

The first freight diesels were painted much like the passenger locomotives. But Seaboard soon adopted a simpler plan, Pullman-green car bodies with a wide yellow stripe, which was applied to all freight and road-switcher units. That basic scheme remained in effect until 1966. In that year, the road took delivery of its first GP40's, dressed in a new livery which retained the old pattern but replaced the dark Pullman green with a bright lime green. Consequently, railroaders began referring to the new units as "Jolly Green Giants." SAL began applying the new color to other locomotives, but relatively few engines had received the new green paint scheme by the time the ACL merger was consummated.

To some minds, SAL reserved its most striking colors for its switch engines. Most railroads painted their lowly switch engines either to match their road units or in some dark utilitarian shade. But Seaboard painted its switchers in an elaborate red and black arrangement that not only was completely different from its road engines, but which may well have been its most colorful paint scheme.

ROLLING STOCK

A large railroad requires a vast amount of rolling stock. At the end of 1962, Seaboard owned over 29,000 cars including 454 passenger cars, 27,560 freight cars and 1,098 pieces of work equipment.

In 1962, Seaboard's passenger fleet comprised 314 standard heavyweight cars and 131 lightweight streamlined cars, plus 9 business cars. The standard cars consisted mainly of 52 coaches, 26 sleepers, 18 combination coach and baggage cars, 10 diners, 36 mail or mail-

Naturally, Seaboard's lightweight passenger cars were "silver," i.e., unpainted stainless steel, and were employed mostly on the *Silver Meteor, Silver Star* and *Silver Comet*. Seaboard normally painted its heavyweight equipment dark green; however, some cars were painted silver to match the streamliners.

The railroad's 1962 freight car fleet included 10,103 boxcars of all types, 4,729 gondolas, 4,329 hoppers, 4,154 covered hoppers, 3,332 wood racks, 556 flats and 321 cabooses. In addition, SAL owned 176 automobile-rack cars which were assigned Trailer Train Co. reporting marks. The road owned only 25 stock cars and a couple of common car types were missing entirely from its roster. Seaboard, like most other railroads, did not possess its own refrigerator cars. Rather SAL used the cars of the Fruit Growers Express Co. in which it had a financial interest. With the exception of a few non-revenue cars, it didn't own any tank cars either. The nations's tank car fleet was, and still is, privately owned, mainly by car companies such as Union Tank Car Co. and General American Transportation.

Most of Seaboard's freight cars were painted boxcar red. That color was applied to gondolas, hoppers and flats, as well as to boxcars. Covered hoppers were generally painted gray, although the phosphate cars were also painted boxcar red. In the sixties, SAL bought a number of custom boxcars fitted with special lading protection equipment which were painted green with aluminum doors and yellow lettering. These cars were promptly dubbed "Green Hornets" by Seaboard hands. As is only right and proper, the railroad painted its cabooses the traditional bright red.

PEOPLE

A railroad is a corporation, a fictitious "person" created by operation of law. And of course it's a lot of material things: tracks and stations and bridges and locomotives and cars. But in the final analysis it's people—thousands of people from the company president down to the lowest gandy dancer.

As an employer, Seaboard was one of the best. Much more so than on most railroads, it was a family. *Trains* magazine once observed that Seaboard was one of the few railroads whose "management-labor relations...traditionally generated more pride than ill will."

I won't pretend that everything was always blissful. The history of labor relations in the railroad industry is much too turbulent for that. Conflict was inevitable in an industry beset by precipitous declines in passenger and merchandise traffic at the same time as technological innovations were rendering numerous jobs obsolete. Dieselization, Centralized Traffic Control and mechanized track repair equipment eliminated the need for thousands of jobs on Seaboard alone. SAL employment declined from a peak of over 20,000 during World War II to only 11,000 by 1965. Certainly Seaboard endured its share of strikes, many of them occasioned simply because it was picked as a representative target in a nationwide dispute. But even now, over 25 years later, former Seaboard men I have talked with remember the railroad with genuine fondness. I doubt that statement could be honestly made about many other railroads.

Seaboard courtesy extended beyond its own "family." "The Route of Courteous Service" was more than just an empty advertising slogan stenciled on its boxcars. I recall once when a clerk in the passenger department in Richmond telephoned the pharmacy where my mom worked in Jacksonville. Someone had left his suitcase on a train. There was no identification, but there was a medicine bottle from the drug store. He had taken the trouble of trying to trace the owner through the prescription.

SAL even tolerated hoboes, although unofficially, of course. When I worked as a yard clerk at West Jax I knew of more than one occasion when a railroader, touched by a sad story, would slip a hobo a buck or two or share a sandwich. I remember one evening when I was out in the yard and a knight of the road asked me where to hop the next freight to Savannah. I told him there wasn't one until the next afternoon and suggested he try the Coast Line. His response was a colorful string of expletives. He'd have nothing to do with the bulls of the ACL—he preferred Seaboard!

CHAPTER SEVEN

SUBSIDIARIES

Over the years, Seaboard controlled several smaller railroads which operated more of less independently. The most important of these was the Macon, Dublin & Savannah RR. But Seaboard's most colorful subsidiary was not a railroad at all, but rather a steamboat company, the Old Bay Line.

MACON, DUBLIN & SAVANNAH RAILROAD

The Macon, Dublin & Savannah RR was chartered in 1885 as the Macon & Dublin RR Co. to construct a line from Macon, Ga., southeastward to Dublin, Ga. Construction began in August of 1885, but was discontinued the following May. It was eventually proposed to build the line all the way to Savannah and the name of the company was changed to Macon, Dublin & Savannah RR Co. in 1890. Work resumed in June of that year and a 54-mile line from Macon to Dublin was completed in December 1891. No further construction was done for almost ten years. In April 1901, work began on a 39-mile extension of the MD&S from Dublin to Vidalia, Ga. The line to Vidalia was completed in April 1902 and a connection was made at that point with Seaboard's Savannah-Montgomery line, thus creating a through route between Macon and Savannah. Vidalia, 80 miles from Savannah, was as close to Georgia's oldest city as the MD&S ever achieved.

In 1904, the Atlantic Coast Line bought control of the 92-mile MD&S. But ACL did not physically connect with the MD&S and had scant need for the property. Thus, in 1907, Coast Line sold its interest to Seaboard. Seaboard eventually acquired all of MD&S's stock in 1945, and the Macon, Dublin & Savannah was finally merged into the SAL on March 1, 1958.

The MD&S connected with the Southern and the Central of Georgia to form a route between points such as Atlanta and Birmingham and Seaboard points in Florida and along the Georgia coast. Important sources of local traffic were several clay and kaolin mines along the line. During the 1940s the road operated two through freight trains in each direction daily, including an overnight run between Macon and Savannah in conjunction with Seaboard. The MD&S also operated a pair of local passenger trains, Nos. 17 and 18, between Macon and Vidalia. It shared the Union Station in Macon with the Central of Georgia, Southern Railway System and the Georgia RR, but its daily locals weren't scheduled to connect with any of the other railroads' passenger trains at Macon or with SAL's passenger service at Vidalia. It finally dropped its passenger service in 1949.

The MD&S bought its last new steam locomotive before World War I. For the most part, the road rostered locomotives purchased from other railroads or hand-me-downs from parent SAL. The ex-Seaboard engines all retained their SAL road numbers on the MD&S. During the closing years of the steam era, its biggest freight locomotives were "Russian" Decapods. MD&S acquired three of these locomotives from the Erie RR in 1937 and three more from the Seaboard in 1949. The road also owned three 2-8-0 Consolidations. Passenger power consisted of a 4-6-0 built in 1920 for the J.F. Darby Lumber Co., and No. 875, an ex-Western Maryland, ex-Seaboard class P-4 4-6-2 which MD&S obtained in 1946. Yard [illegible] 0-6-0 the MD&S bought new in 1906. In addition to its own [illegible] various times.

MACON
FLYER

104
TAVARES & GULF R. R.
104

FACING PAGE,
TOP LEFT:
Working eastbound time freight No. 88, MD&S "Russian" Decapod 46 (ex-Erie 2468) tackles the road's ruling grade west of Dry Branch, Ga., in June 1947. Hugh M. Comer

TOP RIGHT:
Still carrying her SAL road number, Macon, Dublin & Savannah 4-6-2 875 (originally Western Maryland 157) works the daily eastbound local accommodation near Dry Branch, Ga., on September 11, 1949. Seaboard's largest subsidiary, the 93-mile Macon, Dublin & Savannah was absorbed by SAL on March 1, 1958. Hugh M. Comer

MIDDLE LEFT:
MD&S briefly tried a Seaboard doodlebug in passenger service prior to World War II. Relettered MD&S and dubbed the Macon Flyer, *Brill-built motor car 2018 is shown at Macon, Ga., with an SAL trailer in 1940.* Hugh M. Comer

MIDDLE RIGHT:
Carrying white flags, MD&S "Russian" Decapods 47 and 544 work an Extra West through Jeffersonville, Ga., in October 1945. Formerly Erie 2483, No. 47 is one of three ex-Erie "Russians" acquired by the MD&S, while the 544 found its way to the Macon-Vidalia line via Seaboard and Detroit, Toledo & Ironton. Hugh M. Comer

BOTTOM:
One of the last new locomotives acquired by the Tavares & Gulf, 2-6-2 No. 104 poses for a builder's portrait at Alco's Schenectady works in 1916. Alco Historic Photos

THIS PAGE:
Built by Baldwin in 1916, diminutive T&G 2-6-2 No. 100 stands at Tavares, Fla., in October 1950. Harold K. Vollrath collection

The Macon, Dublin & Savannah received its first diesel, Baldwin VO1000 No. 1000, in February 1942. Seven years later, the road began replacing its assortment of hand-me-down Consolidations and Decapods with Alco RS2's and RS3's. MD&S took delivery of its last locomotive, RS3 1706, in February 1956, just two years before the SAL takeover. Seaboard absorbed the Macon, Dublin & Savannah on March 1, 1958, and the road's eight diesels, VO1000 1000, RS2's 1700-1702 and RS3's 1703-1706 were added to the SAL roster.

TAVARES & GULF RAILROAD

A small but valuable subsidiary of the Seaboard was the Tavares & Gulf RR, or "Tug & Grunt" as it was locally called. During the 1940s, one station on the 38-mile short line, Winter Garden, Fla., originated more perishable traffic than any other point on the Seaboard system. The T&G extended from Ellsworth Jct., near Tavares, Fla., on SAL's Wildwood-Orlando branch, south through Winter Garden to Ocoee, Fla., a distance of 28 miles. It also owned a 6-mile branch line from Waits Jct. to Clermont and, in addition, had trackage rights over the Seaboard between Ellsworth Jct. and Tavares, a distance of 3 miles.

The T&G dated back to 1886 when its predecessor, the Tavares, Apopka & Gulf RR Co. was chartered to

TOP:
Prior to her sale to the Unadilla Valley, Jacksonville, Gainesville & Gulf 4-6-0 No. 60 poses with a ramshackle wooden caboose at Gainesville in June 1940. Harold K. Vollrath collection

BOTTOM:
Gainesville, Jefferson & Southern No. 3 was built for the narrow-gauge Jug Tavern Route by the Pittsburgh Locomotive Works in 1883. Alco Historic Photos

By 1888 it had completed a 26-mile line from Ellsworth Jct. to Clermont. The company failed financially and was sold under foreclosure in January 1890 to Henry Jackson, who reorganized the road as the Tavares & Gulf RR Co. In 1894, the T&G built a 6-mile branch line from Waits Jct., about 21 miles from Tavares, south to Oakland. The line was extended from Oakland to Winter Garden in 1899 and, in 1914, from Winter Garden to Ocoee. The line to Ocoee eventually came to be considered the T&G's mainline. Seaboard purchased all of the road's stock in 1926, and the T&G was operated as a separate SAL subsidiary afterward.

Most of the T&G was originally laid with 40-lb rail and the road was dilapidated when Seaboard acquired it. Moreover, the road had numerous curves with about half of its mainline consisting of curved track. Derailments were rife. It was not uncommon for as many as five to occur in a single round trip. As a result, the daily round trip between Tavares and Ocoee sometimes actually required several days. Needless to say, Seaboard proceeded to correct the situation soon after it took over, replacing all the light rail and making other improvements.

The Tavares & Gulf handled perishable traffic almost exclusively, with citrus fruit predominating. Citrus accounted for about 90 percent of its freight and winter vegetables for

TOP:
Neatly attired and well polished, Gainesville & Gulf 4-4-0 No. 344 pauses at Kirkwood, Fla., 3.5 miles north of Micanopy, with a freight train about 1901. H.J. Doherty collection

BOTTOM:
Tampa & Jacksonville's homemade motor car Kathryn *was built by J.A. Whiting about 1916 for service between Gainesville and the Southern Railway connection at Sampson City. Commonly called the "Hoodler," the 41-foot car was powered by two 120-hp engines and could carry 42 passengers.* H.J. Doherty collection

most of the remainder. As a result, the road was highly seasonal, with almost no business for four months out of the year.

Steam locomotives rostered by the T&G included three little 2-6-2's which it had purchased new: No. 100, built by Baldwin in 1916, and Nos. 104 and 105 which came from Schenectady in 1922. In addition it owned two 4-6-0's: No. 106 which had originally belonged to another SAL subsidiary, the Florida Central & Gulf, and No. 661, a Seaboard class L4-S Ten-Wheeler which it obtained in 1942. Its biggest locomotive was No. 874, a Seaboard class P-4 4-6-2 that SAL had acquired from the Western Maryland Ry. during World War II and passed on to the short line in 1946. T&G used Seaboard motive power during the diesel era and never acquired any diesel locomotives of its own.

The Tavares & Gulf was not included in the SAL-ACL merger and continued to operate as a separate railroad. However, its most important station, Winter Garden, was also served by a former ACL branch. As a result, there was little need for the short line after the merger and the T&G was abandoned in 1969.

JACKSONVILLE, GAINESVILLE & GULF RAILWAY

The Jacksonville, Gainesville & Gulf was a Florida short line that connected with the Seaboard at Gainesville. It was originally chartered in 1884 as the Gainesville, Rocky Point & Micanopy Ry., but no construction was undertaken. In 1895 the charter was sold, the name of the company was changed to Gainesville & Gulf Ry. Co., and it was proposed to build the line from Gainesville to either Tampa Bay or the Gulf of Mexico, A 12-mile line from Gainesville south to Micanopy was completed in that year. During the next four years the line was extended south from Micanopy 16 miles to Fairfield, and also north from Gainesville 20 miles to Sampson City. At Sampson City a connection was made with the Georgia Southern & Florida Ry., a subsidiary of the Southern Ry., which operated a line from Macon, Ga., to Palatka, Fla. In 1906 the "Grits & Gravy," as it was sometimes known,

ABOVE: *Perched on the boiler, the fireman and brakeman aboard GM 203 attempt to remedy problems with the sanders as the lanky 2-10-0 eases downgrade with a southbound freight at Belmont, Ga., on March 18, 1950. Built by Baldwin in 1923 as Alabama, Tennessee & Northern Ry. 402, GM 203 is preserved at Tennessee Valley Railroad Museum, Chattanooga, Tenn.* Hugh M. Comer

BELOW: *Working a northbound freight, GM 2-10-0 No. 206 rounds a curve at Belmont on a crisp March 26, 1955. Among six GM steam locomotives to be preserved, the 206, a "Russian" Decapod built as USA 1088 and once employed by DT&I, Seaboard and MD&S, is displayed at Historic Spencer Shops in Spencer, N.C.* Hugh M. Comer

event only 8 more miles were ever added, an extension from Fairfield south to Emathala, giving the road a total length of 56 miles. The little railroad never got close to either Tampa or Jacksonville. Like many a railroad, the aspirations expressed by its corporate title exceeded the wherewithal of its backers.

The Tampa & Jacksonville billed itself as "The Fruit and Vegetable Route of Florida" but locals soon started derisively calling it the "Tug & Jerk," not to be confused with the "Tug & Grunt" sobriquet of the Tavares & Gulf. The line served mainly as a feeder line to the GS&F at Sampson City, hauling mostly produce from the area south of Gainesville and phosphate rock and fuller's earth from around Emaltha.

The railroad also enjoyed a considerable passenger business transporting college students between the then male-only University of Florida at Gainesville and the Florida State College for Women, now Florida State University, at Tallahassee. The eager students rode the T&J between Gainesville and Sampson City, the GS&F between Sampson City and Lake City, and the Seaboard between Lake City and Tallahassee. A tedious journey, no doubt, but hardly a serious impediment to intercollegiate romance. To transport the students, the T&J installed a gasoline-powered rail car on the run between Gainesville and Sampson City. Around 1915 a new car, which resembled a McKeen rail car, was designed and built by a T&J engineer, J.A. Whiting. It was officially named *Kathryn,* but dubbed the "Hoodler" after the sound of its whistle.

In those days when communications were limited, the T&J, like some other Florida railroads, would warn farmers along its line of impending freezing weather. Its trains would periodically blow four short blasts to alert growers to the need to protect their crops.

Seaboard bought the T&J in 1926 and reorganized it as the Jacksonville, Gainesville & Gulf Ry. Co., a name that was no more accurate than its previous designations. Regular passenger service was ended in 1930 and the JG&G was soon abandoned between Sampson City and Gainesville, thus eliminating the connection with the GS&F. The road continued as a feeder to the SAL for several years, but Gainesville was the only place of much consequence on the entire line and Seaboard already served that point. As a result the line was abandoned in 1943. However, a few miles of track in and around Gainesville were sold to the Atlantic Coast Line. The JG&G's motive power had consisted of three Baldwin 4-6-0's, Nos. 60, 70 and 71.

GAINESVILLE MIDLAND RAILROAD

The Gainesville Midland RR operated a 42-mile line from the mill town of Gainesville, Ga., to a connection with the Seaboard at Athens, Ga. This otherwise obscure little line had become famous in the late 1950s as one of the last steam-powered railroads in the country. It continued to operate with an all-steam roster long after almost every other railroad had scrapped its last steam engine.

The Midland began as the Gainesville, Jefferson & Southern RR, the "Jug Tavern Route." In 1883 and 1884 the GJ&S built a 44-mile, 3-foot-gauge road from Gainesville south through Belmont and Jug Tavern (later Winder) to Monroe, Ga., plus a 10-mile branch line from Belmont southeasterly to Jefferson, Ga. In 1884 it acquired the 10-mile-long Walton RR, which extended from Monroe south to a connection with the Georgia RR at Social Circle, Ga., and converted the Walton road from standard to narrow gauge. Soon after its completion, the Georgia RR acquired control of the new line. The Jug Tavern Route entered receivership in 1897 and was sold under foreclosure in 1904, emerging as the Gainesville Midland Ry. The new GM Ry. did not include the old Walton RR, however, as the Georgia RR retained the Monroe-Social Circle line.

In 1906, the Gainesville Midland built a 16-mile standard-gauge extension from Jefferson south to a connection with the Seaboard at Fowler Jct., near Athens. Trackage rights were obtained over SAL for the two miles from the junction into Athens. The slim-gauge line from Gainesville to Jefferson was widened to standard gauge in 1908, and the line from Belmont to Monroe was broadened in 1913.

ABOVE: *Two years after Seaboard diesels killed the fires in GM's famed Decapods, SAL RSC3 No. 1541 is refueled by a C.H. Martin & Son driver at Gainesville in August 1961.* J. Parker Lamb

BELOW: *The Gainesville Midland finally got a diesel to call its own in June 1966 when La Grange delivered SD40 No. 10. A big locomotive for a little railroad, it was GM's first new locomotive since 1906. Still in original paint 14 years later, GM 10 idled at Gainesville on August 23, 1980.* Jim King

The GM remained solvent for a while, helped in part by lumber traffic received from the Gainesville & Northwestern, a little road that built a line from Gainesville northward to Helen in the Georgia mountains in 1913. But the Midland again went bankrupt in 1921, remaining in receivership for 17 years. Seaboard agreed to buy the GM in 1927, provided it could abandon the line from Belmont to Monroe. The Interstate Commerce Commission approved the arrangement at first, but later rescinded its approval of the abandonment application

TOP:
Chesterfield & Lancaster No. 105 on a train at Cheraw, S.C., in June 1935. The Baldwin Ten-Wheeler was built for the Macon, Dublin & Savannah in 1901. Harold K. Vollrath collection

BOTTOM:
Savannah & Statesboro No. 5 at Savannah Union Station in May 1916. The 4-4-0, ex-Georgia Southern & Florida No. 112, was built by the Rhode Island Locomotive Works in 1890. Harold K. Vollrath collection

GM remained independent. In 1938, the Midland was acquired by Forest Greene, proprietor of the Georgia Car & Locomotive Co., a dealer in used railroad equipment, and the line was reorganized as the Gainesville Midland RR.

The GM replaced its steam-powered passenger trains with a fleet of Brill motor cars and a rail bus in 1938. The road operated two daily round trips, one between Gainesville and Athens and the other between Gainesville and Monroe, with that equipment for several years. It finally discontinued its passenger service soon after the end of World War II. The line from Belmont to Monroe was eventually abandoned in 1948.

Seaboard finally bought control of the Midland in 1959, much to the chagrin of rail fans as it promptly dieselized the line. The GM was to be the last addition to the Seaboard system. The little railroad was operated as a separate company and it was not included in the SAL-ACL merger. It continued as a separate subsidiary of Seaboard Coast Line and its successors.

Gainesville was on the Southern Railway's Washington-Atlanta mainline, so that the Midland was confronted with a formidable rail competitor. Moreover, Southern had its own branch line to Athens so there was little opportunity to handle Southern Railway traffic to or from that point. GM existed mainly on traffic interchanged with the Seaboard at Athens and, to a lesser extent, with the Georgia RR and the Central of Georgia, both of which had branch lines to Athens from the south. Its traffic varied. It carried a considerable amount of lumber from the Gainesville & Northwestern until that road pulled up its tracks in 1934. It later handled substantial amounts of textiles, poultry feed and oil, but lost most of that business to trucks or pipelines. By the late fifties its traffic consisted mostly of coal, rock and assorted merchandise.

The Midland was burdened with a rugged saw-toothed profile. The line from Fowler Jct. to Gainesville had no less than 13 summits, one short grade of 2.38 percent and numerous grades of 1 percent or more. Like many a short line, the GM was a rudimentary affair. Most of the line was laid with light 56-lb rail until the late fifties when it was replaced by 75-lb steel. It still had about six miles of 56-lb rail when Seaboard took over. GM's only coaling station, at Belmont, was a simple roof-level platform from which wheelbarrow loads of coal were dumped into a locomotive's tender. And the line clung to steam power almost into the sixties. By 1959, Midland was plagued by frequent breakdowns and had trouble obtaining parts for its anachronistic motive power. Moreover, it had to perform its own locomotive repairs as it could no longer rely on its Class One neighbors for steam repair work.

When Seaboard acquired control of the Midland in 1959, the short line owned seven steam locomotives, most of which had been on SAL's roster at one time or another. It had two 2-8-0's which it used for switching at Gainesville, one of which, No. 301, was originally a Charlotte Harbor & Northern engine that GM bought from SAL in 1951. Its road power consisted of five light 2-10-0's. No. 206 was a "Russian" Decapod that had previously served on the DT&I, SAL and Macon, Dublin & Savannah. It had borne number 544 on the SAL and MD&S. The other four "Dekes" were somewhat newer. No. 203 had been built by Baldwin for the Alabama, Tennessee & Northern Ry. It was similar in design to the Seaboard class D-2 and D-3 2-10-0's. No. 207 had originally been GF&A No. 401, then SAL class D-2 No. 524, and Nos. 208 and 209 were ex-Seaboard class D-3's, Nos. 530 and 533.

Seaboard, of course, dieselized GM as soon as it acquired control of the short line but, fortunately, six of the Gainesville Midland steam locomotives were preserved. No. 116 was placed on display at Jefferson, Ga., No. 203 was given to the Atlanta Chapter of the National Railway Historical Society and No. 206 was donated to the State of Georgia, No. 208 was exhibited at Winder, Ga., No. 209 was placed on display in Gainesville and No. 301 was exhibited in Charlotte, N.C., as Seaboard No. 301.

Initially, Seaboard replaced Midland's steamers with a pair of its own six-axle RSC3's. The Alco's, with their light axle loading, were especially suitable for roads such as the GM. Nevertheless, some improvements had to be made on the short line before even the RSC-3's could be operated. The Midland operated for several years using only Seaboard engines. The short line finally acquired a diesel locomotive of its own in 1966 when it bought No.

Midland since 1906. GM, however, continued to use Seaboard diesels in addition to its own locomotive.

OTHER RAILROAD SUBSIDIARIES

Seaboard controlled several other even more obscure short lines. These included the Raleigh & Charleston RR, the Charlotte, Monroe & Columbia RR and the Chesterfield & Lancaster RR in the Carolinas; the Savannah & Statesboro Ry. in Georgia; and the Florida, Central & Gulf Ry. in Florida. Most were abandoned before World War II.

The Raleigh & Charleston RR owned a 41-mile line extending from Lumberton, N.C., to Marion, S.C. Its predecessor, the Carolina Northern RR Co., was organized in 1899 to build a line from Lumberton to Marion and also from Lumberton north to Goldsboro, N.C. Construction began that year and the line from Lumberton to Marion was completed by December 1901. The Carolina Northern was unsuccessful and the line went into receivership in December 1902. The railroad was sold at foreclosure in 1906 and reorganized as the Raleigh & Charleston. The purchaser of the line was John Skelton Williams, erstwhile president of the Seaboard Air Line. He intended to use the short line as a part of a new trunk line he envisioned to run from Raleigh, N.C., to the Gulf of Mexico. As part of his plan he and his associates also bought six small Georgia railroads which were consolidated into the Georgia & Florida Ry. Williams planned to extend the R&C north to Raleigh and south to Charleston, but in any event the only new line ever actually constructed was a 2-mile spur line from Marion to South Marion. SAL bought all of the R&C's stock in 1911 and the short line was operated as a Seaboard subsidiary from then afterward. A 23-mile segment of the line between Lumberton and Lakeview, S.C., was abandoned in 1933. The remainder of the R&C was abandoned in 1946.

At one time the R&C controlled another short line, the Marion Southern RR. The line was chartered in 1907 and existed principally to haul lumber for the Marion County Lumber Co. Its mainline extended from West Marion, S.C., where the lumber company's mill was located, 2 miles eastward to a connection with the R&C at Marion, and from West Marion to Brownsville, S.C., a distance of about 18 miles. In addition, the line operated a number of logging spurs. The Raleigh & Charleston acquired control of the Marion & Southern in 1912. By 1919, the line from West Marion to Brownsville was no longer in operation. The 2-mile segment from West Marion to Marion remained in service until about 1937, apparently being operated with R&C equipment.

The Charlotte, Monroe & Columbia RR was a 17-mile short line that extended from a connection with SAL at McBee, S.C., northwesterly to Jefferson, S.C. The company was chartered in 1900 to build a line from McBee to Monroe, N.C. In effect, it would have provided the Seaboard with a short route between Charlotte, N.C., and Columbia, S.C., which would have bypassed Hamlet. However, only 17 miles were ever built. Construction began in 1901 and was completed in 1903. The company was reorganized in 1908 and 1909 and, of course, long controlled by Seaboard. The CM&C disposed of its sole locomotive in 1930 and thereafter used SAL motive power. The little line was finally abandoned in 1940.

The Chesterfield & Lancaster RR Co. owned a 35-mile line extending from Cheraw, S.C., westward to Crowburk, S.C. It was chartered in 1887 to build a line from Cheraw to Lancaster, S.C., via Chesterfield Court House, but construction did not begin until 1900. The line was completed to Chesterfield by 1901. It reached Ruby in the next year and in 1907 was extended through Pageland to Crowburk. SAL acquired control of the C&L in 1913 when it purchased three-fifths of its stock, and it bought the remainder of the stock in 1923. Operation of the 3 miles between Pageland and Crowburk was discontinued during the 1920s. The remainder of the Chesterfield & Lancaster was abandoned in 1941. The little railroad had used leased SAL locomotives during the last decade of its existence.

The Savannah & Statesboro Ry. was a Georgia short line that extended from a connection with Seaboard's Savannah-Montgomery line at Cuyler westward to Statesboro, Ga., a total distance of 32 miles. In addition, it had trackage rights over the SAL for the 20 miles from Cuyler into Savannah. The predecessor of the S&S was the Cuyler & Woodburn RR

Co., which was incorporated in 1894. It built a 12-mile line from Cuyler to Hubert, Ga., in that year. The little line failed financially and entered into receivership in 1895. In 1897, it was sold under foreclosure and reorganized as the Savannah & Statesboro. The S&S extended the line to Statesboro in 1899. In 1903, the short line entered into an agreement with the Seaboard whereby SAL became its preferred connection, granted S&S trackage rights into Savannah and agreed to guarantee its bonds. Up until the 1930s, the little road operated two daily passenger trains in each direction between Savannah and Statesboro. The S&S was a victim of the Depression, being abandoned in 1933.

The Florida Central & Gulf Ry. operated a 28-mile line which extended from Hernando, Fla., to Port Inglis, Fla., and connected with the Seaboard at Dunnellon. The FC&G was organized by the Seaboard in 1916 to acquire the Standard & Hernando RR Co. from the Dunnellon Phosphate Co. S&H had existed primarily to transport phosphate rock from the Dunnellon Phosphate Co.'s mine near Hernando. The Standard & Hernando had been organized in 1904 and constructed a 13-mile line from Rockwell to Hernando in 1905. The line was extended to Port Inglis, on the Withlacoochee River near the Gulf of Mexico, in 1911, and dock facilities for loading phosphate were developed at that point. FC&G operated until 1930 when the entire line was abandoned, The road owned three Baldwin 4-6-0's, all of which had originally been built for the S&H.

OLD BAY LINE

Seaboard's longest lived subsidiary was the Baltimore Steam Packet Co. The Old Bay Line, as it was commonly called, operated steam boats on Chesapeake Bay for 122 years. The BSP Co. was organized in 1839, and began service between Baltimore and Norfolk in 1840, replacing the defunct Maryland & Virginia Steam Boat Co. which had operated on the run beginning in 1828. The new company called itself the Bay Line and initiated service with the steamboats *Pocahontas*, *Jewess*, *South Carolina* and *Georgia*. Vessels were scheduled to leave Baltimore at 9:00 A.M. and arrive in Portsmouth at 11:00 P.M., working daily in the summer and three times a week in the winter. The new line continued its predecessor's close cooperation with the Portsmouth & Roanoke RR, soliciting passengers traveling from Baltimore to Weldon, N.C., and points further south.

In 1845, the Bay Line formed an affiliate, the Powhatan Line, which commenced operating on the James River, providing a service from Baltimore to Richmond. The James River line became more important with the demise of the Portsmouth & Roanoke RR's service to Weldon in April of that year. Instead of riding the P&R RR to Weldon, passengers from Baltimore had to be routed to Petersburg, where they caught the Petersburg RR to Weldon and the South. In 1851,

An advertisement for the Old Bay Line's service in January 1940. The company would merge with the rival Chesapeake Steamship Co. in the following year and its "newest-fastest-finest" steamers would be sequestered by the Navy during World War II. Author's collection

TOP:
The State of Maryland *on July 17, 1933. She and her sister the* Virginia *were 320' long, had a beam of 56'6" and a draught of 16'9". The photo was probably taken when she was being converted to an oil burner.* R. Loren Graham; Steamship Historical Society collection, Univ. of Baltimore Library

BOTTOM:
Last new boat built for the Old Bay Line was the President Warfield, *the line's flagship. Built in Wilmington in 1928, she was almost identical to the* Maryland *and* Virginia *but had a slightly greater gross tonnage, 1,814 tons. She too was commandeered by the federal government during World War II. After the war she was sold to the Haganah and renamed* Exodus 1947. *She was caught by the British Navy while attempting to smuggle Jewish settlers into Palestine.* Blakeslee/ Lane; Steamship Historical Society collection, Univ. of Baltimore Library

already controlled the Richmond, Fredericksburg & Potomac and Petersburg Railroads, bought control of the Bay Line, and the steamboat company, in turn, soon bought control of the newly revived Seaboard & Roanoke RR.

The management of the Bay Line was sympathetic to the South before the Civil War. In early 1861, before hostilities actually began, the company refused to transport Union sailors to reinforce the navy yard at Gosport (Portsmouth). Once the war commenced, the Bay Line was prevented from operating to Norfolk by the U.S. Navy, but it was allowed to run between Baltimore and Old Point Comfort, Va., which remained in Union hands. Before the fighting started, Northern authorities allowed the line to operate a small steamer, the *William Selden*, between Old Point Comfort and Norfolk. When the Union declared a blockade, the Confederates seized the *Selden*. She was finally destroyed by the Rebels when they evacuated Portsmouth in 1862. The *William Selden* was the only Bay Line vessel to be lost as a result of the conflict. The Union recaptured Norfolk in 1862, but the Bay Line was not allowed to resume service to the city until after the war was over.

For many years, the BSP Co. had enjoyed a virtual monopoly on the Chesapeake, but soon after the end of the war, Leary Brothers, of New York, inaugurated a competitive service on the Baltimore-Norfolk run. In response the BSP Co. began referring to itself as the "Old Established Bay Line," which eventually became simply the "Old Bay Line." The competition was ended in January 1867 when the Old Bay Line succeeded in buying off the competing firm.

The steamboat company had always been primarily a passenger business but it soon began operating a group of small tramp freighters, which were dubbed the mosquito fleet. The first vessels to be used in this service were war surplus boats that the Union had used as transports or gunboats. The company later bought new freighters especially designed for this type of service. The Old Bay Line operated the mosquito fleet until 1887 when the small freighters were withdrawn due to a combination of increased rail competition and the delivery of new passenger vessels with greater freight capacity.

The BSP Co. faced renewed maritime competition in the 1870s from the Baltimore, Chesapeake & Richmond Steamboat Co. The BC&R, known as the York River Line, was founded in 1874 as an affiliate of the Richmond, York River & Chesapeake RR. The railroad, then controlled by the vast Clyde shipping interests, was a predecessor of the Southern Ry., which operated a line between Richmond and West Point, Va., on the York River. At first the York River Line ran a steamboat service between Baltimore and West Point, but in 1875 the company initiated its People's Line between Baltimore and Norfolk in direct competition with the Old Bay Line. An immediate result was that the Old Bay Line was forced to reduce its fares to match its rival's. On January 11, 1877, Thomas Clyde of the York River Line and John M. Robinson of the Old Bay Line agreed to restrain the competition. Among other things, the Old Bay Line promised not to provide direct service from Baltimore to Richmond or points on the York River. In return, the York River Line terminated its Baltimore-Norfolk service.

Probably the 1890s were the heyday of the Old Bay Line. Rail routes between Baltimore and Norfolk were circuitous, the automobile had yet to appear and the company had no maritime competition. However, competition came to stay in 1896 when the York River Line, by then controlled by the Southern Railway, instituted a new service between Baltimore and Portsmouth. The Old Bay Line protested that this constituted an invasion of its territory in violation of the 1877 agreement between Thomas Clyde and John M. Robinson but to no avail as the original agreement had long since expired. In response the BSP Co. started a rate war and inaugurated a rival service between Baltimore and Richmond in competition with the York River Line's service. But the company was embarrassed when one of its steamers ran hard aground in the James River on its first trip north from Richmond. The new service had to be postponed for two weeks while the vessel was refloated and repaired. The Old Bay Line and the York River Line finally reached an agreement in 1897 and the BSP Co. discontinued its service to Richmond at the end of that year. However, the Baltimore, Chesapeake & Richmond Steamboat Co. continued to operate between Baltimore and Norfolk in direct competition with the Old Bay Line. The BC&R was reorganized in

Chesapeake Steamship Co., with the Southern Railway owning two-thirds of its stock and the Atlantic Coast Line one-third. In that guise the firm competed against the Old Bay Line for years to come.

The Panama Canal Act of 1916 required that railroads divest themselves of competing water carriers. But the Interstate Commerce Commission ruled that the Old Bay Line was an integral component of the Seaboard Air Line so the railroad was permitted to retain control of the steamboat company. Similarly, the ICC allowed the Southern and the Coast Line to continue their ownership of the Chesapeake Line.

Like the railroads, the Old Bay Line was run by the United States Railroad Administration during World War I. During federal control its operations were combined with those of the Chesapeake Line. In 1919, while still under federal management, one of the company's steamers, the *Virginia*, caught fire and was destroyed with the loss of 23 lives. It was the line's only really serious mishap in the twentieth century.

The BSP Co. purchased its last new vessels in the 1920s. The first two boats were sister ships, the *State of Maryland*, built in 1922, and the *State of Virginia*, in 1923. Typical of Chesapeake Bay steamers, each had a steel hull, wooden superstructure and a single screw. They were 320 feet long, 1,783 gross tons, and were powered by a four-cylinder triple-expansion reciprocating steam engine. They could carry 700 tons of cargo and up to 600 passengers. The last boat was the *President Warfield*. Built in 1928, she was slightly larger than the *Maryland* and *Virginia*, and served as flagship of the line. The Old Bay Line usually named its vessels after southern states and it had originally been intended to name the new vessel the *Florida*, but her name was changed when S. Davies Warfield, president of the Old Bay Line as well as the Seaboard Air Line, died while she was under construction. The three vessels had been built as coal burners but all were converted to oil burners during the 1930s.

Normally, the line operated one vessel in each direction nightly between Baltimore and Norfolk and kept a third boat in reserve as a spare. The *Maryland* and the *Warfield* usually made the scheduled runs with the *Virginia* held as the spare boat. The company frequently used the spare in excursion service and at times during the thirties chartered one of the vessels to other lines for use on Long Island Sound or in New England.

The vessels required twelve hours for the run between Baltimore and Norfolk, typically leaving each terminal at 6:30 P.M. and arriving at 6:30 the next morning. They made one stop en route, calling at Old Point Comfort, Va. After discharging passengers and cargo at Norfolk, the vessels would go to Portsmouth for freight loading, returning to Norfolk in time to prepare for the evening departure for Baltimore.

The Old Bay Line steamboats transported, of course, considerable amounts of cargo. During Prohibition some of it was illegal, bootleg liquor that had been smuggled aboard from foreign ships docked at Norfolk. On one occasion in 1929 the *President Warfield* was stopped by an overzealous Coast Guard officer who actually ordered his cutter to fire a shot across the vessel's bow and demanded that she heave to for inspection. Needless to say, the BSP Co.'s management was not amused.

Both the Old Bay Line and the rival Chesapeake Line operated their vessels half empty during the Depression. Of the two firms, the Old Bay Line better survived the hard times. Its vessels were newer than the Chesapeake Line's, and had ample capacity to carry both cargo and passengers' automobiles. In any event, the railroads which owned the two firms decided to merge the steamboat operations. Thus, in 1941, the Chesapeake Steamship Co. was merged into the Baltimore Steam Packet Co. As a result of the consolidation, Seaboard's ownership of the Old Bay Line was reduced to a one-half interest with the Southern Railway owning one-third and the Atlantic Coast Line one-sixth.

The Chesapeake SS Co. had normally operated two vessels on the Baltimore-Norfolk run and two on the West Point line between Baltimore and West Point, Va. In 1911, the company introduced two new steamers in the Norfolk service, the *City of Baltimore* and the *City of Norfolk;* and in 1913 it bought a pair of similar but slightly smaller vessels for the West Point run, the *City of Richmond* and *City of Annapolis*. However, in 1927 the *Annapolis* was rammed and sunk by her sister ship, the *Richmond*. She was replaced by a new vessel, the *Yorktown*. The Chesapeake Line suffered another disaster when the *City of Baltimore* was burned just off Baltimore in 1937. After her loss, the *Yorktown* was transferred to the Norfolk run and Baltimore-West Point service was reduced to three times a week.

Following the merger, the former Chesapeake Line runs to both Norfolk and West Point were discontinued. Only the original Old Bay Line schedules between Baltimore and Norfolk remained in operation.

The Bay Line had inherited four vessels from the Chesapeake Line: the *City of Norfolk, City of Richmond* and *Yorktown,* plus an old tugboat, the *Southern,* which had been used in Baltimore harbor. Of these, the company intended to retain only the *Yorktown.* But World War II intervened and in 1942 the Navy commandeered the *State of Maryland, State of Virginia, President Warfield* and *Yorktown.* The line was left with only the *City of Norfolk* and *City of Richmond.* It used those two old Chesapeake Line steamers to handle a booming business during the war. Both were converted to oil burners in 1944 and an ancient vessel, the *Meteor,* formerly of the Colonial Line, was used as a replacement while they were in the yard.

None of the requisitioned vessels ever returned to Old Bay Line service. The *Yorktown* was sunk by a German U-boat off Greenland on Sept. 27, 1942. The *President Warfield* was sold to a Zionist group, renamed *Exodus 1947* and seized by the British Royal Navy while attempting to smuggle Jewish refugees into Palestine. She was damaged by British destroyers and beached in Haifa where she remained until she was accidentally burned in 1952. The *State of Maryland* was scrapped in 1950 and the *State of Virginia* in 1952.

The Bay Line planned to build two new ships after World War II which would be patterned after cruise liners and, in addition, convert two Navy LSD's into vessels with a capacity for 500 passengers plus the ability to roll vehicles on and off. But the company couldn't raise the capital for the projects and was thus compelled to retain the venerable City of Norfolk and City of Richmond.

The Bay Line did manage to add to its fleet in 1949, when it bought the *District of Columbia* from the Norfolk & Washington Steamboat Co. The N&WSB Co. had provided a nightly service between Norfolk and Washington since 1891. By 1948, it was down to its last vessel, the *District of Columbia,* which operated on alternate nights between the two cities. On October 31, 1948, the *District of Columbia* collided with the tanker *Georgia,* collapsing some 75 feet of the *Columbia's* starboard cabins and killing one passenger. The service had been unprofitable and the N&W decided to terminate its operations. Thus, the Old Bay Line bought the boat, which had been built in 1925, repaired her and converted her to an oil burner. She was returned to the Norfolk-Washington run, but usually withdrawn from that service during the winter and used as a relief boat on the Baltimore run when one of the other vessels was in dry dock. However, the wharf in Washington eventually deteriorated to the point where it was condemned, and the Norfolk-Washington service was finally discontinued on September 30, 1957.

By the 1950s the Old Bay Line was the last operation of its kind remaining in the country. At one time a number of firms had provided overnight steamboat service between various cities. Perhaps the most renowned was the famous Fall River Line which operated between New York and Fall River, Mass., in conjunction with connecting rail service to Boston. But almost all of the lines were out of business by World War II. The Old Bay Line itself began to lose money in 1956. The company continued to enjoy a good freight business but its passenger patronage had become largely seasonal. Service to Old Point Comfort had to be discontinued in 1959 when the dilapidated pier there was closed. Finally, the Old Bay Line terminated its passenger service after Labor Day 1961. Freight service lasted until April 13, 1962, when the Baltimore Steam Packet Co. ceased all operations.

Two of the line's three vessels were destroyed after the company called it quits. The *City of Richmond* was sunk in a hurricane off South Carolina in 1964, while being towed to the Virgin Islands for use as a floating hotel. The *City of Norfolk* was struck by lightning and burned in 1967 while being scrapped in New Jersey. Only the *District of Columbia* long survived. She was sold and renamed the *Provincetown.* She was used between Boston and Provincetown, Mass., during the summers and also served as a spectator vessel for the America's Cup yacht races when they were held off Newport, R.I.

CHAPTER EIGHT

PASSENGER SERVICE

The Seaboard Air Line operated an extensive passenger service. For the most part it was a good one, but it did have its detractors. Some wag once composed the following lines to be sung to the tune of *Sweet Adeline*:

Seaboard Air Line, never on time
Your fret me so 'cause you're so slow.
Your engine steams in all my dreams;
You're the nightmare of my life-
Seaboard Air Line,
Sea-
board
Air
Line

The song may have had some validity at one time, but certainly in the last 25 years of its existence SAL operated some of the best passenger trains in the country.

Seaboard's most important passenger route was from New York City to Florida, especially to the so-called Gold Coast between West Palm Beach and Miami. The New York-Florida trains were handled by the Pennsylvania Railroad between New York and Washington, by the Richmond, Fredericksburg & Potomac RR between Washington and Richmond and, of course, by the Seaboard between Richmond and Florida. Both the Pennsy and the RF&P contributed cars to the equipment pools for the Seaboard trains operating over their lines.

On the SAL, all through passenger trains on the Florida run were normally routed over the line via Columbia, S.C., rather than the longer freight route via Charleston. Prior to the construction of the new Savannah station in 1963, some of the faster Florida trains bypassed Savannah Union Station, making only a brief service stop at West Savannah. Certain trains also bypassed Jacksonville, operating via the Gross Cut-off between Gross and Baldwin, Fla. Most of the New York-Florida trains were divided into East and West Coast sections at Wildwood, Fla., with the East Coast section operating to Miami and the West Coast section to either Tampa or St. Petersburg.

Seaboard also operated a substantial service, in conjunction with the Pennsylvania and the RF&P, between New York or Washington and Atlanta and Birmingham. However, only through Pullman cars, not full consists, were operated to New York prior to the inauguration of the *Silver Comet* in 1947.

Another important route was between Jacksonville and New Orleans, which was operated with the Louisville & Nashville Railroad. SAL handled these trains over the 207 miles between Jacksonville and River Jct. (Chattahoochee), Fla. L&N, in turn, operated the trains over its branch line from River Jct., via Pensacola, Fla., to Flomaton, Ala., and then over its mainline to Mobile and New Orleans. Most of the through equipment used on this run was provided by the L&N The SAL-L&N joint route was the only direct rail link from Florida to New Orleans and points in the Southwest. During the twenties, a through transcontinental Pullman had been operated over this route between Jacksonville and Los Angeles.

A fourth major route was over the original mainline from Portsmouth to a connection with the Richmond-Hamlet mainline at Norlina, N.C. The Portsmouth trains were generally scheduled to connect with mainline trains operating to and from points south, and through coaches and sleepers operated between Portsmouth and Atlanta and Florida points. In later years the southern terminus for the Portsmouth trains was shifted from Norlina to Raleigh.

Unlike its rival, Coast Line, Seaboard was not a major participant in passenger traffic moving between the Midwest and Florida. Its only through Midwestern train was the seasonal *Florida Sunbeam*, which was discontinued in 1949. However, for a while after the *Sunbeam*'s demise, Seaboard did continue to handle a few sleeping cars, in connection with the Southern Railway System, between Midwestern and Florida points.

Historically, the railroad's passenger traffic was heaviest during the Florida winter vacation season. Some of its best trains operated only during that season, generally from mid-December to mid-April. During the 1930s passenger revenues in the peak month of January were, on average, at least twice as much as those in any of the summer or autumn months. In 1939, for example, passenger revenues were well over $700,000 in each of the four months of January, February, March and December, and less than $400,000 in each month from May to October. However, this situation changed over the years so that by the 1950s passenger traffic was fairly evenly distributed throughout the year. Indeed, by 1955, passenger revenues in July actually exceeded those in the peak winter months.

TOP: *In a wild fury of smoke and steel, SAL No. 6, the* Cotton Blossom, *storms out of Birmingham, Ala., behind Mountain 206 on May 23, 1948.* Frank E. Ardrey, Jr.

BOTTOM: *Passing Bellwood Tower, M-class 4-8-2 205 marches into Atlanta with Mail & Express train 11 on an early morning in 1940.* Hugh M. Comer

PREWAR TRAINS

The premier Seaboard passenger train during the 1930s was the sonorously named *Orange Blossom Special,* a crack winter season limited operation on the New York to Florida run. The *Special* was inaugurated in November 1925, soon after the Seaboard's extension to West Palm Beach was completed. Its run was extended to Miami in January 1927, after the line was opened to the "Magic City." Separate East and West Coast sections of the all-Pullman train ran from New York to Miami and St. Petersburg in the late 1920s. But by the 1929-30 season the *Special* was operated as a single train from New York to Miami, with West Coast cars handled by a Wildwood-St. Petersburg connection. The train's personnel were specially selected and at one time a daily report of the *Special*'s performance, occupancy and noteworthy passengers was submitted to Seaboard's president. The emphasis was on comfort and the train included such amenities as a barber, a lady's maid, and shower baths. The train was completely air conditioned beginning January 2, 1934, one of the first trains in the nation to be so equipped. To commemorate the event, the *Special* was re-christened with Florida orange juice in a ceremony at New York's Pennsylvania Station. In 1936, the West Coast train was restored as a separate section of the *Special* all the way between New York and St. Petersburg. Naturally, the *Orange Blossom Special*s were powered by the Seaboard's best steam locomotives, class M-2 4-8-2's equipped with long-distance tenders.

Beginning December 15, 1938, the East Coast section of the *Special* was dieselized, becoming the first train on the Seaboard and, indeed, the first train in the Southeast, to be

Condensed Schedules of the Leaders of the Greatest Fleet to Florida

ORANGE BLOSSOM SPECIAL - (EAST COAST)

8:30 AM	LV	Boston (South Sta.)	NYNH&H	LV	8:45 PM
9:30 AM	LV	Providence	"	AR	7:45 PM
10:15 AM	LV	Springfield	NYNH&H	AR	7:20 PM
10:50 AM	LV	Hartford	"	AR	6:41 PM
11:48 AM	LV	New Haven	NYNH&H	AR	5:27 PM
5:35 PM	AR	Washington	PRR	LV	11:35 AM
1:20 PM	LV	New York (Penn. Sta.)	PRR	AR	3:30 PM
1:35 PM	LV	Newark	"	AR	3:14 PM
2:51 PM	LV	North Philadelphia	"	AR	1:59 PM
3:00 PM	LV	Philadelphia (30th St. Sta.)	"	AR	1:50 PM
4:33 PM	LV	Baltimore	"	AR	12:15 PM
5:55 PM	LV	Washington	RF&P	AR	11:10 AM
g 8:35 PM	LV	Richmond (Main St. Sta.)	SEABOARD	AR	g 8:28 AM
g 9:05 PM	LV	Petersburg	"	AR	g 7:57 AM
g 7:23 AM	LV	Thalmann (Brunswick-Sea Island)	"	AR	g 9:12 PM
Ψ 8:40 AM	AR	Baldwin	"	LV	Ψ 8:05 PM
n11:36 AM	AR	Winter Haven (Florence Villa)	"	LV	n 5:04 PM
•11:45 AM	AR	West Lake Wales-Lake Wales	"	LV	• 4:54 PM
n12:06 PM	AR	Avon Park	"	LV	n 4:32 PM
•12:17 PM	AR	Sebring (Lake Jackson)	"	LV	• 4:22 PM
1:52 PM	AR	West Palm Beach-Palm Beach	"	LV	2:46 PM
n 2:02 PM	AR	Lake Worth	"	LV	n 2:36 PM
n 2:15 PM	AR	Delray Beach	"	LV	n 2:24 PM
n 2:30 PM	AR	Deerfield (Boca Raton)	"	LV	n 2:10 PM
n 2:51 PM	AR	Fort Lauderdale	"	LV	n 1:52 PM
n 3:01 PM	AR	Hollywood	"	LV	n 1:41 PM
3:35 PM	AR	Miami	"	LV	1:10 PM
7:30 PM	LV	Miami .... Hav-MiaSS	For sailing dates	AR	8:00 AM
8:30 AM	AR	Havana .... "	see pages 79-80.	LV	7:00 PM
5:00 PM	LV	Miami	Fla. Motor Lines	AR	11:30 AM
9:30 PM	AR	Key West	" " "	LV	7:00 AM

ORANGE BLOSSOM SPECIAL - (WEST COAST)

8:30 AM	LV	Boston (South Sta.)	NYNH&H	LV	8:45 PM
9:30 AM	LV	Providence	"	AR	7:45 PM
10:15 AM	LV	Springfield	NYNH&H	AR	7:20 PM
10:50 AM	LV	Hartford	"	AR	6:41 PM
11:48 AM	LV	New Haven	NYNH&H	AR	5:27 PM
5:35 PM	AR	Washington	PRR	LV	11:35 AM
1:30 PM	LV	New York (Penn. Sta.)	PRR	AR	3:00 PM
1:40 PM	LV	Newark	"	AR	2:43 PM
2:58 PM	LV	North Philadelphia	"	AR	1:31 PM
3:07 PM	LV	Philadelphia (30th St. Sta.)	"	AR	1:22 PM
4:37 PM	LV	Baltimore	"	AR	11:43 AM
6:10 PM	LV	Washington	RF&P	AR	10:35 AM
r 8:51 PM	LV	Richmond (Main St. Sta.)	SEABOARD	AR	r 7:53 AM
r 9:20 PM	LV	Petersburg	"	AR	r 7:14 AM
6:42 AM	AR	Savannah (Union Sta.)	"	LV	9:33 PM
¢ 7:56 AM	AR	Thalmann (Brunswick-Sea Island)	"	LV	¢ 8:10 PM
9:15 AM	AR	Jacksonville	"	LV	6:55 PM
w10:57 AM	AR	Ocala (Silver Springs)	"	LV	w 5:06 PM
w12:38 PM	AR	Plant City	"	LV	w 3:23 PM
1:15 PM	AR	Tampa	"	LV	2:55 PM
2:18 PM	AR	Clearwater	"	LV	1:55 PM
2:24 PM	AR	Belleair (Belleview-Biltmore Hotel)	"	LV	1:49 PM
3:00 PM	AR	St. Petersburg	"	LV	1:15 PM
3:13 PM	AR	Palmetto-Ellenton	SEABOARD	LV	1:09 PM
3:17 PM	AR	Bradenton-Manatee	"	LV	1:05 PM
3:35 PM	AR	Sarasota	"	LV	12:50 PM
4:20 PM	AR	Venice	"	LV	12:10 PM
3:51 PM	AR	Boca Grande .... Seaboard	"	LV	11:45 AM
4:00 PM	AR	South Boca Grande .... "	"	LV	11:40 AM
4:55 PM	AR	Useppa Island	Yacht	LV	10:00 AM

SILVER METEOR

3:30 PM	LV	New York (Penn. Sta.)	PRR	AR	10:55 AM
3:40 PM	LV	Newark	"	AR	10:39 AM
4:59 PM	LV	North Philadelphia	"	AR	9:24 AM
5:08 PM	LV	Philadelphia (30th St. Sta.)	"	AR	9:14 AM
5:38 PM	LV	Wilmington	"	AR	8:45 AM
6:41 PM	LV	Baltimore	"	AR	7:43 AM
7:30 PM	AR	Washington	"	LV	6:40 AM
7:45 PM	LV	Washington	RF&P	AR	6:40 AM
r10:10 PM	LV	Richmond (Main St. Sta.)	SEABOARD	AR	r 4:15 AM
r10:37 PM	LV	Petersburg	"	AR	r 3:46 AM
4:50 AM	LV	Columbia	"	LV	9:30 PM
7:15 AM	AR	Savannah (Union Sta.)	"	LV	7:05 PM
h 8:21 AM	LV	Thalmann (Brunswick-Sea Island)	"	AR	h 5:50 PM
9:40 AM	AR	Jacksonville	"	LV	4:45 PM
9:45 AM	LV	Jacksonville	"	AR	4:40 PM
z11:19 AM	AR	Ocala (Silver Springs)	"	LV	z 3:05 PM
11:45 AM	AR	Wildwood	"	LV	2:40 PM
▲12:50 PM	AR	Winter Haven	"	LV	▲ 1:28 PM
▼12:59 PM	AR	West Lake Wales	"	LV	▼ 1:20 PM
▲ 1:22 PM	AR	Avon Park	"	LV	▲ 1:01 PM
▼ 1:33 PM	AR	Sebring (Lake Jackson)	"	LV	▼12:52 PM
3:04 PM	AR	West Palm Beach-Palm Beach	"	LV	▲11:19 AM
▲ 3:12 PM	AR	Lake Worth	"	LV	▲11:10 AM
▲ 3:23 PM	AR	Delray Beach	"	LV	▲10:59 AM
▲ 3:35 PM	AR	Deerfield (Boca Raton)	"	LV	▲10:48 AM
▲ 3:53 PM	AR	Ft. Lauderdale	"	LV	▲10:33 AM
▲ 4:01 PM	AR	Hollywood	"	LV	▲10:24 AM
4:30 PM	AR	Miami	"	LV	9:55 AM
11:55 AM	LV	Wildwood	SEABOARD	AR	2:30 PM
▲12:37 PM	AR	Dade City	"	LV	▲ 1:42 PM
▲ 1:07 PM	AR	Plant City	"	LV	▲ 1:11 PM
1:35 PM	AR	Tampa	"	LV	12:40 PM
2:37 PM	AR	Clearwater	"	LV	11:40 AM
3:20 PM	AR	St. Petersburg	"	LV	11:00 AM
1:50 PM	LV	Tampa	SEABOARD	AR	③ 9:40 AM
3:13 PM	AR	Palmetto-Ellenton	"	LV	— — —
3:17 PM	AR	Bradenton-Manatee	"	LV	— — —
3:35 PM	AR	Sarasota	"	LV	③ 8:00 AM
4:20 PM	AR	Venice	"	LV	— — —

FLORIDA SUNBEAM

11:45 PM	LV	Chicago .... (CT)	Big Four	AR	7:35 AM
4:20 AM	LV	Indianapolis	"	AR	1:45 AM
7:55 AM	AR	Cincinnati .... (ET)	"	LV	11:55 PM
11:45 PM	LV	Detroit .... (ET)	Mich. Cent.	AR	7:25 AM
1:40 AM	LV	Toledo	Big Four	AR	5:35 AM
7:05 AM	AR	Cincinnati	"	LV	11:30 PM
12:25 AM	LV	Cleveland .... (ET)	Big Four	AR	7:20 AM
3:50 AM	LV	Columbus	"	AR	3:15 AM
6:50 AM	AR	Cincinnati	"	LV	11:50 PM
8:15 AM	LV	Cincinnati .... (ET)	Sou. Ry.	AR	10:55 PM
2:50 PM	LV	Chattanooga .... (CT)	"	AR	2:00 PM
6:20 PM	AR	Atlanta	"	LV	10:30 AM
6:25 PM	LV	Atlanta	"	AR	10:25 AM
3:45 AM	AR	Hampton .... (ET)	"	LV	2:50 AM
a 4:49 AM	AR	Ocala (Silver Springs)	SEABOARD	LV	a 1:40 AM
a 6:45 AM	AR	Winter Haven	"	LV	a11:35 PM
③ 6:55 AM	AR	West Lake Wales-Lake Wales	"	LV	③11:23 PM
a 7:20 AM	AR	Avon Park	"	LV	a10:57 PM
③ 7:35 AM	AR	Sebring (Lake Jackson)	"	LV	③10:40 PM
9:38 AM	AR	West Palm Beach-Palm Beach	"	LV	8:45 PM
a10:04 AM	AR	Delray Beach	"	LV	a 8:17 PM
a10:18 AM	AR	Deerfield (Boca Raton)	"	LV	a 8:02 PM
a10:41 AM	AR	Fort Lauderdale	"	LV	a 7:44 PM
a10:53 AM	AR	Hollywood	"	LV	7:33 PM
11:30 AM	AR	Miami	"	LV	7:00 PM
7:30 AM	AR	Tampa .... (ET)	SEABOARD	LV	10:40 PM
8:35 AM	AR	Clearwater	"	LV	9:25 PM
8:42 AM	AR	Belleair (Belleview-Biltmore Hotel)	"	LV	9:22 PM
9:20 AM	AR	St. Petersburg	"	LV	8:45 PM
①10:10 AM	AR	Bradenton-Manatee (ET)	SEABOARD	LV	8:31 PM
①10:40 AM	AR	Sarasota	"	LV	8:10 PM
①11:10 AM	AR	Venice	"	LV	7:20 PM
①12:25 PM	AR	Fort Myers	Bus	LV	② 6:30 PM
① 1:45 PM	AR	Naples	"	LV	② 5:10 PM
See Note	AR	Arcadia .... (ET)	SEABOARD	LV	7:30 PM
	AR	Boca Grande	"	LV	6:00 PM
	AR	South Boca Grande	Yacht	LV	5:50 PM
	AR	Useppa Island	"	LV	4:00 PM

Equipment and Explanation of Characters shown on pages 23-26 and 30.

13 14

The schedules of Seaboard's best Florida trains as they appeared in timetables for January 1940. The Silver Meteor *operated throughout the year; the other trains ran only during the winter tourist season.* Author's collection

Ride These Popular-Year 'Round Trains

k12.00M	Lv	Boston (South Sta.) (EST)......	NYNH&H	Ar	p6.15AM
10 30AM	Lv	New York (Penn. Sta.).........	PRR	Ar	5.30PM
12.10PM	Lv	Philadelphia (30th St. Sta.).....	"	Ar	3.49PM
1.42PM	Lv	Baltimore....................	"	Ar	2.15PM
2.50PM	Lv	Washington..................	RF&P	Ar	1.05PM
5 33PM	Lv	Richmond (Main St. Sta.)......	SEABOARD	Ar	10.07AM
4.25PM	Lv	Norfolk......................	Ferry	Ar	11.00AM
4.45PM	Lv	Portsmouth...................	SEABOARD	Ar	10.45AM
9.05PM	Ar	Raleigh (Union Sta.)...........	"	Lv	6.25AM
10.33PM	Ar	Southern Pines (Pinehurst).....	"	Lv	4.45AM
2.10AM	Ar	Columbia....................	"	Lv	1.30AM
5.10AM	Ar	Savannah (Union Sta.).........	"	Lv	10.23PM
8.10AM	Ar	Jacksonville	"	Lv	7.00PM
1.45PM	Ar	West Lake Wales-Lake Wales..	"	Lv	1.45PM
2.31PM	Ar	Sebring (Lake Jackson)........	"	Lv	12.52PM
4.40PM	Ar	West Palm Beach.............	"	Lv	10.36AM
5.48PM	Ar	Fort Lauderdale..............	"	Lv	9.30AM
6.00PM	Ar	Hollywood...................	"	Lv	9.21AM
6.40PM	Ar	Miami......................	"	Lv	8.50AM
1.45PM	Ar	Tampa......................	"	Lv	1.10PM
3.45PM	Ar	St. Petersburg...............	"	Lv	11.20AM
3.35PM	Ar	Sarasota....................	"	Lv	— —
4.30PM	Ar	Venice......................	"	Lv	— —
(S) 4.00PM	Ar	Boca Grande................	"	Lv	— —
(S) 4.55PM	Ar	Useppa Island................	Yacht	Lv	— —

k12 00M	Lv	Boston (South Sta.) (EST).....	NYNH&H	Ar	p6.15AM
10 30AM	Lv	New York (Penn. Sta.)	PRR	Ar	5 30PM
12 10PM	Lv	Philadelphia (30th St. Sta.).....	"	Ar	3.49PM
12 39PM	Lv	Wilmington..................	"	Ar	3.18AM
1.42PM	Lv	Baltimore...................	"	Ar	2.15PM
2.50PM	Lv	Washington..................	RF&P	Ar	1.05PM
5.33PM	Lv	Richmond (Main St. Sta.)......	SEABOARD	Ar	10.07AM
4.25PM	Lv	Norfolk.....................	Ferry	Ar	11.00AM
4.45PM	Lv	Portsmouth..................	SEABOARD	Ar	10.45AM
9 05PM	Ar	Raleigh (Union Sta.)...........	"	Lv	6.25AM
10.33PM	Ar	Southern Pines (Pinehurst).....	"	Lv	4.45AM
12.40AM	Ar	Monroe.....................	"	Lv	2.35AM
2.51AM	Ar	Clinton.....................	"	Lv	12 07AM
3.30AM	Ar	Greenwood..................	"	Lv	11.30PM
5.30AM	Ar	Athens.....................	"	Lv	9 25PM
6.20AM	Ar	Atlanta......(CT)............	"	Lv	6.30PM
6.45AM	Lv	Atlanta.....................	"	Ar	6.10PM
11.10AM	Ar	Birmingham	"	Lv	1 40PM
12 15PM	Lv	Birmingham	FRISCO	Ar	1 30PM
7.00PM	Ar	Memphis....................	"	Lv	7 20AM
1.05PM	Ar	Montgomery (CT)............	A&WP	Lv	7.55AM
5.38PM	Ar	Mobile.....................	L&N	Lv	2.20AM
9.30PM	Ar	New Orleans................	"	Lv	10.15PM
5.45PM	Ar	Tuscaloosa..(CT)............	SOU	Lv	9.40AM
8.50PM	Ar	Meridian...................	"	Lv	6.30AM

Air-Conditioned Modern Convenient Schedules

4 00PM	Lv	Boston (South Sta.) (EST).....	NY &H	Ar	3.00PM
9.45PM	Lv	New York (Penn. Sta.).........	PRR	Ar	8.55AM
11.39PM	Lv	Philadelphia (30th St. Sta.).....	"	Ar	7.12AM
1.25AM	Lv	Baltimore....................	"	Ar	5.05AM
k 2.35AM	Lv	Washington..................	RF&P	Ar	3.55AM
5.33AM	Lv	Richmond (Main St. Sta.)......	SEABOARD	Ar	12.50AM
8.45PM	Lv	Norfolk......................	Ferry	Ar	8.25AM
9.05PM	Lv	Portsmouth..................	SEABOARD	Ar	8.10AM
9.30AM	Ar	Raleigh (Union Sta.)..........	"	Lv	8.45PM
•	Ar	Pinehurst...................	N. S.	Lv	6.00PM
2.25PM	Ar	Columbia....................	SEABOARD	Lv	3.15PM
5.40PM	Ar	Savannah (Union Sta.).........	"	Lv	11.45AM
9.10PM	Ar	Jacksonville.................	"	Lv	8.25AM
5.25AM	Ar	West Palm Beach-Palm Beach..	"	Lv	11.20PM
7.35AM	Ar	Miami......................	"	Lv	9.00PM
5.15AM	Ar	Tampa......................	"	Lv	11.55PM
7.45AM	Ar	St. Petersburg...............	"	Lv	9.15PM
8.00AM	Ar	Sarasota....................	"	Lv	8.10PM
8.45AM	Ar	Venice......................	"	Lv	7.20PM
9 05AM	Ar	Boca Grande................	"	Lv	5.55PM
9.55AM	Ar	Useppa Island................	Yacht	Lv	4.00PM

12 00N	Lv	Boston (South Sta.) (EST).....	NYNH&H	Ar	7.25PM
6.15PM	Lv	New York (Penn. Sta.) (EST)...	PRR	Ar	12.05PM
8.01PM	Lv	Philadelphia (30th St. Sta.).....	"	Ar	10.19AM
9.40PM	Lv	Baltimore...................	"	Ar	8.45AM
10.45PM	Lv	Washington..................	RF&P	Ar	7.30AM
1.35AM	Lv	Richmond (Main St. Sta.)......	SEABOARD	Ar	4.35AM
8.45PM	Lv	Norfolk.....................	Ferry	Ar	8.25AM
9.05PM	Lv	Portsmouth..................	SEABOARD	Ar	8.10AM
5.40AM	Ar	Raleigh (Union Sta.)..........	"	Lv	12.45AM
7.26AM	Ar	Southern Pines (Pinehurst).....	"	Lv	11.12PM
8.00AM	Ar	Pinehurst...................	N. S.	Lv	•
3.00PM	Ar	Athens......................	SEABOARD	Lv	3.50PM
3.55PM	Ar	Atlanta......(CT)............	"	Lv	12.55PM
8.40PM	Ar	Birmingham.................	"	Lv	8.10AM
6.50AM	Ar	Memphis....................	FRISCO	Lv	10.45PM
10 35PM	Ar	Montgomery (CT)............	A&WP	Lv	7.55AM
3.30AM	Ar	Mobile.....................	L&N	Lv	2.20AM
7.45AM	Ar	New Orleans................	"	Lv	10.15PM
10.35PM	Ar	Tuscaloosa..(CT)............	SOU.	Lv	5.18AM
1.10AM	Ar	Meridian...................	"	Lv	2.45AM
7.00AM	Ar	New Orleans................	"	Lv	8.40PM

Explanation of Characters shown on Page 30, Equipment on Pages 23-26.

85 86

The 1940 schedules for the year-round Florida trains and the through Georgia Division runs. In contrast to the Florida operations, the Hamlet-Atlanta-Birmingham schedules changed little from season to season. Author's collection

With a highball from the flagman leaning out the combine door, an A-B of E4's accelerates No. 7, the Orange Blossom Special*, out of Sebring, Fla., in February 1942. Due to the war, operation of the famed all-Pullman train was suspended at the end of the 1942 season, not to be resumed until December 1946.* Sam Appleby, Jr.

powered by diesel locomotives. Nine of the new Electro-Motive E-4's were assigned to the train in three 6,000-horsepower A-B-A sets. The Seaboard diesels operated over the RF&P to Washington so that the train was powered by either electric locomotives on the Pennsy, or diesels on the Seaboard and the RF&P, for the entire run from New York to Miami.

The newly dieselized East Coast section of the *Orange Blossom Special* was substantially faster than the steam-powered train of the previous season. During the 1938-39 season, the running time of the southbound train, No. 7, from New York to Miami was 26 hours 15 minutes, which was 2 hours 50 minutes faster than the previous year. Running time of the northbound train, No. 8, was 26 hours 25 minutes which represented a 3-hour 45-minute improvement. The East Coast train bypassed both Savannah and Jacksonville. Its all-Pullman consist incorporated both a buffet- club-library car and a buffet-lounge-recreation car as well as a diner. A through Boston-Miami sleeper was also included.

The West Coast section of the *Orange Blossom Special,* Nos. 307 and 308, was not dieselized until the following winter season. It was not quite as exclusive as its East Coast running mate. Its consist included coaches as well as sleepers, and it stopped at both Savannah and Jacksonville. The schedules of the West Coast trains were speeded up after they were dieselized for the 1939-40 season. Running time was 1 hour 30 minutes faster southbound and 2 hours faster northbound.

With the increasing popularity of the new *Silver Meteor,* the two sections of the *Orange Blossom Special* were again combined for the 1941-42 season. Only one train ran out of New York. Nos. 307 and 308 operated only as the Wildwood-St. Petersburg connection for the mainline trains, Nos. 7 and 8. The coaches were dropped from the West Coast section, and the *Special* continued to bypass Savannah and Jacksonville. In fact, the train did not make a revenue stop between Richmond and Wildwood. The schedule was again speeded up, to an even 24 hours in both directions between New York and Miami.

The Seaboard's only other winter season limited was the *Florida Sunbeam*, Nos. 5 and 6. It was inaugurated in 1936, as a revival of an earlier train, the *Suwanee River Special,* which had been discontinued during the Depression. The *Sunbeam* was operated by the Southern Railway System from Cincinnati, through Atlanta, to a connection with the SAL at Hampton, Fla., a point on the Jacksonville-Wildwood mainline 33 miles south of Baldwin. It ran over the Seaboard between Hampton and Miami, with a West Coast connection, Nos. 305 and 306, operating between Wildwood and St. Petersburg. Through sleeping cars from points such as Detroit, Cleveland, Chicago and Toledo were handled by the New York Central System north of Cincinnati. The *Sunbeam's* January 1939 schedule was typical of its

operation: it departed Cincinnati at 7:30 A.M., arriving at Hampton at 3:00 the next morning and Miami at 10:45 A.M. Northbound, No. 6 left Miami at 7:00 P.M., Hampton at 2:50 A.M., and reached Cincinnati at 10:55 P.M., with through cars arriving at Detroit and Cleveland the next morning. By the beginning of World War II, the *Sunbeam* was diesel powered for most of its run over the Southern, but not over the Seaboard.

Trailing a sleek consist of stainless-steel Budd equipment, E4A 3006 departs Savannah with the newly launched Silver Meteor *in March 1939.* Hugh M. Comer

The streamliner era on the Seaboard began in 1939 with the introduction of the *Silver Meteor*, the train that would ultimately become the flagship of its fleet. Streamlining was all the rage during the late thirties, a concept ushered in by, among other things, the phenomenally ugly Chrysler Airflow. Everything from ocean liners to office buildings to refrigerators was streamlined, and trains were no exception.

The *Silver Meteor* began rather modestly as a single train set with one E-4 and seven cars. The lightweight stainless-steel cars, which were designed by Paul Cret and built by the Budd Co., comprised an observation-lounge-coach, a diner, a tavern-coach, a baggage-dormitory-coach and three chair cars. It was to be the first streamliner in the Southeast. A contest was held to name the new train and over 76,000 entries were received. Thirty people submitted the winning name and shared the $500 prize, no doubt to their individual disappointment. The *Meteor* was officially dedicated at the New York World's Fair Grounds as the "Train of Tomorrow," a bit of advertising hyperbole which for once was pretty much on the mark.

The inaugural run of the new streamliner was from New York on February 2, 1939, less than two months after the *Orange Blossom Special* began diesel operation. Initially, the train left New York every third day, running alternately to Miami and St. Petersburg. It thus departed each southern terminus on every sixth day. As originally scheduled, the southbound *Silver Meteor*, No. 43, left New York at 3:30 P.M., and arrived in St. Pete at 4:15 P.M., or Miami at 6:00 P.M., the next day. Northbound, No. 44 departed Miami at 9:05 A.M., or St. Pete at 11:00 A.M., and reached New York at 12:05 P.M. the following day. All seats were reserved and the train, following the airline practice of the day, featured a stewardess-registered nurse. To assist passengers, the train also carried a traveling passenger agent, a service rarely provided on other railroads. As with the *Orange Blossom Special*, the *Silver Meteor*'s Seaboard diesel was operated over the RF&P into Washington.

The *Silver Meteor* was an immediate success, operating at or near full capacity on every trip. By the summer of 1939, the train was scheduled to operate to and from both Miami and St. Petersburg every third day. Two new seven-car train sets, plus one additional diner and two additional chair cars for the West Coast section, went into service in December of that year. The new equipment permitted the *Meteor* to operate on a daily basis between New

York and Miami while continuing to provide every third day service between New York and St. Pete. Running time was also reduced in December 1939 to 25 hours in each direction between New York and Miami.

Additional equipment received in late 1940 permitted daily operation of the *Meteor* to both the East and West Coasts of Florida. To power the Wildwood-St. Petersburg connection, Seaboard assigned elderly class P 865-868 4-6-2's which were adorned with streamlined shrouds. The streamers were painted in a green, yellow and orange scheme similar to "citrus" colors worn by the E4's. The streamlined Pacifics lasted into World War II when class M-2 4-8-2's had to take over due to heavy wartime traffic. In the spring of 1941, Pullman cars, albeit standard heavyweight ones, were added to the *Silver Meteor* for the first time. By then, the consist of the train had grown to thirteen cars, including three lounge cars, two diners and three sleepers. The heavyweight sleeping cars were painted silver to match the train's stainless-steel equipment. The *Meteor* wasn't to receive lightweight sleepers until 1949.

Before the advent of the *Silver Meteor*, the railroad's best year-round train was the *Southern States Special*, Nos. 107 and 108. Nos. 107 and 108 ran between New York and St. Petersburg with a Wildwood-Miami connection, Nos. 807 and 808. It also handled the through Atlanta and Birmingham cars of the *Cotton States Special* between New York and Hamlet. Although it was essentially a limited train, the *Southern States Special* served almost all local stations south of Jacksonville. In the years prior to World War II, it was diesel powered between Richmond and Miami during the off season. Running time between New York and Miami was reduced by more than 2 hours and 30 minutes when the train was powered by the diesels. The *Southern States Special* was renamed the *Sun Queen* in December 1941. There was little change in the train's schedule, although the *Sun Queen* was diesel powered during the winter season and no longer handled the *Cotton States Special* cars north of Hamlet.

The secondary mainline train was the *New York-Florida Limited,* Nos. 191 and 192. It operated under a rather leisurely two nights out schedule between its namesake city and Miami, providing an overnight service between Manhattan and North Carolina points as well as between Jacksonville and Miami. For the most part it operated as a limited train during the winter season making relatively few stops. However, during the warmer months, it frequently served as a local between Hamlet and Jacksonville. In addition to its through New York to Florida cars, the train carried a sleeping car between Tampa and Miami, which it handled between West Lake Wales and Miami. The cross-state Pullman cars were carried in connecting trains, Nos. 427 and 428, between Tampa and West Lake Wales. During the winter seasons in the late thirties, Nos. 191 and 192 were regularly pulled by R class 2-6-6-4's between Richmond and Hamlet. The *New York-Florida Limited* was also renamed in December 1941, becoming the *Palmland,* a name which it would bear until after the 1967 SAL-ACL merger. The *Palmland* was renumbered to 9 and 10 in 1946.

The *New York-Florida Limited*'s running mates were Nos. 1 and 2. During most winter seasons they ran between Washington and St. Petersburg, although for all practical purposes they were completely different trains north and south of Jacksonville. They made relatively few scheduled stops in Virginia and North Carolina which they transited at night, but they provided local service between Hamlet and Jacksonville, relieving the *New York-Florida Limited* of that duty. They also served as the *Limited*'s West Coast connection, carrying its through cars between Jacksonville and St. Petersburg. During the off season, however, Nos. 1 and 2 frequently operated only between Wildwood and St. Pete, carrying the *Limited*'s cars between those points. While these were the typical schedules for the trains, their actual operation varied greatly from year to year and season to season. For example, during the summer of 1939, No. 1 ran from Washington to Savannah, while No. 2 ran from Jacksonville to Washington, and they both, of course, operated between Wildwood and St. Petersburg. And in the warm months of 1941, No. 1 operated from Washington to Hamlet as well as from Wildwood to St. Petersburg, while No. 2 did not operate at all north of Wildwood. The only certainty was that these trains always served as the West Coast connection for the *Limited,* running from St. Petersburg to at least as far north as Wildwood. During most of World War II, however, these trains did operate all the way between Washington and St. Petersburg.

Dressed in a modified version of the "citrus" colors worn by Seaboard E4's, shrouded Pacific 868—one of three 4-6-2's streamlined in 1940 for service on the West Coast section of the Silver Meteor*—prepares to depart Wildwood, Fla., with No. 343 in the early forties.* Railway Negative Exchange

TOP:
The northbound Robert E. Lee, *No. 6, eases to a stop at Emory University, Ga., in 1940 behind a pair of E4 diesels. At the time, the northbound* Lee *and the southbound* Cotton States Special *were diesel powered during the summer months.* Hugh M. Comer

BOTTOM:
Swinging through an S-curve, E7A's 3026 and 3027 hurry No. 6, the Robert E. Lee, *toward Atlanta on December 15, 1946. While hardly one of the road's premier trains, Seaboard management thought at least enough of Nos. 5 and 6 to stencil "Route of the* Robert E. Lee*" on a few boxcars.* R.D. Sharpless; F.E. Ardrey, Jr., collection

Hardly showing her age, 20-year-old M-2 263 simmers at Columbia, S.C., while southbound local No. 1 loads mail and express on June 14, 1942. George E. Votava

The other locals on the main line were passenger, mail and express trains 3 and 4 between Washington and Jacksonville. The trains made all local stops between Richmond and Hamlet, which they served during the daytime, but very few stops south of Hamlet. Unlike Nos. 1 and 2, the schedule of these trains remained almost unchanged from 1939 to 1949.

In addition to the mainline trains, a number of connecting trains operated between Tampa and various branch lines of the South Florida Division. Nos. 509 and 510 ran between Tampa and Venice, connecting with the West Coast section of the *New York-Florida Limited* and carrying a through Pullman from New York. Another pair of trains, Nos. 507 and 508, operated between Tampa and Venice during the winter season as a connection to the *Orange Blossom Special.* Nos. 509 and 510 were rescheduled during World War II to connect with the *Silver Meteor,* an arrangement which persisted with little interruption for many years. No. 509 was later renumbered to 26 from Tampa to Valrico, Fla., and 257 from Valrico to Venice. Similarly, 510 was renumbered to 258 and 25.

On the Boca Grande branch, Nos. 409 and 410 ran between Tampa and South Boca Grande (Port Boca Grande). These trains also connected with the *New York-Florida Limited* and carried a through sleeping car from either New York or Jacksonville, but only during the winter season. They were renumbered to 30 and 321, and 322 and 29, after the war. In later years their through cars were included in the *Silver Star.* Before World War II, additional trains, 407 and 408, operated between Plant City and South Boca Grande during the winter with through sleepers from the *Orange Blossom Special.*

On the Georgia Division line between Hamlet and Birmingham, the better trains were the *Robert E. Lee*, Nos. 5 and 6, and the *Cotton States Special*, Nos. 9 and 10. The *Robert E. Lee* was the only Georgia Division train to operate over the mainline north of Hamlet. Its December 1938 schedule was typical. No. 5 left Washington at 10:45 P.M. and arrived in Atlanta at 4:55 the next afternoon and Birmingham at 8:40 that evening. Northbound, No. 6 departed Birmingham at 8:10 A.M.. and Atlanta at 1:55 P.M., arriving in Washington at 7:35 the next morning. Its consist included a New York-Memphis sleeper, which was handled beyond Birmingham by the Frisco, and a winter season Pullman between New York and the golfing resort of Southern Pines, N.C. However, its coaches operated only as far north as Washington.

The *Cotton States Special* ran only between Hamlet and Birmingham in the prewar years. Its through cars were included in the *Southern States Special* north of Hamlet. In the winter of 1938-39, No. 9 was scheduled to leave Hamlet at 10:55 P.M. and arrive in Birmingham at 11:00 A.M. No. 10 left Birmingham at 1:45 P.M. and arrived in Hamlet at 4:05 A.M. The *Special* handled a through Pullman between New York and Birmingham, but its coaches, like those of the *Robert E. Lee,* did not run beyond Washington. A Portsmouth-Atlanta sleeping car was added to its consist in 1941 and, in December of that year, the *Special* began operating as a separate train between Washington and Hamlet. However, its schedule over the Georgia Division was little changed from prior years. Beginning in 1939, the

TOP:
Big M-2 class Mountain 249 heads No. 191, the Palmland, *at Columbia, S.C., in the early months of World War II. Many a new recruit rode that train, shown here on April 26, 1942, to basic training at nearby Fort Jackson.* George E. Votava

MIDDLE:
Passing heavyweight Pullman Demosthenes, *Brill motor car 2015 and a trailer coach depart Savannah, Ga., with a local passenger run in March 1939.* Hugh M. Comer

BOTTOM:
Seaboard's first diesel-powered trains were the local runs on the North Carolina Division line between Wilmington and Rutherfordton. Electro-Motive power car No. 2027 is in charge as one of the locals loads mail and express at Hamlet in November 1937. Harold K. Vollrath collection

southbound *Cotton States Special* and the northbound *Robert E. Lee* were diesel powered between Hamlet and Atlanta during the warmer months, when the diesels weren't otherwise engaged on the *Orange Blossom Special*. In subsequent summer seasons both trains were diesel powered in each direction north of Atlanta.

A third pair of trains also operated over the Georgia Division, locals 11 and 12, which provided an overnight service between Hamlet and Atlanta. They connected at Hamlet with mainline locals 3 and 4 from and to northern points. These trains did not run to Birmingham. Only two trains, the *Robert E. Lee* and the *Cotton States Special* were operated between Atlanta and Birmingham. During the early forties, 11 and 12 carried merchandise freight cars behind their passenger cars.

The Seaboard operated two through trains over the Tallahassee Sub-Division between Jacksonville and River Junction: the *New Orleans-Florida Limited*, Nos. 36 and 37, and passenger, mail and express trains Nos. 38 and 39. The westbound *Limited* departed Jacksonville at 11:35 A.M. and arrived at New Orleans at 7:45 A.M., the next day. Eastbound, the train left New Orleans at 10:15 P.M. and arrived in Jacksonville at 6:00 P.M. It carried a through sleeping car between Jacksonville and New Orleans and a dining car between Jacksonville and Pensacola. No. 39 left Jacksonville at 9:20 P.M. and reached New Orleans at 7:00 P.M. No. 38 left New Orleans at 8:45 A.M., arriving in Jacksonville at 6:15 A.M. Nos. 38 and 39 carried a Jacksonville-Pensacola sleeping car as well as a Jacksonville-New Orleans Pullman. The through cars of both the *Limited* and Nos. 38 and 39 were handled in other L&N trains west of Flomaton, Ala., and none of these trains carried through coaches all the way between Jacksonville and New Orleans. The operation of these trains remained relatively unchanged until the inauguration of the *Gulf Wind* in 1949. An additional schedule, Nos. 34 and 35, the *Tallahassee Flyer*, was operated on the Jacksonville-River Junction line with a "doodlebug," a self-propelled rail car which was the railroad equivalent of a motor bus. However, the *Flyer* was terminated before World War II.

During the late thirties, three daily trains operated in each direction over the Portsmouth Sub-Division between Portsmouth and Norlina, N.C. The best trains were Nos. 17 and 18, which connected with the *Southern States Special* at Norlina. These trains carried a diner plus—a rarity on the Seaboard—a parlor car. Beginning in 1941, they also handled a Portsmouth-Atlanta sleeping car. Nos. 13 and 14 were locals which connected with mainline locals 3 and 4. Their passenger accommodations were limited to coaches. The third pair

Doubleheading Birmingham-Atlanta local No. 16, P-2 Pacific 823 and an M-class Mountain tear through Powder Springs, Ga., in August 1950.
R.D. Sharpless; F.E. Ardrey, Jr., collection

of trains were Nos. 15 and 16, which connected with locals 1 and 2 and carried a Portsmouth-Hamlet sleeping car. They were discontinued in 1940.

In addition to the mainline trains, Seaboard operated local passenger trains over most of its longer branch lines. At one time or another many of these schedules were operated by doodlebugs. Perhaps the most noteworthy of the branch line locals were the two sets of trains which ran over the line between Wilmington and Rutherfordton, N.C. Nos. 13 and 14 provided a daily round trip between Wilmington and Charlotte, and Nos. 21 and 22 ran between Hamlet and Rutherfordton. The Wilmington-Charlotte trains should not be confused with the trains of the same numbers which operated on the Portsmouth-Norlina run. SAL sometimes persisted in the confusing practice of assigning the same number to separate trains operating on different divisions. Beginning in 1936, Nos. 13 and 14 and Nos. 21 and 22 were each assigned one of the two Electro-Motive "power cars" which the railroad purchased that year. Winton-powered motor cars 2027 and 2028 contained mail and baggage compartments in addition to their 600-hp diesel engines and were capable of pulling up to three standard passenger cars. Each power car made a daily round trip on its assigned run. These obscure locals were thus the first true diesel-powered trains on the Seaboard, although technically their motive power wasn't locomotives. Nos. 21 and 22 were no longer diesel powered by 1940. But Nos. 13 and 14 continued to be pulled by a power car until early 1942 when increased wartime traffic exceeded the capacity of the diesel and it was replaced by a steam engine. However, when traffic returned to normal after the war, a power car was again assigned to the Wilmington-Charlotte run.

Other locals included a daily doodlebug, Nos. 25 and 26, which was the only passenger service over the freight line between Hamlet, Charleston and Savannah. These trains were informally known as the "Boll Weevil." On the Alabama Division, daily locals 11 and 12 were operated between Savannah and Montgomery. They were the only trains serving the hometown of future president Jimmy Carter, Plains, Ga. All or portions of Nos. 11 and 12 were variously operated at different times with doodlebugs, diesel-electric power cars and conventional steam locomotives. SAL ran yet another pair of trains numbered 13 and 14, on the Alabama Division between Savannah and Americus, Ga. The Alabama Division Nos. 13

3051

THIS AND FACING PAGES: *Making light work of her eight-car train, E8A 3051 breezes though a cut near Weems, Ala., with the* Silver Comet, *at 3:15 P.M., July 3, 1959. At Atlanta, the* Comet *will pick up cars for Portsmouth, Washington and New York, and the 3051 will require the assistance of two additional E-units to further No. 34 eastward.* J. Parker Lamb

and 14 were discontinued in 1939. Another doodlebug, operating as train Nos. 17 and 18, provided the passenger service over the former GF&A line between Tallahassee and Cuthbert, Ga. It was irreverently dubbed the "Butthead." At one time a through Tallahassee-Atlanta sleeping car had operated over this route in connection with the Central of Georgia, but service was reduced to the daily doodlebug by the late thirties.

Although at least some passenger service was still provided on most of the railroad's major branch lines in the early forties, a few significant lines were devoid of passenger trains. The Orlando branch was provided only with mixed-train service. The line between Albany and Columbus, Ga., and the Brooksville Sub-Division between Tampa and Waldo, Fla., were limited to freight service only, as was the line between McBee and Poston, S.C. Passenger service over the ill-starred Fort Myers extension had been discontinued in the early thirties.

WORLD WAR II

World War II had an enormous impact on the nation's railroads. A huge increase occurred in military traffic, while other means of civilian transportation were severely curtailed. Gasoline and tires were stringently rationed and a 30 mph nationwide speed limit was imposed. (The Florida East Coast even dubbed one of its wartime trains *The Tiresaver.*) Americans were forced to temporarily suspend their love affair with the automobile. As a result, railroad service was at a premium, and resources were stretched to the limit. Tired old coaches were reprieved from the rip track and pressed into service. Lounge cars, per se, disappeared. Instead, they were drafted for use as coaches. Sleeping-car runs of less than 200 miles were suspended. "Standing room only" was the order of the day on many trains, and railroad stations across the land blossomed with posters inquiring, "Is this trip necessary?"

The impact on the Seaboard was no less dramatic. For one thing, the Southeast was replete with military bases. Numerous troop trains were run and extra sections of regularly scheduled trains proliferated. Seaboard's passenger count quadrupled, from 1.6 million passengers carried in 1940, to an all time high of 6.6 million in 1944. Moreover, the miles traveled by the average passenger also increased, from 277 to 333.

Naturally, the railroad's schedules were affected by the emergency. The *Orange Blossom Special* and the *Florida Sunbeam,* vacation-oriented seasonal trains, were both suspended at the close of the 1941–42 winter season. It was just as well. Many of the South Florida resort hotels, which had been the destinations of their passengers, were commandeered as barracks or military hospitals. But other trains were added to the time card. Beginning in 1942, the *Silver Meteor* was regularly scheduled to operate in two sections between New York and Miami, a regular and an advance section. Later in the war, instead of two New York-Miami sections, a separate West Coast section of the *Meteor,* Nos. 31 and 32, ran all the way between New York and St. Petersburg. An additional mail and express train, Nos. 45 and 46, operated between Washington and Hamlet.

But the wartime passenger schedule was not greatly different from the prewar timetable. For example, in July 1944 nine passenger trains were scheduled in each direction over the mainline between Richmond and Hamlet: the East and West Coast sections of the *Silver Meteor*, the *Sun Queen, Palmland, Cotton States Special* and *Robert E. Lee,* and locals 1 and 2, 3 and 4, and 45 and 46. Six trains were scheduled each way between Hamlet and Jacksonville, and three operated between Hamlet and Atlanta. Of course, the published timetable did not reflect all the extra trains and multiple sections of regular trains that were operated during the war.

POSTWAR TRAINS

Passenger operations returned to normal soon after World War II ended in August 1945. Beginning in 1946, the *Cotton States Special* was again combined with the *Sun Queen* north of Hamlet and the southbound *Robert E. Lee* was combined with the *Palmland.* Nos. 45 and 46, the additional mail and express trains, were discontinued even before the end of the

Led by an A-B of E7's, the southbound Robert E. Lee *nears Greenwood, S.C., on March 16, 1947.* Hugh M. Comer

war. However, both the East and West Coast sections of the *Silver Meteor* continued to run to New York until December 1946, and locals 1 and 2 remained in year-round service between Richmond and Jacksonville, although No. 2 was combined with the *Robert E. Lee*, north of Hamlet, in the summer season of 1946.

Both the *Orange Blossom Special* and the *Florida Sunbeam* returned to service for the 1946-47 season. There were some changes, however. The *Special* was assigned new numbers, 45 and 46, and ran through Jacksonville rather than over the Gross Cut-off. As in the 1941-42 season, it ran as a single New York-Miami train with a connecting West Coast section between Wildwood and St. Petersburg. Once again, it was all-Pullman. However, its New York-Miami running time was eased to about 26 hours 40 minutes, some 2 hours 30 minutes slower than the 1941–42 schedule. The West Coast section of the *Special*, Nos. 145 and 146, operated for only two seasons after resuming postwar service. The *Sunbeam* did not have a West Coast section at all after the war. It operated for only three postwar seasons, being permanently discontinued after the conclusion of the 1948–49 season.

The late forties and early fifties were a period of transition for the Seaboard's passenger service. New trains were introduced and old ones terminated. The *Silver Meteor* was completely re-equipped and three new streamliners were inaugurated, the *Silver Star*, *Silver Comet* and *Gulf Wind*. New lightweight baggage-dormitory, coach, dining and observation-lounge cars entered service on the *Meteor* and the *Silver Comet* in 1947. Although ordered in 1946, delivery of new sleeping cars was delayed until 1949.

During the winter of 1946–47, the schedule of the *Silver Meteor* was changed so that there were two New York-Miami trains: the regular *Meteor*, Nos. 57 and 22, and the advance *Meteor*, Nos. 21 and 58, each with its own Wildwood-St. Petersburg connection. Nos. 21 and 22 were dropped at the conclusion of the winter season and Nos. 57 and 58, and their West Coast connections, 157 and 158, continued to operate as the *Silver Meteor* on a schedule that was similar to the *Meteor*'s prewar schedule. In the following winter, Nos. 21 and 22 reappeared on essentially the same schedule as the previous year but as a new train, the *Silver Star*.

The *Silver Star* was equipped mostly with the *Meteor*'s original prewar cars. Initially, the train ran only during the winter season, not beginning year-round operation until the summer of 1949; the *Star*'s West Coast section, Nos. 121 and 122, never operated during the off

Resplendent in the green, yellow and orange "citrus" colors, a legacy of her days on the St. Petersburg section of the Silver Meteor, *EMC motor car 2028 heads Savannah-Montgomery local No. 11 at Pitts, Ga., on December 1, 1946.* David W. Salter

ing in St. Petersburg at around 9:30 A.M. the next day and Miami at about 11:00 A.M. Northbound, it left Miami at 4:40 P.M. and St. Pete at 5:30 P.M., arriving in New York at 6:25 the following afternoon. During the winter season, the *Star* bypassed both Savannah and Jacksonville, operating via the Gross Cut-off. In the off season, the northbound *Star* departed Miami about four hours earlier than in the winter, and the train operated through Jacksonville. For many years the *Star*'s winter consist included a New York-Port Boca Grande Pullman. During the warmer months No. 22 carried a Portsmouth coach and sleeper from Jacksonville to Norlina or, later, Raleigh. It also handled the *Silver Comet*'s northbound Portsmouth cars from Hamlet to Norlina for several years. Like the *Meteor*'s, the *Star*'s crew included a stewardess-nurse and a traveling passenger agent, and coach seats were reserved.

The *Silver Comet,* Nos. 33 and 34, made its inaugural trip on the New York-Birmingham run, May 18, 1947, replacing the *Cotton States Special.* The train began operation with new lightweight coaches, observation and dining cars, but conventional heavyweight sleepers. It did not receive lightweight Pullman cars until SAL finally took delivery of its long-awaited new sleeping cars in 1949. Most of the train's consist, including its coaches, ran all the way from New York to Birmingham. The *Comet* also carried a Portsmouth-Atlanta Pullman and coach, which it handled south of Hamlet. Since the new train was not scheduled to stop at Norlina, the Portsmouth cars were handled by other trains between Norlina and Hamlet for many years. The *Comet* was scheduled to leave New York at 12:45 P.M., arriving in Atlanta at 7:40 the next morning and Birmingham at 10:45 A.M. Northbound, it left Birmingham at 2:45 P.M. and Atlanta at 7:55 P.M., and arrived in New York at 2:50 P.M. This schedule remained basically unchanged over the years. The *Silver Comet* featured amenities similar to those on its "Silver" sisters: a nurse, passenger agent and reserved coach seats. The *Comet* was usually powered by three diesel units north of Atlanta, but in later years much of the consist was cut out at Atlanta and a single diesel was adequate for the Atlanta-Birmingham segment of the train.

Simultaneously with the inauguration of the *Comet*, the *Robert E. Lee* was renamed the *Cotton Blossom.* It continued to carry a sleeping car and a diner for a time, but lost its premium accommodations in 1949. During the late forties and early fifties the *Blossom* did not run beyond Atlanta, and a separate train, Nos. 14 and 15, was operated between Atlanta and Birmingham. In some years, Nos. 5 and 6 were operated only between Hamlet and Atlanta, but by 1952 the train was restored to operation between Washington and Birmingham. The name *Cotton Blossom* was dropped in the early fifties, and the once proud *Robert E. Lee* was reduced to a nameless passenger, mail and express train. Finally, the northbound train, No. 6, was terminated, first at Richmond and, beginning in 1958, at Hamlet. However, the southbound train, No. 5, continued to operate from Washington to Birmingham until after the 1967 merger.

Other changes were made to the timetables in May 1947; the *Sun Queen* was renamed the *Camellia.* It had previously been renumbered to 7 and 8, and its West Coast terminus cut back from St. Petersburg to Tampa. The *Camellia*'s schedule was similar to its predecessor's, except that it was no longer combined with any Georgia Division train north of Hamlet. Its consist included a Portsmouth-Jacksonville sleeper as well as through cars between New York, Washington and Florida points. No. 7 also handled the *Silver Comet's* southbound Portsmouth-Atlanta sleeper and coach from Norlina to Hamlet. In the summer of 1948 service was reinstated to St. Petersburg, but only until the next winter. The name *Camellia* didn't last long. In December 1948 the train was again renamed, becoming the *Sunland.*

At first the *Sunland* was relatively unchanged, but over the years it was downgraded to

Alabama Division train No. 11 is wheeled by No. 654, a class L-2S Ten-Wheeler, on Thanksgiving Day 1948, in what the photographer accurately called a "typical American branch line scene of the forties." David W. Salter

little more than a mail and express train. By 1952, the *Sunland* ran only as far north as Washington and carried no sleeping cars south of Jacksonville; by 1955 it was devoid of lounge or dining cars. In some years the Wildwood-Miami segment of the train operated only during the winter season. At times when it did run, No. 108, the ostensible Miami-Wildwood segment of the *Sunland,* operated completely independently of the Tampa-Washington train and didn't remotely come close to making a connection with it at Wildwood. Beginning in 1958, No. 7 ran only south of Hamlet. Its through cars were carried by the *Silver Comet* north of Hamlet. However, No. 8 continued to operate from Tampa to Washington and it handled Georgia Division train No. 6's through cars from Hamlet to Washington. No. 7 did continue to carry the southbound Portsmouth-Jacksonville Pullman and coach until 1967, but that one sleeping car was the only luxury equipment handled by the *Sunland* in either direction. Throughout the sixties, the *Sunland* did not carry any passenger cars through Jacksonville. For all practical purposes it was really two distinct trains, one between Tampa and Jacksonville, and one between Jacksonville and Hamlet or Washington.

The last of the streamliners to enter service was the *Gulf Wind,* Nos. 38 and 39. It made its maiden trip on the Jacksonville-New Orleans run on July 31, 1949. The new train made the 612-mile run in about 15 hours, some 5 hours faster than the previous best time. The *Gulf Wind* left each terminal at 5:00 P.M., arriving the next morning. The train was scheduled so that South Florida passengers could connect to and from the *Silver Meteor* at Jacksonville. On the L&N, the consist of the *Gulf Wind* was handled in the *Pan American* from Flomaton, Ala., to New Orleans, and in the *Piedmont Limited* in the opposite direction. The *Gulf Wind* was the one Seaboard streamliner that wasn't "Silver." Most of its cars were

Seaboard AIR LINE RAILROAD
ROUTE OF THE SILVER FLEET

SEABOARD AIR LINE RAILROAD — THROUGH THE HEART OF THE SOUTH

BETWEEN EASTERN CITIES AND FLORIDA.

The Palmland	Silver Meteor ⊡	The Sunland	Silver Star ⊡	Pas., Mail and Express	Daily Schedules. Eastern Standard time. See Equipment of Trains, pages 606 and 608.	The Palmland	Silver Meteor ⊡	Silver Star ⊡	The Sunland	Pas., Mail and Express	The Tide-water
171	175	173	173	173	*New Haven*	188	22	170	170	.....	.....
143	113	123	127	173	*P. R.R.*	112	114	128	170	.....	.....
9	57	107	21	93	*R. F. & P.*	110	58	22	108	.....	.....
9-1	57-157	7-107	21-121	3	*Seaboard Air Line Railroad Co.*	2-10	158-58	122-22	108-8	4	16-34-18
3 00 PM	8 30 AM	‡11 00 PM	‡11 00 PM	‡11 00 PM	lve. **Boston**.........(*New Haven*) arr.	3 10 PM	5 15 PM	11 50 PM	11 50 PM	Passengers destined to stations on R F & P and beyond may transfer to Broad St. Sta. for R F & P train No. 16 from Richmond 5 20 p.m., due Washington 7 35 p.m	....
3 58 PM	9 35 AM	‡11 56 PM	‡11 56 PM	‡11 56 PM	lve. **Providence**......... » arr.	2 19 PM	4 20 PM	10 48 PM	10 48 PM		....
t4 15 PM	a10 00 AM	..... 5 00	..... 5 00	:12 12 AM	lve. **Springfield**.....(*New Haven*) arr.	t3 53 PM	t3 53 PM	l11 50 PM	l11 50 PM		....
t4 50 PM	a10 48 AM	..... 5 35	..... 5 35	:1 02 AM	lve. **Hartford**............ » arr.	t3 13 PM	t3 13 PM	l11 01 PM	l11 01 PM		....
6 03 PM	11 55 AM	†2 06	†2 06	†2 06 AM	lve. **New Haven**.....(*New Haven*) arr.	12 00 Noon	2 19 PM	8 33 PM	8 33 PM		....
....	....	....	....	....	arr. New York (*G. C. Sta.*).. » lve.	....	1 00 PM	....	....		....
7 30 PM	1 30 PM	†3 35 8 00	†3 35 8 00	†3 35 AM	arr. New York (Penna. Sta.)...(*P. R.R.* lve.	10 30 AM	....	7 00 PM	7 00 PM		....
11 40 PM	5 38 PM	†8 30 AM	†8 30 AM	†8 30 AM	arr. **Washington**........ » lve.	....	....	3 00 PM	3 00 PM		....
8 30 PM	2 55 PM	*11 30 AM	*10 00 AM	*3 50 AM	lve. New York (Penna. Sta.)...(*P. R.R.*) arr.	9 20 AM	10 20 AM	6 15 PM	6 45 PM		....
8 45 PM	3 10 PM	11 45 AM	10 15 AM	4 03 AM	lve. **Newark**.............. » arr.	9 03 AM	10 04 AM	5 57 PM	6 29 PM		....
9 29 PM	3 55 PM	12 28 PM	11 06 AM	4 54 AM	lve. **Trenton**.............. » arr.	8 15 AM	9 19 AM	5 13 PM	o5 48 PM		....
9 58 PM	4 24 PM	12 56 PM	11 35 AM	5 29 AM	lve. **North Philadelphia**. » arr.	7 45 AM	8 50 AM	4 44 PM	5 22 PM		....
10 08 PM	4 34 PM	1 05 PM	11 45 AM	5 55 AM	lve. Philadelphia (30th St. Sta.). » arr.	7 25 AM	8 40 AM	4 34 PM	5 12 PM		....
10 39 PM	5 03 PM	1 35 PM	12 17 PM	6 30 AM	lve. **Wilmington**......... » arr.	6 50 AM	8 10 AM	4 05 PM	4 42 PM		....
11 45 PM	6 05 PM	2 35 PM	1 17 PM	7 45 AM	lve. **Baltimore**........... » arr.	5 40 AM	7 10 AM	3 05 PM	3 41 PM		....
12 25 AM	6 45 PM	3 15 PM	2 00 PM	8 30 AM	arr. **Washington**.......... » lve.	5 00 AM	6 30 AM	2 25 PM	3 00 PM		....
b1 00 AM	7 10 PM	3 35 PM	2 25 PM	9 15 AM	lve. **Washington**......(*R. F. & P.*) arr.	c4 25 AM	6 05 AM	2 00 PM	2 35 PM		....
3 40 AM	i9 35 PM	6 20 PM	4 48 PM	12 10 PM	lve. **Richmond** (Main St. Sta.)(*S. A. L.*) arr.	1 00 AM	□3 32 AM	11 25 AM	11 30 AM	3 40 PM	....
4 15 AM	i9 59 PM	6 50 PM	i5 13 PM	12 58 PM	lve. **Petersburg**.......... » arr.	12 30 AM	□3 00 AM	□10 45 AM	11 00 AM	2 35 PM	....
f5 38 AM	— —	8 00 PM	— —	2 22 PM	lve. **Norlina**............. » lve.	11 00 PM	— —	— —	9 40 AM	12 50 PM	....
5 56 AM	— —	8 17 PM	— —	2 40 PM	lve. **Henderson**.......... » arr.	10 40 PM	— —	— —	9 10 AM	12 27 PM	....
6 50 AM	12 15 AM	9 10 PM	7 30 PM	3 45 PM	arr. **Raleigh**............. » lve.	9 50 PM	12 45 AM	8 15 AM	8 20 AM	11 30 AM	....
....	....	4 00 PM	....	....	lve. **Norfolk**.........(*Tunnel Bus*) arr.	....	....	....	....	....	8 40 AM
....	....	4 30 PM	....	....	lve. **Portsmouth**........(*S. A. L.*) arr.	....	....	....	....	....	8 15 AM
....	....	7 30 PM	....	....	lve. **Norlina**............. » arr.	....	....	....	....	....	5 15 AM
....	....	7 50 PM	....	....	lve. **Henderson**.......... » arr.	....	....	....	....	....	4 45 AM
....	....	8 45 PM	....	....	arr. **Raleigh**............. » lve.	....	....	....	....	....	4 00 AM
7 00 AM	12 20 AM	9 20 PM	7 35 PM	4 10 PM	lve. **Raleigh**............. » arr.	9 35 PM	12 40 AM	8 10 AM	8 05 AM	11 05 AM	3 20 AM
7 49 AM	— —	10 08 PM	— —	5 10 PM	arr. **Sanford**............. » lve.	8 30 PM	— —	— —	7 02 AM	10 00 AM	— —
8 18 AM	— —	10 38 PM	— —	5 45 PM	arr. Southern Pines (Pinehurst) » lve.	8 00 PM	— —	— —	6 32 AM	9 22 AM	— —
8 26 AM	— —	q10 43 PM	— —	5 54 PM	arr. **Aberdeen**............ » lve.	7 47 PM	— —	— —	— —	9 10 AM	— —
9 00 AM	2 05 AM	11 20 PM	9 15 PM	6 50 PM	arr. **Hamlet**.............. » lve.	7 20 PM	11 00 PM	6 25 AM	5 55 AM	8 40 AM	1 35 AM
9 45 AM	2 15 AM	11 45 PM	9 30 PM	Coach Train—Handles No Sleeping Cars.	lve. **Hamlet**.............. » arr.	6 35 PM	10 50 PM	6 15 AM	5 35 AM	Coach Train—Handles No Sleeping Cars.	11 50 PM
11 27 AM	— —	12 57 AM	₼10 39 PM		arr. **Camden**.............. » lve.	4 40 PM	e9 25 PM	— —	3 28 AM		— —
12 25 PM	4 05 AM	1 45 AM	11 30 PM		arr. **Columbia**............ » lve.	3 55 PM	8 50 PM	3 55 AM	2 50 AM		9 45 PM
....	....	....	j1 55 AM		arr. **West Savannah**..... » lve.	....	....	....	....		....
4 25 PM	6 38 AM	5 00 AM	....		arr. Savannah (*Union Sta.*). » lve.	12 15 PM	6 28 PM	1 35 AM	11 45 PM		7 25 PM
f6 12 PM	d7 43 AM	f6 27 AM	d2 58 AM		arr. Thalmann (Bruns.-Sea Isl.). » lve.	f10 28 AM	d5 15 PM	— —	f10 14 PM		— —
8 20 PM	9 10 AM	8 00 AM	....		arr. **Jacksonville**........ » lve.	8 55 AM	4 05 PM	....	9 00 PM		5 00 PM
10 00 PM	9 20 AM	9 40 AM	....		lve. **Jacksonville**........ » arr.	6 59 AM	3 55 PM	....	8 15 PM		....
f10 21 PM	— —	r10 03 AM	— —		lve. **Baldwin**............. » arr.	f6 05 AM	— —	— —	♮7 24 PM		....
10 55 PM	— —	10 27 AM	— —		arr. **Starke**.............. » lve.	5 35 AM	— —	— —	7 00 PM		....
11 15 PM	n10 14 AM	10 40 AM	y4 50 AM		arr. **Waldo** (Gainesville)... » lve.	5 15 AM	n2 45 PM	z10 35 PM	6 42 PM		....
12 05 AM	n10 54 AM	11 25 AM	y5 30 AM		arr. **Ocala** (Silver Springs). » lve.	4 20 AM	n2 06 PM	z9 56 PM	5 58 PM		....
12 50 AM	11 25 AM	11 55 AM	6 00 AM		arr. Wildwood (Homosassa Springs) » lve.	3 25 AM	1 40 PM	9 30 PM	5 25 PM		....
2 25 AM	⊙12 40 PM	1 33 PM	△7 07 AM		arr. Winter Haven (Cypress Gardens) » lve.	1 25 AM	⊙12 25 PM	h8 10 PM	3 06 PM		....
2 50 AM	√12 52 PM	1 58 PM	△7 20 AM		ar. W. Lake Wales-Lake Wales. (Bok Tower) » lve.	1 15 AM	√12 18 PM	h8 01 PM	2 55 PM		....
3 10 AM	▼1 12 PM	2 20 PM	△7 40 AM		arr. **Avon Park**.......... » lve.	12 40 AM	■11 54 AM	h7 41 PM	2 20 PM		....
3 30 AM	▼1 23 PM	2 45 PM	△7 50 AM		ar. Sebring (Highlands Hammock St. Pk.) » lve.	12 28 AM	▼11 44 AM	h7 30 PM	2 09 PM		....
5 20 AM	2 56 PM	5 00 PM	9 25 AM		arr. West Palm Beach-Palm Beach » lve.	10 35 PM	10 18 AM	6 00 PM	12 28 PM		....
u5 28 AM	‡3 05 PM	f5 08 PM	△9 34 AM		arr. **Lake Worth**........ » lve.	u10 20 PM	‡10 09 AM	h5 52 PM	f12 10 PM		....
u5 45 AM	‡3 16 PM	f5 30 PM	△9 45 AM		arr. **Delray Beach**....... » lve.	u10 04 PM	‡9 58 AM	h5 41 PM	f11 53 AM		....
u5 58 AM	‡3 28 PM	f5 50 PM	△9 55 AM		arr. Deerfield Beach (Boca Raton). » lve.	u9 54 PM	‡9 48 AM	h5 31 PM	f11 39 AM		....
6 35 AM	3 47 PM	6 20 PM	10 15 AM		arr. **Fort Lauderdale**.... » lve.	9 35 PM	9 34 AM	5 16 PM	11 19 AM		....
6 48 AM	☽4 00 PM	6 40 PM	△10 25 AM		arr. **Hollywood**.......... » lve.	9 15 PM	☽9 25 AM	h5 08 PM	11 04 AM		....
8 10 AM	4 40 PM	7 50 PM	11 10 AM		arr. **Miami**............... » lve.	8 30 PM	9 00 AM	4 40 PM	10 30 AM		....
10 00 AM	6 00 PM	9 15 PM	1 00 PM	....	lve. **Miami** (Southeastern Greyhound Lines) arr.	7 10 PM	4 25 AM	10 30 AM	....	....	....
2 10 PM	9 30 PM	1 10 AM	5 10 PM	....	arr. **Key West**...... » lve.	3 00 PM	12 30 AM	7 00 AM	....	....	....
10 00 PM	9 20 AM	9 40 AM	....	....	lve. **Jacksonville**........(*S. A. L.*) arr.	6 59 AM	3 55 PM	....	8 15 PM	....	....
f10 21 PM	— —	r10 03 AM	— —	....	lve. **Baldwin**............. » arr.	f6 05 AM	— —	— —	♮7 24 PM	....	....
10 55 PM	— —	10 27 AM	— —	....	arr. **Starke**.............. » lve.	5 35 AM	— —	— —	7 00 PM	....	....
11 15 PM	n10 14 AM	10 40 AM	y4 50 AM	....	arr. **Waldo** (Gainesville)... » lve.	5 15 AM	n2 45 PM	z10 35 PM	6 42 PM	....	....
12 05 AM	n10 54 AM	11 25 AM	y5 30 AM	....	arr. **Ocala** (Silver Springs). » lve.	4 20 AM	n2 06 PM	z9 56 PM	5 58 PM	....	....
12 50 AM	11 25 AM	11 55 AM	6 00 AM	....	arr. Wildwood (Homosassa Springs » lve.	3 25 AM	1 40 PM	9 30 PM	5 25 PM	....	....
3 11 AM	w12 51 PM	1 16 PM	△7 18 AM	....	arr. **Plant City**.......... » lve.	12 35 AM	g11 59 AM	h7 45 PM	3 30 PM	....	....
4 10 AM	1 30 PM	2 15 PM	8 00 AM	....	arr. **Tampa**.............. » lve.	11 59 PM	11 30 AM	7 15 PM	3 00 PM	....	....
See Note ◈	2 40 PM	See Note ◈	9 07 AM	....	arr. Clearwater (Bellv.-Biltmore Hotel) » lve.	See Note ◈	10 20 AM	6 05 PM	See Note ◈	....	....
	w —		△ —	....	arr. **Belleair**............ » lve.		g —	h —		....	....
	3 25 PM		9 45 AM	....	arr. **St. Petersburg**...... » lve.		9 45 AM	5 30 PM		....	....
◆7 30 AM	1 45 PM	◆4 00 PM	◆11 45 AM	....	lve. **Tampa**.............(*S. A. L.*) arr.	◆9 50 PM	11 10 AM	●6 55 PM	11 10 AM	....	....
◆8 35 AM	f3 15 PM	◆5 20 PM	◆12 50 PM	....	arr. **Palmetto-Ellenton**. » lve.	◆8 15 PM	f9 26 AM	◆5 50 PM	f9 26 AM	....	....
◆8 45 AM	3 25 PM	◆5 30 PM	◆1 00 PM	....	arr. **Bradenton**.......... » lve.	◆8 05 PM	9 20 AM	◆5 40 PM	9 20 AM	....	....
◆9 20 AM	3 45 PM	◆5 55 PM	◆1 25 PM	....	arr. **Sarasota**........... » lve.	◆7 40 PM	9 00 AM	◆5 15 PM	9 00 AM	....	....
◆9 50 AM	4 40 PM	◆6 30 PM	◆2 40 PM	....	arr. **Venice**............. » lve.	◆7 00 PM	8 15 AM	Ψ —	8 15 AM	....	....
8 25 AM	....	....	8 25 AM	....	lve. **Tampa**.............(*S. A. L.*) arr.	6 30 PM	....	6 30 PM	....	....	....
10 22 AM	....	....	10 22 AM	....	arr. **Arcadia**............ » lve.	4 25 PM	....	4 25 PM	....	....	....
11 45 AM	....	....	11 45 AM	....	arr. **Boca Grande**........ » lve.	3 09 PM	....	3 09 PM	....	....	....
11 55 AM	....	....	11 55 AM	....	arr. **Port Boca Grande**.. » lve.	3 00 PM	....	3 00 PM	....	....	....
12 40 PM	....	....	12 40 PM	....	lve. **Boca Grande**.......(*Yacht*) arr.	2 50 PM	....	2 50 PM	....	....	....
1 55 PM	....	....	1 55 PM	....	arr. **Useppa Island**....... » lve.	2 10 PM	....	2 10 PM	....	....	....

For Explanation of Signs, see page 608.

Seaboard's New York-Florida schedules as of January 1958. The road's winter schedules changed little over the next few years. Note that SAL billed itself as the "Route of the Silver Fleet." Ironically, rival Eastern Airlines had once boasted of its "Great Silver Fleet." Author's collection

Seaboard AIR LINE RAILROAD
ROUTE OF THE SILVER FLEET

BETWEEN EASTERN CITIES AND FLORIDA.

The Palmland	Silver Meteor ⊡	The Sunland	Silver Star ⊡	Pas., Mail and Express	Daily Schedules. Eastern Standard time. See Equipment of Trains, pages 606 and 608.	The Palmland	Silver Meteor ⊡	Silver Star ⊡	The Sunland	Pas., Mail and Express	The Tide-water
171 143 9 9-1	175 113 57 57-157	173 123 107 7-107	173 127 21 21-121	173 173 93 3	*New Haven* *P. R.R.* *R. F. & P.* *Seaboard Air Line Railroad Co.*	188 112 110 2-10	22 114 58 158-58	170 128 22 122-22	170 170 108 108-8	 4	 16-34-18
3 00 P M	8 30 A M	‡11 00 P M	‡11 00 P M	‡11 00 P M	lve. **Boston**.........(*New Haven*) arr.	3 10 P M	5 15 P M	11 50 P M	11 50 P M	Passengers destined to stations on R F & P and beyond may transfer to Broad St. Sta. for R F & P train No. 16 from Richmond 5 20 p.m., due Washington 7 35 p.m	....
3 58 P M	9 35 A M	‡11 56 P M	‡11 56 P M	‡11 56 P M	lve. **Providence**.......... » arr.	2 19 P M	4 20 P M	10 48 P M	10 48 P M		....
t4 15 P M	a10 00 A M	.... 5 00	.... 5 00	:12 12 A M	lve. **Springfield**.....(*New Haven*) arr.	t3 53 P M	t3 53 P M	l11 50 P M	l11 50 P M		....
t4 50 P M	a10 48 A M	.... 5 35	.... 5 35	:1 02 A M	lve. **Hartford**............ » arr.	t3 13 P M	t3 13 P M	l11 01 P M	l11 01 P M		....
6 03 P M	11 55 A M	†2 06	†2 06	†2 06 A M	lve. **New Haven**.....(*New Haven*) arr.	12 00 Noon	2 19 P M	8 33 P M	8 33 P M		....
....	....	....	....	....	arr. New York (*G. C. Sta.*).. » lve.	....	1 00 P M	....			....
7 30 P M	1 30 P M	†3 35 8 00	†3 35 8 00	†3 35 A M	arr. New York (Penna. Sta.)...(*P. R.R.* lve.	10 30 A M	....	7 00 P M	7 00 P M		....
11 40 P M	5 38 P M	†8 30 A M	†8 30 A M	†8 30 A M	arr. **Washington**......... » lve.	....	....	3 00 P M	3 00 P M		....
8 30 P M	2 55 P M	*11 30 A M	*10 00 A M	*3 50 A M	lve. New York (Penna. Sta.)...(*P. R.R.*) arr.	9 20 A M	10 20 A M	6 15 P M	6 45 P M		....
8 45 P M	3 10 P M	11 45 A M	10 15 A M	4 03 A M	lve. **Newark**............ » arr.	9 03 A M	10 04 A M	5 57 P M	6 29 P M		....
9 29 P M	3 55 P M	12 28 P M	11 06 A M	4 54 A M	lve. **Trenton**............ » arr.	8 15 A M	9 19 A M	5 13 P M	o5 48 P M		....
9 58 P M	4 24 P M	12 56 P M	11 35 A M	5 29 A M	lve. **North Philadelphia**. » arr.	7 45 A M	8 50 A M	4 44 P M	5 22 P M		....
10 08 P M	4 34 P M	1 05 P M	11 45 A M	5 55 A M	lve. Philadelphia (30th St. Sta.). » arr.	7 25 A M	8 40 A M	4 34 P M	5 12 P M		....
10 39 P M	5 03 P M	1 35 P M	12 17 P M	6 30 A M	lve. **Wilmington**........ » arr.	6 50 A M	8 10 A M	4 05 P M	4 42 P M		....
11 45 P M	6 05 P M	2 35 P M	1 17 P M	7 45 A M	lve. **Baltimore**.......... » arr.	5 40 A M	7 10 A M	3 05 P M	3 41 P M		....
12 25 A M	6 45 P M	3 15 P M	2 00 P M	8 30 A M	arr. **Washington**......... » lve.	5 00 A M	6 30 A M	2 25 P M	3 00 P M		....
b1 00 A M	7 10 P M	3 35 P M	2 25 P M	9 15 A M	lve. **Washington**.....(*R. F. & P.*) arr.	c4 25 A M	6 05 A M	2 00 P M	2 35 P M		....
3 40 A M	i9 35 P M	6 20 P M	4 48 P M	12 10 P M	lve. **Richmond** (Main St. Sta.)(*S.A.L.*) arr.	1 00 A M	□3 32 A M	11 25 A M	11 30 A M	3 40 P M	....
4 15 A M	i9 59 P M	6 50 P M	i5 13 P M	12 58 P M	lve. **Petersburg**......... » arr.	12 30 A M	□3 00 A M	□10 45 A M	11 00 A M	2 35 P M	....
f5 38 A M	– –	8 00 P M	– –	2 22 P M	lve. **Norlina**............ » lve.	11 00 P M	– –	– –	9 40 A M	12 50 P M	....
5 56 A M	– –	8 17 P M	– –	2 40 P M	lve. **Henderson**.......... » arr.	10 40 P M	– –	– –	9 10 A M	12 27 P M	....
6 50 A M	12 15 A M	9 10 P M	7 30 P M	3 45 P M	arr. **Raleigh**............ » lve.	9 50 P M	12 45 A M	8 15 A M	8 20 A M	11 30 A M	....
....	....	4 00 P M	....	....	lve. **Norfolk**.........(*Tunnel Bus*) arr.	....	....	....	....	....	8 40 A M
....	....	4 30 P M	....	....	lve. **Portsmouth**.........(*S. A. L.*) arr.	....	....	....	....	....	8 15 A M
....	....	7 30 P M	....	....	lve. **Norlina**............ » arr.	....	....	....	....	....	5 15 A M
....	....	7 50 P M	....	....	lve. **Henderson**.......... » arr.	....	....	....	....	....	4 45 A M
....	....	8 45 P M	....	....	arr. **Raleigh**............ » lve.	....	....	....	....	....	4 00 A M
7 00 A M	12 20 A M	9 20 P M	7 35 P M	4 10 P M	lve. **Raleigh**............ » arr.	9 35 P M	12 40 A M	8 10 A M	8 05 A M	11 05 A M	3 20 A M
7 49 A M	– –	10 08 P M	– –	5 10 P M	arr. **Sanford**............ » lve.	8 30 P M	– –	– –	7 02 A M	10 00 A M	– –
8 18 A M	– –	10 38 P M	– –	5 45 P M	arr. Southern Pines (Pinehurst) » lve.	8 00 P M	– –	– –	6 32 A M	9 22 A M	– –
8 26 A M	– –	q10 43 P M	– –	5 54 P M	arr. **Aberdeen**........... » lve.	7 47 P M	– –	– –	– –	9 10 A M	– –
9 00 A M	2 05 A M	11 20 P M	9 15 P M	6 50 P M	arr. **Hamlet**............. » lve.	7 20 P M	11 00 P M	6 25 A M	5 55 A M	8 40 A M	1 35 A M
9 45 A M	2 15 A M	11 45 P M	9 30 P M	Coach Train—Handles No Sleeping Cars.	lve. **Hamlet**............. » arr.	6 35 P M	10 50 P M	6 15 A M	5 35 A M	Coach Train—Handles No Sleeping Cars.	11 50 P M
11 27 A M	– –	12 57 A M	↑10 39 P M		arr. **Camden**............. » lve.	4 40 P M	e9 25 P M	– –	3 28 A M		– –
12 25 P M	4 05 A M	1 45 A M	11 30 P M		arr. **Columbia**........... » lve.	3 55 P M	8 50 P M	3 55 A M	2 50 A M		9 45 P M
....	....	....	j1 55 A M		arr. **West Savannah**..... » lve.	....	....	....	....		....
4 25 P M	6 38 A M	5 00 A M	....		arr. Savannah (*Union Sta.*). » lve.	12 15 P M	6 28 P M	1 35 A M	11 45 P M		7 25 P M
f6 12 P M	d7 43 A M	f6 27 A M	d2 58 A M		arr. Thalmann (Bruns.-Sea Isl.). » lve.	f10 28 A M	d5 15 P M	– –	f10 14 P M		– –
8 20 P M	9 10 A M	8 00 A M	....		arr. **Jacksonville**....... » lve.	8 55 A M	4 05 P M	....	9 00 P M		5 00 P M
10 00 P M	9 20 A M	9 40 A M	....		lve. **Jacksonville**....... » arr.	6 59 A M	3 55 P M	....	8 15 P M		....
f10 21 P M	– –	r10 03 A M	– –		lve. **Baldwin**............ » arr.	f6 05 A M	– –	– –	♮7 24 P M		....
10 55 P M	– –	10 27 A M	– –		arr. **Starke**............. » lve.	5 35 A M	– –	– –	7 00 P M		....
11 15 P M	m10 14 A M	10 40 A M	y4 50 A M		arr. **Waldo** (Gainesville)... » lve.	5 15 A M	n2 45 P M	z10 35 P M	6 42 P M		....
12 05 A M	m10 54 A M	11 25 A M	y5 30 A M		arr. **Ocala** (Silver Springs). » lve.	4 20 A M	n2 06 P M	z9 56 P M	5 58 P M		....
12 50 A M	11 25 A M	11 55 A M	6 00 A M		arr. Wildwood (Homosassa Springs) » lve.	3 25 A M	1 40 P M	9 30 P M	5 25 P M		....
2 25 A M	⊙12 40 P M	1 33 P M	△7 07 A M		arr. Winter Haven (Cypress Gardens) » lve.	1 25 A M	⊙12 25 P M	h8 10 P M	3 06 P M		....
2 50 A M	√12 52 P M	1 58 P M	△7 20 A M		ar. W. Lake Wales-Lake Wales. (Bok Tower) » lve.	1 15 A M	√12 18 P M	h8 01 P M	2 55 P M		....
3 10 A M	▼1 12 P M	2 20 P M	△7 40 A M		arr. **Avon Park**.......... » lve.	12 40 A M	■11 54 A M	h7 41 P M	2 20 P M		....
3 30 A M	▼1 23 P M	2 45 P M	△7 50 A M		ar. Sebring (Highlands Hammock St. Pk.) » lve.	12 28 A M	▼11 44 A M	h7 30 P M	2 09 P M		....
5 20 A M	2 56 P M	5 00 P M	9 25 A M		arr. West Palm Beach-Palm Beach » lve.	10 35 P M	10 18 A M	6 00 P M	12 28 P M		....
u5 28 A M	‡3 05 P M	f5 08 P M	△9 34 A M		arr. **Lake Worth**........ » lve.	u10 20 P M	‡10 09 A M	h5 52 P M	f12 10 P M		....
u5 45 A M	‡3 16 P M	f5 30 P M	△9 45 A M		arr. **Delray Beach**....... » lve.	u10 04 P M	‡9 58 A M	h5 41 P M	f11 53 A M		....
u5 58 A M	‡3 28 P M	f5 50 P M	△9 55 A M		arr. Deerfield Beach (Boca Raton). » lve.	u9 54 P M	‡9 48 A M	h5 31 P M	f11 39 A M		....
6 35 A M	3 47 P M	6 20 P M	10 15 A M		arr. **Fort Lauderdale**.... » lve.	9 35 P M	9 34 A M	5 16 P M	11 19 A M		....
6 48 A M	☽4 00 P M	6 40 P M	△10 25 A M		arr. **Hollywood**......... » lve.	9 15 P M	☽9 25 A M	h5 08 P M	11 04 A M		....
8 10 A M	4 40 P M	7 50 P M	11 10 A M		arr. **Miami**............. » lve.	8 30 P M	9 00 A M	4 40 P M	10 30 A M		....
10 00 A M	6 00 P M	9 15 P M	1 00 P M	....	lve. **Miami** (Southeastern Greyhound Lines) arr.	7 10 P M	4 25 A M	10 30 A M	....	....	....
2 10 P M	9 30 P M	1 10 A M	5 10 P M	....	arr. **Key West**...... » lve.	3 00 P M	12 30 A M	7 00 A M	....	....	....
10 00 P M	9 20 A M	9 40 A M	....	....	lve. **Jacksonville**........(*S. A. L.*) arr.	6 59 A M	3 55 P M	....	8 15 P M	....	....
f10 21 P M	– –	r10 03 A M	– –	....	lve. **Baldwin**............ » arr.	f6 05 A M	– –	– –	♮7 24 P M	....	....
10 55 P M	– –	10 27 A M	– –	....	arr. **Starke**............. » lve.	5 35 A M	– –	– –	7 00 P M	....	....
11 15 P M	m10 14 A M	10 40 A M	y4 50 A M	....	arr. **Waldo** (Gainesville)... » lve.	5 15 A M	n2 45 P M	z10 35 P M	6 42 P M	....	....
12 05 A M	m10 54 A M	11 25 A M	y5 30 A M	....	arr. **Ocala** (Silver Springs). » lve.	4 20 A M	n2 06 P M	z9 56 P M	5 58 P M	....	....
12 50 A M	11 25 A M	11 55 A M	6 00 A M	....	arr. Wildwood (Homosassa Springs » lve.	3 25 A M	1 40 P M	9 30 P M	5 25 P M	....	....
3 11 A M	w12 51 P M	1 16 P M	△7 18 A M	....	arr. **Plant City**......... » lve.	12 35 A M	g11 59 A M	h7 45 P M	3 30 P M	....	....
4 10 A M	1 30 P M	2 15 P M	8 00 A M	....	arr. **Tampa**.............. » lve.	11 59 P M	11 30 A M	7 15 P M	3 00 P M	....	....
See Note ◈	2 40 P M	See Note ◈	9 07 A M	....	arr. Clearwater (Bellv.-Biltmore Hotel) » lve.	See Note ◈	10 20 A M	6 05 P M	See Note ◈	....	....
	w –		△ –	....	arr. **Belleair**........... » lve.		g –	h –		....	....
	3 25 P M		9 45 A M	....	arr. **St. Petersburg**...... » lve.		9 45 A M	5 30 P M		....	....
◆7 30 A M	1 45 P M	◆4 00 P M	◆11 45 A M	....	lve. **Tampa**..............(*S. A. L.*) arr.	◆9 50 P M	11 10 A M	●6 55 P M	11 10 A M	....	....
◆8 35 A M	f3 15 P M	◆5 20 P M	◆12 50 P M	....	arr. **Palmetto-Ellenton**. » lve.	◆8 15 P M	f9 26 A M	◆5 50 P M	f9 26 A M	....	....
◆8 45 A M	3 25 P M	◆5 30 P M	◆1 00 P M	....	arr. **Bradenton**.......... » lve.	◆8 05 P M	9 20 A M	◆5 40 P M	9 20 A M	....	....
◆9 20 A M	3 45 P M	◆5 55 P M	◆1 25 P M	....	arr. **Sarasota**........... » lve.	◆7 40 P M	9 00 A M	◆5 15 P M	9 00 A M	....	....
◆9 50 A M	4 40 P M	◆6 30 P M	◆2 40 P M	....	arr. **Venice**............. » lve.	◆7 00 P M	8 15 A M	Ψ –	8 15 A M	....	....
8 25 A M	....	....	8 25 A M	....	lve. **Tampa**..............(*S. A. L.*) arr.	6 30 P M	....	6 30 P M	....	....	....
10 22 A M	....	....	10 22 A M	....	arr. **Arcadia**............ » lve.	4 25 P M	....	4 25 P M	....	....	....
11 45 A M	....	....	11 45 A M	....	arr. **Boca Grande**........ » lve.	3 09 P M	....	3 09 P M	....	....	....
11 55 A M	....	....	11 55 A M	....	arr. **Port Boca Grande**.. » lve.	3 00 P M	....	3 00 P M	....	....	....

Schedules on the Georgia Division line to Atlanta and Birmingham as advertised in August 1960. Georgia Division schedules were essentially unchanged from season to season.
Author's collection

3074

1104

FACING PAGE, TOP: *Just as fast as the* Meteor, *if not quite as posh, the* Silver Star *was an excellent train in its own right. With E6A 3014, E8A 3056 and E7B 3105 and 18 cars, No. 21, the southbound* Star, *strides down the Virginia Division main-line at Gill, N.C., in September 1963.* Curt

FACING PAGE, BOTTOM: *Headed up by SDP35's 1104 and 1102, No. 10, the northbound* Palmland, *rattles across the Trout River draw-bridge at Jacksonville, Fla., on August 5, 1966. Although the* Palmland *rarely missed a stop south of Hamlet, the train nonetheless carried from Miami to New York for those in no particular hurry.* David W. Salter

THIS PAGE: *Operating "elephant style" in the Seaboard tradition, E8 3049 and a pair of E7's stride into Atlanta with No. 33, the* Silver Comet, *in July 1965.* David W. Salter

On the final approach to Municipal Airport, a Convair airliner drones overhead as Seaboard E8A 3051 accelerates the eastbound Silver Comet *out of Birmingham Terminal Station on July 3, 1961.*
J. Parker Lamb

after observation cars were out of favor with most railroads. Nor, for that matter, was the *Gulf Wind* totally streamlined. For many years it carried a heavyweight SAL dining car between Jacksonville and Tallahassee. Unlike its predecessors, the new train operated through coaches all the way between Jacksonville and New Orleans. The *Wind* was not a long train; it normally had about seven cars and was powered by a single 3000-series diesel locomotive. With the advent of the *Gulf Wind,* the remaining train on the run, the *New Orleans-Florida Limited,* Nos. 36 and 37, was demoted to a nameless local between Jacksonville and Flomaton.

Other changes to existing trains were made in the late forties and early fifties. In the spring of 1949, locals 3 and 4 were discontinued on the overnight run between Hamlet and Jacksonville. However, they remained in service as the daylight locals between Washington and Hamlet. Eventually, in 1958, these trains were combined with Georgia Division locals 11 and 12 so that 3 and 4 ran through from Washington to Atlanta. Nos. 3 and 4 continued to operate between Washington and Atlanta until after the 1967 merger.

The *Palmland*'s West coast connection, Nos. 1 and 2, was discontinued between Tampa and St. Petersburg, February 11, 1951, leaving only two trains serving St. Pete, the *Silver Meteor* year round plus the *Silver Star* in the winter. Nos. 1 and 2 were also permanently terminated north of Jacksonville in the early fifties. The *Palmland,* Nos. 9 and 10, thus became the only train providing local service between Hamlet and Jacksonville, and Nos. 1 and 2 were limited to operation between Wildwood and Tampa. Nos. 427 and 428, the Tampa-West Lake Wales connection for the *Palmland*'s overnight cross-Florida service, were discontinued in April 1953, although for a while afterward a Miami-Tampa coach and Pullman continued to be operated, via Wildwood, in Nos. 10 and 1, and 2 and 9. Pullman service to Tampa by the *Palmland* ceased altogether by the mid- fifties, but the train continued to handle sleeping cars from New York to Hamlet and Miami. For many years the *Palmland* carried a full diner between Raleigh and Hamlet. However, between Hamlet and Jacksonville, the train carried only a grill car, a converted coach with a lunch-counter section that could be operated by a single attendant. It was the only train on the Seaboard with such equipment.

The decade of the fifties witnessed the demise of almost all of the branch-line locals. Portsmouth-Norlina locals 13 and 14 were discontinued October 1, 1950, leaving only Nos. 17 and 18 to provide passenger service on the Portsmouth Sub-Division. The Hamlet-Rutherfordton locals, which had been renumbered to 19 and 20 after the war, were dropped in December of the same year. The Alabama Division lost all of its passenger trains in 1951 when both the Savannah-Montgomery locals, Nos. 11 and 12, and the Tallahassee-Cuthbert "Butthead" were killed. The "Boll Weevil" over the freight line between Hamlet and Savannah was withdrawn south of Charleston in 1952 and eliminated entirely in 1956. The Wilmington-Charlotte trains, Nos. 13 and 14, were among the last to go. They survived until 1958, when they too were discontinued. Finally, service on the run from Tampa to Port Boca Grande was restricted to the winter season and then eliminated completely after the conclusion of the 1958-59 season. Of the shorter branch lines, only the line to Venice, which served the burgeoning retirement communities of Sarasota and Bradenton, retained passenger service until after the Seaboard-Coast Line merger.

But the saddest cut of all came in 1953 with the last run of the *Orange Blossom Special*. The famous train was terminated at the conclusion of the 1952-53 winter season. During the last years of its operation the *Special* ran only between New York and Miami. It bypassed Savannah, but stopped at Jacksonville. In its final season the *Special*'s consist ran to 15 cars, including 2 dining cars and 2 Pullman buffet-lounge cars. Two through Boston-Miami and two Washington-Miami Pullman cars were handled in addition to the train's New York-Miami cars. During the summers, many of the *Special*'s cars were used in the *Bar Harbor Express*, a luxury train between New York and Maine resorts. The train's heavyweight Pullman cars had been rebuilt in 1949 with streamliner-type accommodations such as roomettes and bedrooms and refurbished in 1951 with a special light-gray and maroon paint scheme. But the *Orange Blossom Special* was never equipped with streamlined cars. It became obvious that new streamlined equipment would be required if the *Special* was to remain competitive. Seaboard's management decided that the investment wasn't justified for a train which ran only four months a year, and so the *Orange Blossom Special* passed into history.

The *Orange Blossom Special* had indeed been "special." Before the arrival of the "Silver" streamliners, it had been the one really outstanding train in an otherwise mediocre fleet. In its heyday it was unquestionably one of the finest trains in the nation. It was also one of the most romantically named, the train with a "name like a cocktail." The *Special* was the inspiration for a tune that became a country music classic, a ditty that was a fiddler's *tour de force*. The name was too good to languish in oblivion. Years later, in 1982, Seaboard System revived the name for a crack freight train, a redball from Florida to the Northeast devoted, naturally, to the transportation of citrus fruit. And the freight was worthy of its heritage. At the time, it was the fastest long-distance freight train in the United States.

With the demise of the *Orange Blossom Special,* the *Silver Meteor* reigned as the undisputed queen of the Seaboard passenger fleet. When its heavyweight sleeping cars were replaced by new cars in 1949, the *Meteor* once again had an all-lightweight stainless-steel consist. More new cars were added to the train in 1955 and 1956. The most notable of the additions were unique Sun-Lounge cars, sleeper-lounges with wide picture windows and glass roof panels. They were acquired in lieu of vista dome cars, which were precluded by tunnel clearance restrictions at Washington. Not that the inability to handle vista domes was all that tragic; most of the terrain traversed by the *Silver Meteor* was considerably less than spectacular anyway. The train regularly carried as many as 18 cars, with 11 cars operating between New York and Miami, 5 between New York and St. Petersburg, and 2 between New York, Tampa and V

With a business car on the rear, No. 10, the Palmland, *makes a stop at Raleigh on a frigid night in January 1962.*
J. Parker Lamb

Lounge in midtrain, plus a tavern-observation car at the rear. The round-end observation car continued to grace the rear of the *Silver Meteor*, as God intended, until long after the Seaboard-Coast Line merger. Normally, three diesel units handled the train between Richmond and Wildwood, with two units operating between Wildwood and Miami and one between Wildwood and St. Petersburg. The diesels usually ran all the way between Richmond and Miami or St. Petersburg without change.

For years the *Silver Meteor*'s schedule was virtually unaltered. It departed New York in mid-afternoon, arriving in Jacksonville the next morning and Miami in the afternoon. Northbound, the *Meteor* left Miami in the morning and Jacksonville in the afternoon, arriving in New York in the late morning of the next day. It was one of the fastest trains in the country, scheduled to operate at over 75 mph for part of its run. Total running time between New York and Miami was about 25 hours 30 minutes in each direction.

Another change in the fifties involved the remaining Portsmouth trains, Nos. 17 and 18. They finally received a name, becoming the *Tidewater*. They carried a diner as well as through cars between Portsmouth and Atlanta and Jacksonville. In late 1957, the *Tidewater*'s southern terminal was changed from Norlina to Raleigh. To handle the northbound Jacksonville-Portsmouth cars during the winter when the *Silver Star* bypassed Jacksonville, a new seasonal train from Jacksonville to Hamlet, No. 16, was inaugurated for the 1953–54 season. This train was also called the *Tidewater* and continued to operate each year through the 1966–67 winter season.

By 1958, Seaboard's mainline passenger operations had settled into the pattern they would follow for most of the next decade. Six trains were operated in each direction daily between Richmond and Hamlet: the *Meteor, Star, Comet* and Palmland, the northbound *Sunland,* and locals 3, 4 and 5. Four trains, the *Meteor, Star, Palmland* and *Sunland,* operated between Hamlet and Florida, with the addition of No. 16 during the winter season. Three Georgia Division trains ran between Hamlet and Atlanta and two between Atlanta and Birmingham. And two trains, the *Gulf Wind* and locals 36 and 37, served the Tallahassee Sub-Division between Jacksonville and Chattahoochee.

The railroad's passenger count had dropped steadily throughout the fifties, from 2,200,000 passengers carried in 1947 to a low of 894,000 in 1959. But the impact was ameliorated somewhat by a continuing increase in the number of miles traveled by the average passenger, from 315 miles per passenger in 1947 to 498 in 1959. In other words Seaboard was carrying fewer passengers, but transporting them farther. At any rate, the passenger count stabilized after 1959 and never again dropped below 900,000 per year. It even improved a bit during the sixties. SAL's passenger total in 1966, its last full year before the merger, was the greatest since 1958. Moreover, the average miles traveled per passenger continued to increase during the sixties so that the total passenger miles in 1965 was the highest of any year since 1952.

Seaboard's passenger operations received an unexpected boost in 1963 when the employees of the Florida East Coast Railway began a protracted strike on January 23rd. As a result, three Atlantic Coast Line passenger trains, which had been handled by the East Coast between Jacksonville and Miami, were switched to an alternate ACL-SAL route. The Coast Line operated the trains over its Jacksonville-Tampa line to Auburndale, Fla., and Seaboard handled the trains the remaining 220 miles from Auburndale to Miami. The trains were the *Florida Special, East Coast Champion* and a Chicago-Miami streamliner which alternately operated as the *South Wind* and the *City of Miami.*

The *Florida Special,* ACL Nos. 87 and 88, was a *grande dame* of American railroading. A posh winter-season train between New York and Miami, it was in its 75th season in 1963. It operated over the Pennsylvania RR from New York to Washington, the RF&P from Washington and Richmond, and Coast Line from Richmond to Jacksonville. For many years an all-Pullman train, the *Orange Blossom Special* had been its rival for the carriage trade between New York and the Florida Gold Coast. By 1963, it included coaches as well as sleepers in its consist, but it provided amenities such as fashion shows, movies and complimentary champagne, and charged an extra fare. On the Seaboard, the *Special* was scheduled to leave Auburndale at 7:25 A.M. and reach Miami at 11:25. Northbound, it departed Miami at 5:25 P.M. and arrived in Auburndale at 9:20.

The *East Coast Champion,* ACL Nos. 1 and 2, was a New York-Miami streamliner which operated on a schedule that was competitive with the *Silver Meteor.* Indeed, it was inaugurated as the *Champion,* in December 1939, nine months after the *Meteor* began operating. Like its rival, the *Champion* had grown from a seven-car coach streamliner to be one of the premier trains in the nation. On the SAL, the *Champion* left Auburndale at about 1:00 P.M. and arrived in Miami at 5:45. No. 2 left Miami at 9:30 A.M., arriving in Auburndale at 1:35 P.M.

The *South Wind* operated every other day between Chicago and Miami. Most of its tuscan-red equipment was provided by the Pennsylvania Railroad, and it was operated by the Pennsy between Chicago and Louisville, the Louisville & Nashville between Louisville and Montgomery, Ala., and the ACL between Montgomery and Jacksonville, via Waycross, Ga. The *City of Miami* was primarily an Illinois Central train, painted in IC's striking chocolate-and-orange color scheme. It was routed over the IC from Chicago to Birmingham, the Central of Georgia from Birmingham to Albany, Ga., and Coast Line from Albany, via Waycross, to Jacksonville, alternating operating days with the *South Wind.* The two trains shared the same schedule over the ACL between Waycross and Jacksonville, as well as over the FEC. Thus, one Chicago streamliner operated each way daily between Waycross and Miami. On the ACL-SAL joint route, the Chicago trains used their FEC operating numbers, 5 and 6. They were [illegible] 1:45 P.M., arriving in Miami

The FEC strike dragged on for years. Although a reluctant East Coast was eventually compelled by the Florida Supreme Court to run a token passenger train between Jacksonville and Miami for a while, FEC never again ran a through passenger train. The temporary detour became a permanent route and the Coast Line trains continued to operate over Seaboard up to the merger. By 1966, the *Champion* and the Chicago trains were combined into a single train south of Jacksonville during the off season, but all three trains were separately scheduled each winter through the 1966–67 season. Operation via Auburndale was continued by SCL after the merger and the route was adopted by Amtrak when it took over passenger service in 1971. Curiously, Seaboard never acknowledged the existence of the ACL trains in its public timetables or in the *Official Guide*, but the schedules were listed in its employee timetables.

By 1967, many railroads had severely curtailed their passenger service. Some had gotten out of the passenger business altogether, while others had allowed their trains to deteriorate. The Interstate Highway Act had been passed in 1956, authorizing construction of the Interstate Highway System, and, in 1959, the first successful jetliner, the Boeing 707, had entered airline service. Those two events were not exactly conducive to the health of the passenger train. To make matters worse, the Post Office began a nationwide diversion of mail from passenger trains in 1967. The days of the privately operated passenger train were dwindling. Amtrak, the nationalization of rail passenger service, was only a few years away.

Although its passenger revenues had held up better than most railroads', Seaboard was not immune from these trends. It began discontinuing some of its passenger trains in the mid-sixties. The *Palmland*'s Wildwood-Tampa connection, which had been renumbered to 11 and 12, was halted November 13, 1965, due to diversion of its mail traffic to trucks. Nos. 36 and 37, the Jacksonville-Chattahoochee local, disappeared in 1966. Seaboard also sought to cancel the *Tidewater* between Portsmouth and Raleigh, in 1966, but was required by the Interstate Commerce Commission to operate the train until at least November 1, 1967. The railroad did drop the *Tidewater*'s diner and sleeping cars, although it continued to operate through coaches between Portsmouth and Atlanta and Jacksonville. Other schedule changes reflected the exigencies of the time. The *Palmland* cut out a number of local stops with the result that many small communities lost their only passenger service. And the westbound *Gulf Wind* was rescheduled so as to arrive in Jacksonville in the early afternoon, a move necessitated by L&N reducing its passenger service out of New Orleans.

To its credit, Seaboard's mainline passenger service remained largely intact at the time of the merger. Four daily trains still operated between the Northeast and Florida and three were still running on the Georgia Division. The *Gulf Wind*, of course, continued on the Jacksonville-New Orleans run. Moreover, the quality of service remained high. The *Silver Meteor*, *Comet* and *Star* were about as good as ever. Even the *Palmland*, never the best of trains, maintained a decent level of service. The extent of Seaboard's commitment to quality passenger service may be gauged by the fact that it bought 20 new passenger locomotives in 1964, albeit dual-service SDP35's, and picked up 36 lightweight cars from the FEC in 1965.

Not surprisingly, many of the Seaboard Air Line trains did not long survive the merger. The *Tidewater* was soon discontinued. The West Coast section of the *Silver Meteor* was dropped in 1968. The *Silver Comet* disappeared in 1969 and the former SAL Georgia Division was reduced to freight service only. Nor did the *Gulf Wind* survive until the Amtrak takeover of passenger service in 1971. The East Coast *Meteor* and the *Silver Star* lived on under Seaboard Coast Line colors, however, and were adopted by Amtrak. With the probable exception of the West Coast section of the *Silver Meteor*, Seaboard would no doubt have discontinued these trains had there been no merger. But at least it can be said that up to July 1, 1967, the Seaboard Air Line Railroad Company provided a passenger service of which it could well be proud—one of the finest in the nation.

CHAPTER NINE

FREIGHT SERVICE

Passenger trains may have been interesting to watch and fun to ride but, as on every other railroad in America, freight paid Seaboard's bills, typically providing about 80 percent of the road's revenues and almost all of its profits.

TRAFFIC

As would be expected of a 4,000-mile railroad system, Seaboard hauled a wide variety of commodities. The glamorous freight was perishable traffic, especially citrus fruit and vegetables moving from Florida to Northern markets. Yet in a typical year, 1951, agricultural commodities of all kinds accounted for less than 5 percent of the total Seaboard freight tonnage. In that year, manufactures and miscellaneous commodities comprised 28 percent of Seaboard traffic and forest products 16 percent. By far the biggest single category of Seaboard traffic was mineral products, accounting for almost 51 percent of the railroad's freight tonnage. Of course the average carload of rock no doubt weighed considerably more than a load of oranges.

Seaboard's Florida perishable traffic was seasonal, being concentrated in the winter months. Most of the traffic originated in Central Florida at towns along the Wildwood-Miami line and the Tampa and Orlando Sub-Divisions. Important shipping points included Winter Haven, Auburndale, West Lake Wales and Pompano Beach on the Miami line; Plant City and Clearwater on the Tampa Sub-Division; Palmetto on the Sarasota branch; and Zellwood and Oviedo on the Orlando line. In addition, the little Tavares & Gulf RR was an important source of perishable traffic.

Seaboard owned an interest in the Fruit Growers Express Co., and most of the perishables were shipped in yellow FGEX refrigerator cars. As Fruit Growers was closely affiliated with the Great Northern Railway's Western Fruit Express and the Chicago, Burlington & Quincy's Burlington Refrigerator Express Co., cars of the latter two firms were also commonly used in Seaboard perishable service. In earlier years, ventilated boxcars, sometimes called watermelon cars, were also widely used to handle perishables. But by the fifties, the vents were mostly relegated to general merchandise service, and, by 1963, Seaboard's ventilated boxcar fleet, which had numbered almost 3,000 units in 1948, had dwindled to a mere 46 cars.

Ordinarily the reefers would be iced at Wildwood, Tampa or West Lake Wales before being loaded for the trip north. The cars would be re-iced at various points en route, primarily at Hamlet or the RF&P's Potomac Yard near Washington. Beginning in the fifties, refrigerator cars were increasingly equipped with mechanical refrigeration units which, of course, did not require icing. Carloads of perishables were routinely shipped north without a specific destination designated. The perishables would be sold en route and diverted at Savannah to their ultimate destination. As many as 250 cars a day were reconsigned at Savannah Yard.

Over the years, SAL lost much of its perishable business to truckers. In 1946, 70 percent of Florida perishable moved by rail. By 1960, only 30 percent was handled by the railroads.

THIS PAGE, CLOCKWISE FROM TOP LEFT: *Georgia Division freights meet east of Rockingham, N.C., as No. 46, with two GP30's, an F3 and a GP9, encounters No. 89, the* Tar Heel, *on April 15, 1966.* Bruce R. Meyer

Leaning into a well-banked curve, B-1 class 2-10-2 No. 2499 works an eastbound time freight near Winder, Ga., on January 8, 1950. Hugh M. Comer

Laborers on the icing platform at Baldwin, Fla., replenish the ice bunkers of refrigerator cars loaded with northbound perishables. The advent of mechanical refrigerator cars doomed this and other major SAL ice docks at Tampa, West Lake Wales, Wildwood and Tallahassee, Fla., Savannah, Ga., and Hamlet, N.C. CSX Transportation collection

FACING PAGE: *His work interrupted by the yard engine, a lone track worker takes a break while SAL 0-6-0 No. 1058 switches wooden reefers in downtown Jacksonville, Fla.* James G. LaVake

HOTEL
MAYFLOWER
CONDITIONED
1058
1058

concentrates became popular after World War II. Several carloads of fresh oranges would be replaced by a single car of concentrated orange juice.

In any event, fruit and vegetables accounted for only a fraction of the agricultural tonnage handled by SAL. As early as 1950, perishables constituted less than half of the road's traffic in farm commodities. Other important agricultural commodities included cotton and cotton products, wheat and flour, and other grains and grain products.

The manufactures and miscellaneous commodities category naturally included a bit of just about everything going to almost everywhere. Traditionally the traffic was predominantly southbound, from the industrial Northeast and Midwest to the agrarian Southeast. That pattern changed somewhat with the increased industrialization of the South after World War II. Fertilizer and cement were the two biggest categories of manufactured freight tonnage in 1951. But reflecting the proliferation of pulp mills in the Southeast, paperboard had become the biggest single class of miscellaneous freight revenue by 1960.

FACING PAGE, TOP: *One of eight Wabash Mikes acquired by Seaboard during World War II, Q-4 487 works a westbound drag near Lake City, Fla., on the line from Jacksonville to River Junction in February 1946. Tied to the 1912 Baldwin's Vanderbilt tank (a Seaboard addition) are a pair of ancient Frisco stock cars and a cut of pulpwood racks.* Hugh M. Comer

FACING PAGE, BOTTOM LEFT: *Although Seaboard served no on-line mines, the road hauled a significant amount of coal. Snaking through Petersburg, Va., in August 1945, Q-3 Mike 324 works southbound with a train of black diamonds.* D. Wallace Johnson

FACING PAGE, BOTTOM RIGHT: *Toting one of the staples of South Florida Division tonnage, RS3 1676, a pair of modified RSC2's and a Baldwin RS12 lug a westbound phosphate train near Valrico, Fla., in March 1960.* David W. Salter

THIS PAGE: *Piggybacks and brand-new Fords blur past shiny second-generation Geeps as southbound hotshot No. 27, the* Capital, *meets No. 280, led by GP30 504, at Boylan Avenue Tower in Raleigh, N.C., in January 1963.* J. Parker Lamb

Forest products transported by Seaboard included logs, posts and finished lumber. But the most important category of forest product, by far, was pulpwood, again a reflection of the importance of the pulp and paper industry. Most of the pulpwood came from pine trees. Pines were the predominant trees in the forests of the coastal South and were also raised commercially in tree farms. In 1960, pulpwood accounted for over 11 percent of Seaboard's total freight tonnage and 6 percent of its freight revenue. Pulpwood was normally transported in wood racks. But by the sixties, the raw pine was increasingly moving to the mills in the form of wood chips, shipped in special large-volume hopper cars.

A rather unusual forest commodity handled by SAL was pine stumps. They were shipped in high-side gondolas to plants where they yielded pine oil and turpentine. One of the largest consumers of the stumps was a plant located, off line, in Brunswick, Ga.

Seaboard's heaviest mineral traffic was in phosphate. The substance is utilized to make phosphoric acid, ammunition and matches, but its principal use is as an ingredient in fertilizer. Over the years the phosphate loaded on the SAL increased from less than 3 million tons in 1938 to over 12 million tons in 1963. Seaboard's phosphate traffic originated mostly in the Bone Valley of Florida, an area east of Tampa centered around Mulberry and Bartow. Bone Valley, so called for the many fossils found in the vicinity, contains some of the biggest and most important phosphate deposits in the world. Other phosphate deposits on the Seaboard were located at Dunnellon and Arcadia, Fla., but the Bone Valley deposits were by far the leading source. Only two railroads served the Valley, Seaboard and ACL. The heavy phosphate traffic was probably the main reason why the relatively small South Florida Division remained as a separate operating division.

The Dunnellon and Arcadia deposits were of hard rock phosphate, while the Bone Valley beds consisted mostly of pebble phosphate. The hard rock has a higher phosphorous

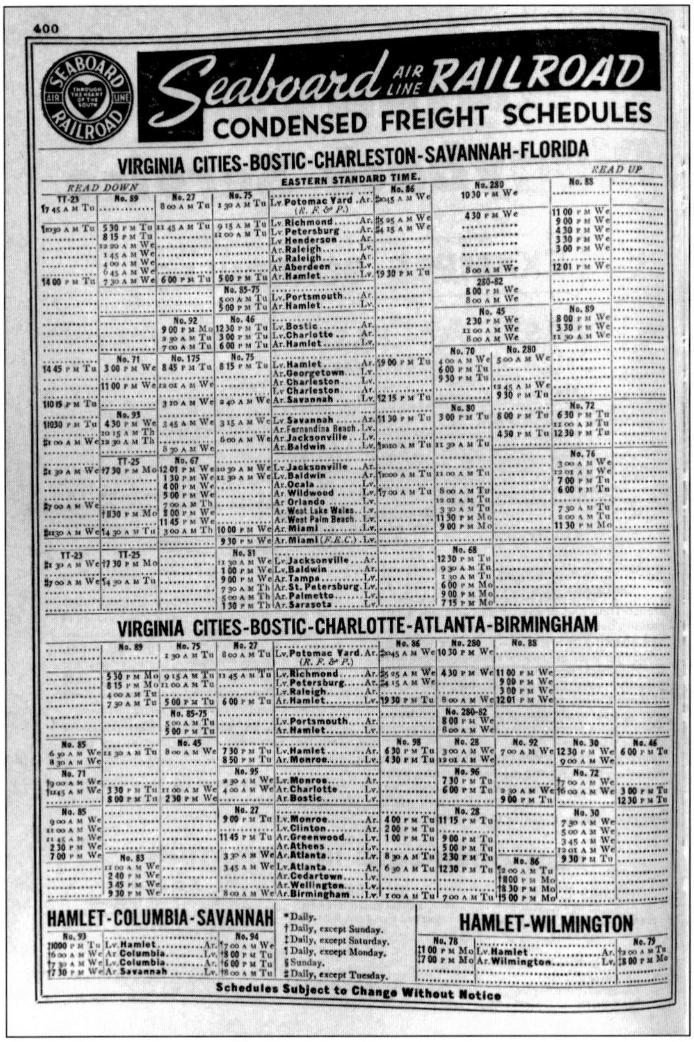
400

Seaboard AIR LINE RAILROAD

CONDENSED FREIGHT SCHEDULES

VIRGINIA CITIES-BOSTIC-CHARLESTON-SAVANNAH-FLORIDA

EASTERN STANDARD TIME.

READ DOWN — READ UP

VIRGINIA CITIES-BOSTIC-CHARLOTTE-ATLANTA-BIRMINGHAM

HAMLET-COLUMBIA-SAVANNAH

HAMLET-WILMINGTON

*Daily. †Daily, except Sunday. ‡Daily, except Saturday. ‡Daily, except Monday. §Sunday. ‡Daily, except Tuesday.

Schedules Subject to Change Without Notice

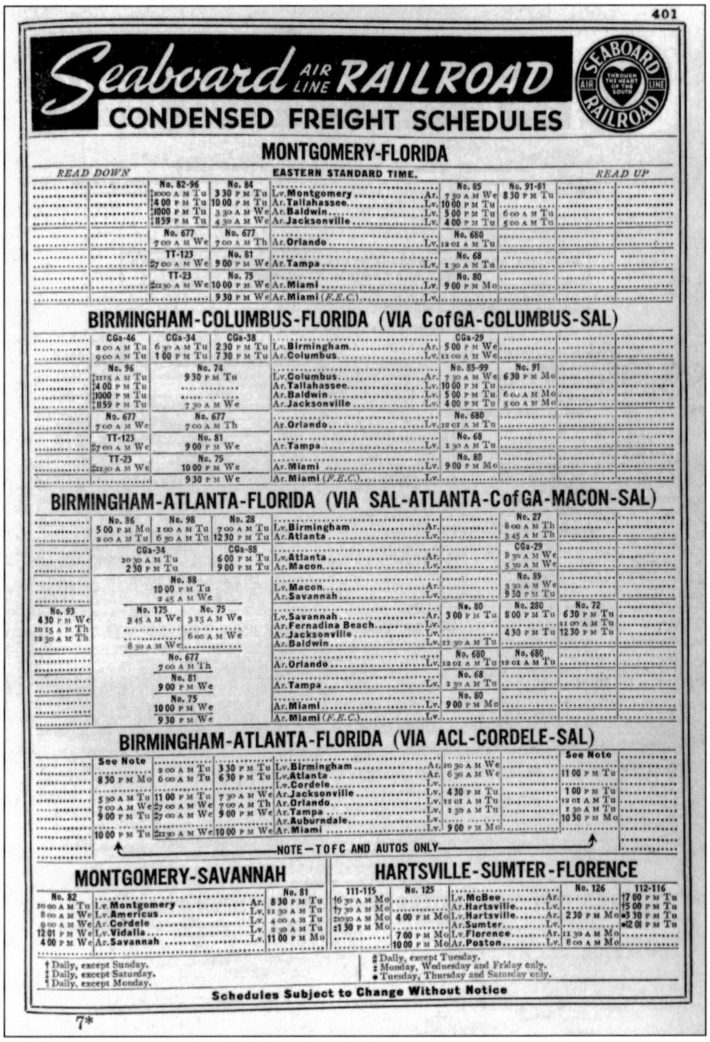
401

Seaboard AIR LINE RAILROAD

CONDENSED FREIGHT SCHEDULES

MONTGOMERY-FLORIDA

EASTERN STANDARD TIME.

READ DOWN — READ UP

BIRMINGHAM-COLUMBUS-FLORIDA (VIA CofGA-COLUMBUS-SAL)

BIRMINGHAM-ATLANTA-FLORIDA (VIA SAL-ATLANTA-CofGA-MACON-SAL)

BIRMINGHAM-ATLANTA-FLORIDA (VIA ACL-CORDELE-SAL)

NOTE—TOFC AND AUTOS ONLY

MONTGOMERY-SAVANNAH

HARTSVILLE-SUMTER-FLORENCE

†Daily, except Sunday. ‡Daily, except Saturday. ‡Daily, except Monday.

‡Daily, except Tuesday. ‡Monday, Wednesday and Friday only. •Tuesday, Thursday and Saturday only.

Schedules Subject to Change Without Notice

Seaboard's freight schedules as advertised in June 1965. A northbound piggyback train was not listed in these summer schedules. The advertised schedules were usually more accurate than these shown in employee timetables. Author's collection

content, but pebble phosphate is cheaper to mine. Pebble phosphate is extracted from open-pit mines. Huge walking drag lines remove the matrix of sand, clay and phosphate, which is then slurried to washing plants where the extraneous material is removed. The resulting granular raw phosphate, or wet rock, is then transported to treatment plants by rail. The treated product is called, not surprisingly, dry rock. To transport the wet rock, Seaboard used open-top hoppers. Given the nature of the lading, the cars tended to rust out rather quickly. Dry rock was handled in distinctive squat covered hoppers especially built for phosphate service. For long-distance shipments the railroad also used converted box cars which were modified with roof-top loading hatches.

Most of the phosphate traffic was short haul. The wet rock usually moved only from the mines to nearby processing plants and much of the dry rock from Bone Valley to Seaboard's marine terminals at Port Boca Grande and Seddon Island, Tampa. Mulberry Yard, the heart of SAL's Bone Valley operations, was only about 30 miles from Tampa and 100 miles from Port Boca Grande. However, the phosphate that wasn't exported or moved by ship to ports in the Northeast, moved in interior trade by rail to fertilizer plants throughout the U.S. and Canada.

Other important minerals transported by Seaboard included coal, iron ore, clay, sand and gravel, and rock. They came from mines and quarries around the system. Among others, kaolin, a high-quality fine white clay, was loaded in large amounts at Attapulgas, Ga., on the old GF&A line, and enormous quantities of rock were shipped from the area around Brooksville, Fla. Much of Seaboard's ballast came from Greystone, N.C., on the Virginia

Division mainline. Although SAL handled large quantities of coal, it was virtually all interchange traffic received from other railroads. No coal mines were located on the Seaboard.

The late fifties and early sixties witnessed a revolution in railroading: the development of piggyback, the hauling of highway trailers on specially equipped railroad flatcars. This marriage of railroading and trucking enabled the railroads to recover a lot of perishable and general merchandise traffic they had previously lost to highway carriers, and was eventually to render the traditional railroad boxcar almost obsolete. At about the same time, the railroads also developed the auto-rack car. Capable of carrying up to 15 automobiles at a time, the new type of rolling stock permitted the railroads to successfully compete for new auto traffic for the first time in years. But if they were to prevail against the highway carriers, the railroads had to offer service at speeds comparable to that of the truckers. As a result, piggyback flats and auto racks were given priority treatment and handled in the fastest trains, in some cases special high-speed runs restricted to "pigs" and auto racks.

Seaboard inaugurated trailer-on-flatcar (TOFC) service late in 1959 and auto-rack service in the latter part of the next year. To obtain the necessary rolling stock, SAL joined Trailer Train, the national pool of piggyback and auto-rack equipment. Beginning in 1960, SAL started operating special high-speed piggyback trains. The traffic increased rapidly. By 1965, the road handled over 52,000 carloads of TOFC and new autos, which accounted for almost seven percent of the company's total revenues.

Another important new development in the sixties was the unit train, the movement of an entire train for a single shipper at a special low rate to reflect the high volume. Unit trains were eventually to have an important impact on the railroad industry, but mostly after SAL had merged into Seaboard Coast Line. Seaboard handled its first unit train, of coal to a power plant in Virginia, in January 1965.

FREIGHT ROUTES

For the most part, Seaboard freight trains followed the same routes as the passenger trains. But several lines which were inconsequential from a passenger standpoint were important freight routes. The paramount example was the East Carolina line. All through freight trains between Hamlet and Savannah ran over the low-level line via Charleston, a route that never enjoyed more than local passenger service. Another example was the line from Monroe to Charlotte and Bostic (Rutherfordton), which supported heavy freight operations. In Florida, the Orlando Sub-Division from Wildwood to Orlando was an important freight line. Other freight routes, which never had through passenger service, were from Montgomery, Ala., and Columbus, Ga., over the old GF&A line to Tallahassee. Also in Florida, the Gross Cut-off north out of Baldwin was an important freight route, permitting traffic moving between South Florida and the Northeast to bypass Jacksonville. Heavy phosphate traffic moved over the line from Mulberry Yard to Tampa and over the old CH&N route south to Port Boca Grande.

On the other hand, a few major passenger lines were relatively insignificant in terms of freight operations. The original Hamlet-Savannah mainline via Columbia, transited by all the Richmond-Florida passenger trains, was provided with only limited freight service. The line between Tallahassee and Chattahoochee (River Jct.) Fla., over which the Jacksonville-New Orleans passenger trains operated, received only local freight service. Only traffic destined to or from the Florida Panhandle was interchanged with the L&N at Chattahoochee. Through SAL-L&N freight moving between Florida and points farther west was routed via Montgomery. The line between Tampa and St. Petersburg was another important line that normally was scheduled to receive only daily local freight service.

CONNECTING RAILROADS

Seaboard interchanged freight with numerous other railroads, large and small, at junction points all over its system. In 1948, SAL maintained connections with 56 other railroads.

Comprising one-third of Seaboard's Alco cab fleet, FA1 4200 and FB1 4300 work No. 88 through Floyd, Ga., in April 1950. Railway Negative Exchange

Naturally, the largest number of junction points were with railroads that also served Seaboard's territory. The most with a single railroad, 55, were with the Atlantic Coast Line. Next was Southern with 32, followed by Central of Georgia with 13. But most of the more important connections were with railroads at the periphery of its system with which Seaboard maintained only a few junction points.

Seaboard's leading freight connection was undoubtedly with the Richmond, Fredericksburg & Potomac at the little road's Acca Yard in Richmond. Almost all traffic between Seaboard points and the Northeast moved over the RF&P. The two railroads cooperated closely and RF&P preblocked SAL traffic at Potomac Yard, Alexandria, Va., eliminating the need for Seaboard to classify incoming RF&P interchange traffic at Richmond.

In addition to RF&P, an important connection at Richmond was the Chesapeake & Ohio with which SAL interchanged traffic at Brown Street Yard, just north of Main Street Station. C&O provided Seaboard with a connection to Cincinnati, Detroit and Chicago. An alternative connection to Cincinnati and the Midwest was with the Norfolk & Western Ry. at Petersburg, Va. N&W's Norfolk-Cincinnati mainline crossed SAL's main stem at that point. Alberta, Va., was an additional major junction point in the Old Dominion, where SAL connected with the Virginian Ry.'s line to the coal fields of West Virginia.

In the Carolinas, a valuable connecting line was the Clinchfield RR, which interchanged with SAL at Bostic Yard, near Rutherfordton, N.C. A relatively small bridge line extending from a connection with the Chesapeake & Ohio at Elkhorn City, Ky., south to Spartanburg, S.C., Clinchfield handled large quantities of freight from Ohio, Indiana, Michigan and Illinois, as well as a heavy volume of coal from mines on its own line. A small but important connection in North Carolina was the little Durham & Southern Ry., which connected with SAL's Virginia Division mainline at Apex, N.C. The D&S functioned as a bridge line connecting the Norfolk & Western's line to Cincinnati with Seaboard's line to the Southeast.

Enjoying the breeze, the conductor and brakeman of an SAL transfer job ride the pilot beam of H-1 2-8-0 No. 917 as the pre-World War I Baldwin stomps past Bellwood Tower in Atlanta in 1940. Hugh M. Comer

On the Georgia Division, Atlanta and Birmingham were the major junction points. At Atlanta, Seaboard connected principally with the Nashville, Chattanooga & St. Louis Ry. (later Louisville & Nashville) line to Chattanooga and Nashville; the L&N line to Knoxville and Cincinnati; the West Point Route to Montgomery, Ala., and points west; the Georgia RR to Augusta, Ga.; and the Southern Ry., which went from Atlanta in just about every direction. Freight interchanged at Atlanta included some bridge traffic to and from the west which moved over SAL between Birmingham and Atlanta, Central of Georgia between Atlanta and Macon, Ga., and SAL (or Macon, Dublin & Savannah) again between Macon and Savannah or Florida points.

In Birmingham, Seaboard connected with the Frisco (St. Louis-San Francisco Ry.) to Memphis, St. Louis and Kansas City; the Illinois Central to St. Louis and Chicago; the Louisville & Nashville to Montgomery, Mobile and New Orleans, as well as almost everywhere else in Alabama; and the Southern Railway System to Memphis, Mobile and New Orleans. SAL had little local business in Birmingham. Most of its traffic handled to that city was interchanged with other railroads.

Montgomery, Ala., and Columbus, Ga., were the principal junction points on the Alabama Division. SAL routed most of its traffic between Florida and the Midwest via Baldwin, Tallahassee and either Montgomery or Columbus. At Columbus, Seaboard connected with the Central of Georgia's line to Birmingham. Central, in turn, connected at Birmingham with the Frisco, Illinois Central and L&N lines to the north and west. In Montgomery, the major connections were the Gulf, Mobile & Ohio's line to St. Louis and Chicago and the L&N's lines west to New Orleans and north to Nashville. During the sixties, SAL also promoted a connection with the Atlantic Coast Line at Cordele, Ga., on the Savannah-Montgomery line. Coast Line handled the traffic from Birmingham or Atlanta south to Cordele, and Seaboard from Cordele to Florida points.

The important gateway in Florida was Jacksonville, where the major connecting carri-

TOP:
With an A-B-B-A of ice-encrusted FT's sandwiched between a pair of GP9's, southbound No. 75 pauses for a quick crew change at Raleigh, N.C., at dusk on a stormy December 1962 day. The aging FT's are experiencing their final winter and will soon be retired and traded in to EMD on GP30's. J. Parker Lamb

BOTTOM:
Nicknamed "Jolly Green Giants" for their handsome green garb, Seaboard GP40's 609, 608 and 610 thunder through Henderson, N.C., with the 92-car Merchandiser *in June 1966.* Curt Tillotson, Jr.

ers were the Southern Railway System and the Florida East Coast. SAL interchanged South Florida traffic with the Southern, which handled it north of Jacksonville. Traffic moving to and from the north via Seaboard, as well as traffic from other points in Florida, was interchanged with the FEC for movement from Jacksonville south. East Coast wouldn't enter into favorable tariff agreements for traffic interchanged with Seaboard in South Florida. As a result almost all SAL-FEC traffic was interchanged at Jacksonville. The East Coast interchange was conducted near downtown at the romantically named "Honeymoon" Yard.

THE TRAINS

Most of Seaboard's through freights ran as scheduled trains and many of them bore names. A few of the hotter freights were even rated as first-class trains, with timetable rights equal to those of passenger schedules. Almost all of the first-class freights were southbound, however. Only one eastbound train was accorded this status, probably because north and eastbound trains normally have superior rights over south and westbound trains of the same class. Although the freights operated as scheduled trains, the schedules didn't seem to be adhered to very closely. Seaboard's freight schedules served mostly as approximations of actual practice. The freight schedules published in the *Official Guide* usually advertised later arrivals and slower running times than those shown in the employee timetables. For the most part, the advertised schedules were actually closer to the mark. However, in discussing freight operations I have used the times shown in the employee timetables since they were, after all, official.

I am focusing on Seaboard's schedules during the mid-sixties. There had of course been changes over the years, but the sixties were fairly representative of the level of the road's operations during the diesel era. There was one exception, however: the introduction of special piggyback trains during the last years of SAL's existence.

The premier freight train on the run from Virginia to Florida for many years was No. 75, the *Merchandiser.* Rated as a first-class train, it was frequently pulled by passenger diesels between Richmond and Jacksonville. In 1964 it was scheduled, according to the employee timetables, to leave Hermitage Yard, Richmond at 8:00 A.M. and Hamlet at 6:00 P.M., arriving in West Jax at 3:30 the next morning and Hialeah at 7:30 that evening. Actually, almost all of the cars handled into Jacksonville were either local traffic for that city or interchange for the Florida East Coast. Through traffic for South Florida moved in No. 175, the *Merchandiser*'s Hamlet-Baldwin section which operated over the Gross Cut-off bypassing Jacksonville. Also a first-class train, No. 175 followed No. 75 out of Hamlet at 6:30 P.M. reaching

Continuing the long-standing Seaboard practice of assigning passenger power to fast freights, E7A's 3045, 3029 and an E7B team up with a pair of Geeps, wheeling southbound hotshot 27 through Aberdeen, N.C., in August 1962.
J. Parker Lamb

Timecarded as a First Class train, redball No. 27 storms through Henderson, N.C., with GP35 538, GP30 517, GP9 1980, F3A 4030 and 110 cars in November 1964. Carefully making his way along the gangway of the 538, No. 27's fireman is heading back to investigate problems with one of the trailing units. Curt Tillotson, Jr.

Baldwin at 4:00 A.M. No. 75 out of Jacksonville would stop at Baldwin to pick up Hialeah traffic from No. 175. Traffic for the South Florida Division was handled in No. 81, the *Cavalcade,* which also picked up cars at Baldwin. It left West Jax at 11:45 A.M. and arrived at Yeoman Yard, Tampa, at 7:00 P.M.

Northbound, the principal train out of South Florida was No. 80, the *Marketer,* which ran from Hialeah to Hamlet via the Gross Cut-off. In 1964, it was officially scheduled to leave Hialeah at 7:35 P.M. and Baldwin at 8:30 A.M., arriving at Hamlet at 7:30 that evening. The Tampa section of the *Marketer* was No. 68, which departed from Yeoman Yard at 8:15 P.M., arrived at Baldwin at 3:55 A.M. and West Jax at 4:50 A.M. North out of Jacksonville the primary train was No. 280. Much of its consist was interchange from the FEC, a large portion of which was perishables. No. 280 departed West Jax at 3:00 P.M. and arrived in Hamlet at 2:00 the next morning. After classification at Hamlet, it left that point at 5:30 A.M., reaching Richmond at 2:00 P.M. The hottest conventional train out of Florida was No. 86, the "advance perishable service," which operated from Wildwood to Hermitage via the Gross Cut-off. It departed Wildwood at 3:00 A.M., arrived in Hamlet at 3:00 P.M. and Richmond at 2:20 A.M., less than 24 hours after its departure. At one time this train had been called the *Red Fox.*

On the run from Richmond to Atlanta and Birmingham, the top train was No. 27, the *Capital.* Like the *Merchandiser,* it was a first-class train, rated as such between Hermitage and Howells Yard, Atlanta. Long the pride of the operating department, the *Capital* may well have been the fastest conventional train on the system. Its scheduled running time between Hermitage and Hamlet was the same as No. 75's, but in actual practice it was normally faster than the *Merchandiser* as it made fewer stops to pick up traffic along the way. On the Georgia Division it was permitted a maximum speed of 60 mph while all other freights were limited to 50 mph. The *Capital* was scheduled to leave Richmond at 10:00 A.M. and Hamlet at 5:37 P.M. arriving at Howells at 1:30 the next morning and Birmingham at 5:40 A.M., eastern time.

The other major southbound train on the Georgia Division was No. 85, a through freight which at one time had been scheduled to operate all the way from Portsmouth to Birmingham. But by the sixties, it was restricted to the run from Hamlet to Atlanta, departing Hamlet at 5:10 A.M. and arriving in Atlanta at 4:00 P.M. Another through freight, No. 83, operated from Atlanta to Birmingham, leaving Howells at 9:00 A.M. and arriving in the Alabama city at 2:30 that afternoon.

While only two through freights were scheduled southbound over the Georgia Division, three were listed in the opposite direction. Northbound, two trains operated all the way from Birmingham to Hamlet, Nos. 98 and 28. The earlier train, No. 98, left Birmingham at midnight and Atlanta at 7:30 a.m, arriving at Hamlet at 4:00 P.M. The premier train was No. 28, which was rather confusingly called the *Iron Master* from Birmingham to Atlanta and the *Courier* from Atlanta to Hamlet. It departed Birmingham at 7:00 A.M. and Howells at 12:30 P.M., arriving in Hamlet at 10:25 that evening. An additional train, No. 86, operated from Birmingham to Atlanta, departing Birmingham at 3:00 each afternoon. The third train from Atlanta to Hamlet was No. 30, which left Howells at 7:30 P.M. and arrived in Hamlet at 4:30 the next morning.

On the Virginia Division three through freights were scheduled in each direction between Richmond and Hamlet. The southbound trains included the first-class hotshots, the *Capital* and the *Merchandiser*, plus an additional train, No. 89, the *Tar Heel*. The *Tar Heel* operated from Richmond to Charlotte and Bostic on a less than spectacular schedule. It departed Richmond at 5:35 P.M., arrived in Hamlet at 5:00 the next morning, left that point at 10:00 A.M., reached Charlotte at 1:00 P.M. and Bostic at 5:00 that afternoon. The northbound runs included two redballs from Florida, No. 280 and No. 86, plus No. 88. The latter served mostly as a clean-up train. Operating on a leisurely schedule, No. 88 departed Hamlet at 10:30 A.M. and arrived in the Virginia capital at 7:00 that evening. In addition two other trains, Nos. 60 and 61, operated each morning between Hamlet and Raleigh. The northbound train, No. 60, was designated as the *Courier*.

The Portsmouth Sub-Division in the mid-sixties was served by a single through freight in each direction daily between Portsmouth and Raleigh. No. 85, the southbound train, was scheduled to leave Portsmouth at 5:45 A.M., and the northbound train, No. 82, arrived in town at 3:40 P.M. At one time the Portsmouth trains terminated at Norlina, but their southern terminus, like that of the Portsmouth passenger trains, had been moved to Raleigh. The Wilmington Sub-Division was also served by a single pair of trains. No. 78, the eastbound train, ran from Hamlet over to Wilmington each afternoon, and the return train, No. 77, left Wilmington at 8:00 each evening.

On the Monroe Sub-Division, two through freights ran daily from Hamlet to Bostic Yard, the *Tar Heel* and No. 45. The latter was scheduled to depart Hamlet at 5:00 A.M., arriving in Charlotte at 6:50 A.M. and Bostic at 9:30 A.M. Eastbound, the premier redball out of Bostic was No. 46. Rated as a first-class train, it was the only even-numbered first-class freight on the system. It left Bostic at 8:30 A.M. and arrived in Hamlet at 1:00 P.M. Another train, No. 94, ran from Bostic to Charlotte each evening. It connected with No. 92, which was scheduled to leave Charlotte at 2:00 each morning and arrive in Hamlet at 4:30 A.M. Two additional freights were scheduled to operated daily in each direction on the short run between Charlotte and Monroe. Westbound, No. 95 was the Charlotte connection from the *Capital* and No. 71 served as the connection from No. 85. They arrived in Charlotte at 11:30 P.M. and 9:00 A.M. respectively. Eastbound, No. 96 departed Charlotte at 5:00 P.M. with cars for No. 28, the *Courier*, and No. 72 was scheduled to leave Charlotte at 5:30 A.M. It was advertised as connecting with No. 30, even though according to the employee timetable, No. 30 would have already left Monroe before No. 72 even departed Charlotte—an indication of the unreliability of the employee time cards.

Carolina Division through freights between Hamlet and Savannah were, of course, all routed over the low line via Charleston. Two through freights were operated southbound

RICHMOND STEEL CO.

1109
1109
SEABOARD
1109

from Hamlet to Savannah daily, Nos. 75 and 175, the two sections of the *Merchandiser.* And three were scheduled northbound: No. 80, the *Marketer,* out of Miami; No. 86, the "advance perishable service," out of Wildwood; and No. 280 from Jacksonville. In addition, a through freight was operated between Hamlet and Charleston in each direction, six days a week. The southbound train, No. 71, was scheduled to leave Hamlet at 2:30 P.M. and arrive at Cooper Yard, Charleston at 7:30 P.M. Northbound, No. 70 departed Charleston at 7:30 P.M. and arrived in Hamlet at 1:10 A.M. Only a single pair of trains operated over the line via Columbia, Nos. 93 and 94, and they performed a lot of local work along the way.

South of Savannah, four freights ran daily in each direction on the Carolina Division mainline, with two each serving Baldwin and Jacksonville. The premier southbound trains were, of course, the two *Merchandiser*s, No. 75 to West Jax and No. 175 to Baldwin. The secondary trains were No. 93 to Jacksonville and No. 99, the *Migrator,* to Baldwin, both of which were scheduled to leave Savannah in the early afternoon. Northbound, the through freights out of Baldwin were No. 80, the *Marketer,* and No. 86, the "advance perishable service." From West Jax, the principal train was No. 280 and the secondary run was No. 72, scheduled to leave the Florida gateway at 11:30 each morning.

A single pair of freights operated daily on the old Alabama Division line between Savannah and Montgomery. The westbound train, No. 81 the *Clipper,* left Savannah at 10:00 P.M. and arrived at Clisby Park Yard in Montgomery at 5:45 P.M. eastern time. Eastbound, No. 82, the *Alaga,* was scheduled to depart Clisby Park at 8:00 A.M. and reach Savannah at 12:35 P.M. the next day, after a lengthy lay-over in Americus. The *Alaga* was rated as only a third-class train from Montgomery to Americus. Another set of trains were operated each evening between Savannah and Macon: No. 89, the *Tropical Trader,* westbound and No. 88, the *Acme,* eastbound. The latter may have been named in homage to Acme Fast Freight, a freight forwarder that was closely associated with Seaboard. Two additional freights were scheduled over the former MD&S line between Macon and Vidalia, Ga., No. 281, which departed Vidalia at 7:00 A.M., and No. 282, which was scheduled out of Macon at 5:00 each afternoon.

Seaboard operated three through freights in each direction between Jacksonville, Tallahassee and the west-end gateways at Columbus and Montgomery. From Montgomery the eastbound train was No. 84, the *Pioneer,* which was due to leave at 1:30 P.M. eastern time and arrive at West Jax at 12:50 A.M. Westbound, No. 85 departed Jacksonville at 3:10 P.M., and reached the Alabama capital at 3:45 the next morning. It had a Richland-Columbus connection, No. 99, which was scheduled to arrive in Columbus at 6:00 A.M. On the Columbus-Jacksonville run, the premier eastbound train was No. 74, the *Cavalcade.* It left Columbus at 5:00 P.M. and arrived in West Jax at 2:00 the next morning. A second train, No. 96, departed at 10:15 A.M. and arrived in the Florida city at 9:00 that evening. Westbound, No. 91 left Jacksonville at 1:50 A.M. and arrived in Columbus at 2:50 P.M. The third train out of Florida, No. 95 ran from West Jax only as far as Richland, departing at 8:00 P.M. and arriving at 11:00 A.M. The west-end trains all picked up or set out South Florida traffic at Baldwin.

On the North Florida Division mainline, three through freights were scheduled in each direction between Jacksonville, Baldwin and South Florida points. No. 75, the *Merchandiser,* ran from Jacksonville to Hialeah and No. 81, the *Cavalcade,* to Tampa. The additional southbound train was No. 67, the *Migrator,* which operated from West Jax to Hialeah. It was due to depart at 10:45 A.M. and arrive at 9:15 P.M. The northbound trains out of Wildwood were, of course, Nos. 80 and 68, the Hialeah and Tampa sections of the *Marketer,* and No. 86, the "advance perishable service." Of these trains, only Nos. 68 and 86 ran into Jacksonville. A second freight was operated from Hialeah to Wildwood, No. 76, which was scheduled to depart the Miami area at 9:35 each evening.

Elsewhere on the North Florida Division, two trains were operated each way between Wildwood and Orlando. The eastbound trains were Nos. 677 and 607 which departed Wildwood at 1:00 A.M. and 7:00 A.M. respectively, and the return trains were Nos. 686 and 608 which left Orlando at 11:00 in the morning and 10:00 at night.

Few through freights were scheduled on the South Florida Division, most notably

FACING PAGE, TOP: *The piggyback revolution arrived with the sixties. A TOFC extra speeds south of Richmond behind three passenger diesels and an EMD road switcher.* CSX Transportation Collection

FACING PAGE, BOTTOM: *Piggyback hotshot TT23 pulls into Raleigh for a brief stop in 1967. Two dual service SDP35's and two GP30's have 77 cars in tow.* Curt Tillotson, Jr.

Flying soiled white flags, SDP35 1117 and GP35 544 highball through Gill, N.C., in February 1966, Florida-bound with TT-23, the pride of the fleet. Curt Tillotson, Jr.

the *Cavalcade* and *Marketer* between Wildwood and Yeoman Yard. Connecting sections of the *Marketer* were scheduled on the Sarasota and Boca Grande Sub-Divisions, but most other freights operated as locals or extras.

During the sixties, the railroad's fastest freights were the piggyback trains. In 1960, Seaboard inaugurated the twice-weekly *Piggyback Special*, a TOFC extra which left Auburndale in Central Florida at 5:00 P.M. and arrived in Richmond by 2:00 the next afternoon. Two years later the company initiated TT-23, the *Razorback*, a joint effort with the Pennsy and the RF&P, which operated six days a week on the run from Kearny, N.J., to Hialeah. It was originally scheduled to make the run from the New York area to Jacksonville in 29 hours 30 minutes. The *Razorback* was substantially faster than No. 75, SAL's swiftest conventional freight train on the Virginia to Florida run. In June 1965, the piggyback train made the run from Potomac Yard to Jacksonville in 17 hours 15 minutes, while No. 75 required 28 hours 30 minutes, and the trip from Potomac Yard to Hialeah needed 27 hours 45 minutes, versus 44 hours 30 minutes for the *Merchandiser*. In 1963 and 1964, TT-23 was considered the fastest scheduled freight train in the country, and the only one scheduled at over 60 mph. It was supposed to cover the 136.9 miles from Savannah to West Jax in 135 minutes for an average speed of 60.8 mph. Certainly it was not unusual for it to run hard on the heels of the *Silver Star* between those terminals. Paradoxically, the train actually ran as an extra. Although its schedule was widely advertised, neither TT-23 nor any of Seaboard's other piggyback trains were ever listed in the railroad's employee timetables.

In 1965, TT-23 was advertised as leaving Kearny at 11:00 P.M. and Potomac Yard at 7:45 A.M., arriving at West Jax at 1:30 the second morning and Hialeah at 11:30 A.M. Its Tampa connection, TT-123, arrived at Yeoman Yard at 7:00 A.M. TT-23's northbound counterpart, TT-24, was also called the *Razorback*. The train was discontinued after only two runs during the 1962-63 winter season due to a poor citrus crop following a freeze in December, but later the train operated on a regular basis. In 1965, TT-24 was advertised as leaving Hialeah at 8:00 P.M. and Jacksonville at 10:30 the next morning, arriving at Potomac Yard at 10:00 the second morning and Kearny at 11:45 that evening. The northbound *Razorback* did not have a Tampa section. Its piggyback cars out of Tampa were handled in No. 68, the *Marketer*. During the mid-sixties, Seaboard also operated piggyback cars on the southbound *Palmland* from Jacksonville to Miami, advertising the TOFC schedule as TT-25.

Seaboard never advertised any exclusively piggyback trains on the Georgia Division. TOFC traffic on the run to Atlanta and Birmingham was handled in Nos. 27 and 28, the Georgia Division hotshots, south of Hamlet, and in TT-23 and 24 north of that point.

TOP LEFT:
Baldwin DS4-4-1000 1459 idles with wooden caboose 5298 at Hamlet, N.C., in May 1962. J. Parker Lamb

TOP RIGHT:
One of ten RS11's on the Seaboard roster, SAL 104 reposes at Hialeah, Florida, with C420 133 and RS3 1631 on July 21, 1967. Ken Ardinger; collection of F.E. Ardrey, Jr.

MIDDLE LEFT:
switcher, SW1 1200, rests at Hialeah, Florida, July 18, 1963. Ken Ardinger

MIDDLE RIGHT:
Steam generator-equipped RS12 1473 switches at Hamlet, N.C., August 5, 1967. J.H. Wade; collection of F.E. Ardrey, Jr.

BOTTOM LEFT:
Operating behind the Meteor, *No. 7, the* Sunland, *made all local stops between Jacksonville and Tampa. On*
the eve of her retirement, Baldwin DR6-4-1500 2702 leads No. 7 through Bushnell, Fla., at 1:30 P.M., April 14, 1964. David W. Salter

BOTTOM RIGHT:
Seaboard's first GE diesels, U30B's 800-814, were among the last locomotives purchased by the railroad. Sisters 807 and 810 stand at Jacksonville on July 18, 1967. J.H. Wade; collection of F.E. Ardrey, Jr.

APPENDIX I

SEABOARD AIR LINE STEAM LOCOMOTIVE ROSTER (1938–1959)

The following roster details the steam locomotive fleets of the Seaboard Air Line; Gainesville & Midland; Jacksonville, Gainesville & Gulf; Macon, Dublin & Savannah; as well as the Tavares & Gulf, from 1938 until complete dieselization in 1959. Specifications are for locomotives in 1938 and thereafter.

BUILDERS

Alco	American Locomotive Co., Schenectady, N.Y.
Alco-B	American Locomotive Co., Brooks Works, Dunkirk, N.Y.
Alco-C	American Locomotive Co., Cooke Works, Paterson, N.J.
Alco-P	American Locomotive Co., Pittsburgh Works, Pittsburgh, Pa.
Alco-R	American Locomotive Co., Richmond Works, Richmond, Va.
BLW	Baldwin Locomotive Works, Philadelphia and Eddystone, Pa.
SAL	Seaboard Air Line Portsmouth Shops, Portsmouth, Va.

M CLASS 4-8-2

No.	Class	Cyl.	Driv.	WT	Pres.	T.E.	Builder/Date	Note
200-209	M	27x28	69	316,000	190	47,800	Alco-R 1914	1
210-214	M	27x28	69	316,000	190	47,800	Alco 1917	1
215-219	M-1	27x28	69	315,000	190	47,800	Alco 1922	2
221-224	M-1	27x28	69	315,000	190	47,800	Alco 1922	2
235-270	M-2	27x28	72	320,500	200	47,800	BLW 1924-26	3, 4, 5

M Class Notes

1. Class M 4-8-2's retired 1948–50.
2. M-1 220 wrecked in 1931 and scrapped; remainder of M-1 class retired 1950–52.
3. The following engines were re-equipped with large tenders in the mid-1930s: 235, 239, 242-244, 249, 253, 254, 257, 259, 261, 263-265 and 267.
4. The following engines were converted to oil burners after World War II: 242, 253, 254, 257, 261 and 267.
5. M-2 class retired 1952–55.

Q CLASS 2-8-2

No.	Class	Cyl.	Driv.	WT	Pres.	T.E.	Builder/Date	Note
300-318	Q	26x30	63	282,000	200	54,700	Alco-R 1914	1, 2
319-333	Q-2	26x30	63	283,000	200	54,700	Alco 1922	1, 2
334-356	Q-3	26x30	63	300,000	200	54,700	Alco 1923	3, 4
357-376	Q-3	26x30	63	300,000	200	54,700	BLW 1924	3
377-396	Q-3	26x30	63	300,000	200	54,700	Alco-R 1925	3
397-400	Q-3	26x30	63	300,000	200	54,700	BLW 1925	3
401-410	Q-3	26x30	63	300,000	200	54,700	BLW 1925	3
411-440	Q-3	26x30	63	300,000	200	54,700	BLW 1926	3, 5
442-450	Q-3	26x30	63	300,000	200	54,700	BLW 1926	3, 6
451	Q-3	26x30	63	300,000	200	54,700	SAL 1931	3, 6
480-481	Q-4	26x30	64	266,840	200	53,870	Alco-R 1912	7
482-487	Q-4	26x30	64	266,840	200	53,870	BLW 1912	8
490-499	Q-1	26x30	63	292,000	200	54,700	Alco 1918	9

Notes:

1. Engines 301, 304, 306, 317, 325, 330, 332 and 333 had 27x30 cylinders, 185 psi boiler pressure and 54,590 lb tractive effort.
2. Class Q and Q-2 locomotives retired 1950–52.
3. Class Q-3 locomotives were equipped with Franklin trailer boosters which increased starting tractive effort to 65,200 lb.
4. Engine 356 was scrapped in 1945, the remainder of the Q-3 class survived until retirement between 1952 and 1955.
5. Locomotives 418, 433 and 434 were converted to oil burners.
6. Engine 441 was destroyed by a boiler explosion in 1930. SAL Portsmouth shops built Q-3 451 as a replacement, utilizing a new boiler from Baldwin, along with the frame and running gear from the 441.
7. Ex-Wabash 2414-2415, acquired July 1942. 480 wrecked and scrapped in 1946; 481 retired in 1949.
8. Ex-Wabash 2424, 2427, 2434, 2436, 2439 and 2440; acquired July 1942 and retired 1949–50.
9. Q-1 class were USRA light 2-8-2's. All retired in 1950.

D CLASS 2-10-0

No.	Class	Cyl.	Driv.	WT	Pres.	T.E.	Builder/Date	Note
500-520	D	25x28	52	207,000	180	51,500	Alco-R 1918	1, 2
521-522	D-1	25x28	52	207,000	180	51,500	BLW 1918	1, 3
523-528	D-2	24x28	56	212,000	190	46,150	BLW 1924–26	4
529-536	D-3	24x28	56	212,000	190	46,150	BLW 1930	5
537-546	D-4	25x28	52	207,700	180	51,500	Alco-B 1917–18	1, 6
547, 550	D-5	25x28	52	207,700	180	51,500	BLW 1918	1, 7
548	D-5	25x28	52	207,700	180	51,500	Alco-R 1918	1, 7
549	D-5	25x28	52	207,700	180	51,500	Alco-B 1918	1, 7

Notes:

1. Classes D, D-1, D-4 and D-5 were originally built for Czarist Russia, but never delivered.
2. 520 ex-Georgia Northern 111. 508 to Gainesville Midland 204, Dec. 1949. 518 to MD&S 518, Dec. 1949, ultimately to GM 205. Rest of class retired 1946–51, with most removed from service 1949–50.
3. Nos. 521-522 were ex-GF&A 300-301; scrapped 1949–50.
4. Nos. 523-528 were ex-GF&A 400-405. 524 to Gainesville Midland 207, Apr. 1953. Remainder of D-2 class retired 1951–53.
5. 530 and 533 to Gainesville Midland 208-209. Remainder of D-3 class retired 1952–53.
6. 537-546 were ex-DT&I 303-312, acquired in 1935. 537 and 544 to MD&S 537 and 544 in 1949. 544 later sold to Gainesville Midland 206. Remainder of class retired 1949–50.
7. 547-550 were ex-Erie 2454, 2472, 2481 and 2484, acquired 1935; retired 1949–51.

I, K, L CLASS 4-6-0

No.	Class	Cyl.	Driv.	WT	Pres.	T.E.	Builder/Date	Note
601, 607	L-2	20x28	67	152,500	200	28,400	Alco-R 1902	1
614-615	L-2	20x28	67	165,090	200	28,400	BLW 1903–07	1
617	L-2	20x28	67	165,090	200	28,400	BLW 1903–07	1
624	L-2	20x28	67	165,090	200	28,400	Alco-R 1905	1
630	L-2	20x28	67	165,090	200	28,400	BLW 1903–07	1
631, 634	L-2	20x28	67	165,090	200	28,400	BLW 1903–07	1
643, 649	L-2	20x28	67	165,090	200	28,400	BLW 1903–07	1
650-651	L-4S	19x28	60	172,000	200	28,640	BLW 1910	2
652-654	L-2S	19x28	67	176,130	200	25,700	BLW 1910	3
658	K	21x28	72	173,700	200	29,200	BLW 1910	4
659	L-2S	19x28	67	176,130	200	25,700	BLW 1910	3
655-657	L-4S	19x28	60	172,000	200	28,640	BLW 1910	2
660-664	L-4S	19x28	60	172,000	200	28,640	BLW 1910	2
671-673	I-12	18x26	57	128,800	180	22,600	BLW 1909–12	5
675-676	I-12	18x26	57	128,800	180	22,600	BLW 1909–12	5
678	I-12	18x26	57	128,800	180	22,600	BLW 1909–12	5
681-683	I-13	19x26	62	139,200	185	23,800	BLW 1915	6
704-705	L-4	19x28	60	161,050	200	28,640	BLW 1903–07	7
708, 712	L-4	19x28	60	161,050	200	28,640	BLW 1903–07	7
715, 718	L-4	19x28	60	161,050	200	28,640	BLW 1903–07	7
734, 752	L-4	19x28	60	161,050	200	28,640	Alco-R 1905–07	7
756	L-4	19x28	60	161,050	200	28,640	Alco-R 1906	7
760, 784	L-4	19x28	60	161,050	200	28,640	BLW 1903–07	7
775	L-4	19x28	60	161,050	200	28,640	Alco-R 1907	7
789	L-4	19x28	60	161,050	200	28,640	BLW 1903-07	7
795	L-4	19x28	60	161,050	200	28,640	Alco-R 1907	7

Notes:

1. Entire L-2 class retired by 1946, except for 630, which lasted until 1950.
2. Class L-4S rebuilt 1933–36, 1942 from class K passenger engines for branch-line freight service. 661 to Tavares & Gulf in 1942. Most of class scrapped 1948–50.
3. Class L-2S rebuilt 1934, 1937–38 from class K; retired 1948–50.
4. 658 last unrebuilt class K, retired in 1940.
5. Nos. 671-673, 675-676 and 678 were ex-Carolina, Atlantic & Western 2-4, 6-7 and 9. 671 to St. Marys RR 207 in 1940. 673 to St. Marys RR 308 in 1946. Last I-12 class locomotives retired in 1948.
6. Ex-Carolina, Atlantic & Western 14-16; retired 1940–46.
7. 715 wrecked in 1944. Most remaining L-4's retired by the late forties.

P CLASS 4-6-2

No.	Class	Cyl.	Driv.	WT	Pres.	T.E.	Builder/Date	Note
800-803	P-3	22x28	69	227,917	200	33,389	BLW 1912	1
804-805	P-1	22x28	63	220,000	185	33,826	BLW 1912	2
807	P-1	22x28	63	220,000	185	33,826	BLW 1912	2
809	P-3	22x28	69	227,917	200	33,389	BLW 1912	1
810, 813	P-1	22x28	63	220,000	185	33,826	BLW 1912	2
814	P-3	22x28	69	227,917	200	33,389	BLW 1912	1
815-831	P-2	23x28	69	230,600	195	36,000	Alco-R 1913	3
833-849	P-2	23x28	69	230,600	195	36,000	Alco-R 1913	3
851-858	P	23x28	72	214,400	195	34,100	Alco-R 1911	4
859-863	P	23x28	72	214,400	195	34,100	BLW 1912	4
864-870	P	23x28	72	223,000	195	34,100	Alco-R 1913	4, 5
871-880	P-4	23x28	68	201,700	200	37,030	BLW 1909–11	6

Notes:

1. Class P-3 4-6-2's rebuilt from class P-1 for dual service. 809 retired 1938; 803 in 1945 and remainder retired by 1950.
2. The last five class P-1 engines were retired 1948–50.
3. Class P-2 rebuilt from class P-1 for dual service. Nos. 815, 818, 820, 825, 827, 830, 835, 836, 839, 842, 845 and 846 re-equipped with Vanderbilt tenders from class M-2 4-8-2's. The following locomotives converted to oil burners: 819, 829, 836, 845, 847. Most of P-2 class retired between 1948–50.
4. Nos. 858-863 had Baker valve gears. The remainder of the class was equipped with Walschaerts. Nos. 865, 867 and 868 were streamlined; 869 and 870 were retired before World War II. Most of the remainder of the class were retired between 1946 and 1951.
5. Engines 865, 867 and 868 streamlined and painted in "citrus" colors similar to E-units in late 1940, for use on Wildwood-St. Petersburg section of the *Silver Meteor*.
6. Ex-Western Maryland (K-1 class) 152, 154-158, 160, 151, 153 and 159, acquired in 1943. 874 to Tavares & Gulf April 1946; 875 to MD&S March 1946. Remainder retired 1950–52.

H CLASS AND UNCLASSED 2-8-0'S

No.	Class	Cyl.	Driv.	WT	Pres.	T.E.	Builder/Date	Note
900-918	H-1	23x30	56	217,000	195	46,995	BLW 1911	1
919	H-1	25x30	56	214,700	170	48,450	BLW 1911	1
920-924	GF&A	20x26	56	147,800	180	28,410	BLW 1906–13	2
927-928	CH&N	20x26	54	164,500	180	29,400	Alco-R 1913	3
929-932	CH&N	21x28	54	177,000	180	35,000	BLW 1920	4
933-937	H-2	25x32	61	243,500	185	51,600	Alco 1910–12	5
976, 981	L-3	20x28	57	145,000	200	33,403	Alco-R 1902–03	6
990, 992	H	21x30	57	178,940	200	39,500	BLW 1904	7
995-997	H	21x30	57	178,940	200	39,500	BLW 1904	7
999	H	21x30	57	178,940	200	39,500	BLW 1904	7

Notes:

1. Most of class H-1 retired 1946–50.
2. Ex-Georgia, Florida & Atlantic 200-204. Retired 1946–49.
3. Ex-Charlotte Harbor & Northern 50-51. 928 scrapped 1941; 927 scrapped 1949.
4. Ex-Charlotte Harbor & Northern 71-74. Originally built as oil burners, but converted to burn coal by SAL. 930 to Gainesville Midland 301 in 1951; remainder retired 1950–51.
5. Ex-C&NW 1744, 1787, 1806, 1843 and 1859; acquired during World War II. Retired 1948–49.
6. 976 to Georgia Northern 976 in 1945. 981 to Aberdeen & Rockfish 45 in 1941.
7. 993 and 998 to MD&S 993 and 997 in 1937. Remainder of class scrapped 1938.

ODD CLASS 0-4-0T'S

No.	Class	Cyl.	Driv.	WT	Pres.	T.E.	Builder/Date	Note
1001	ODD	16x24	48	108,000	180	22,400	BLW 1936	1
1003	ODD	16x24	50	86,500	160	16,710	BLW 1913	2

Notes:

1. 1001 retired in 1959; last steam locomotive on SAL roster.
2. Originally built with trolley-type carbody for use on street trackage in Columbus, Ga. Sold in 1949.

F, L CLASS 0-6-0

No.	Class	Cyl.	Driv.	WT	Pres.	T.E.	Builder/Date	Note
1030-1059	L-5	19x28	51	144,280	190	32,000	BLW 1907–13	1
1090-1099	F-5	21x28	51	165,000	190	39,100	Alco-C 1918	2
1101-1125	F-7	23x28	51	180,000	205	45,000	BLW 1927	3
1126-1150	F-7	23x28	51	180,000	205	45,000	BLW 1928	3

Notes:

1. 1057 to Atlantic & East Carolina 10 in March 1952. Remainder of class retired 1945–52.
2. F-5 class were USRA 0-6-0's; scrapped 1950–52.
3. 1129 to Norfolk & Portsmouth Belt Line 80 in October 1953. Remainder of class scrapped 1952–53.

F CLASS 0-8-0

No.	Class	Cyl.	Driv.	WT	Pres.	T.E.	Builder/Date	Note
1175	F-9	22x28	51	184,500	200	45,173	Alco-P 1904	1
1176-1179	F-9	22x28	51	187,900	200	45,173	Alco-P 1905	1

Notes:

1. Ex-Elgin, Joliet & Eastern 545, 549, 550, 553 and 568. Built for EJ&E predecessor Chicago, Lake Shore & Eastern as 2-8-0's and converted to 0-8-0's by EJ&E. 1179 retired in 1944; rest of class scrapped in 1949.

B CLASS 2-10-2

No.	Class	Cyl.	Driv.	WT	Pres.	T.E.	Builder/Date	Note
2400-2409	B	27x32	63	336,000	190	59,800	BLW 1918	1
2485-2499	B-1	27x32	57	352,000	200	69,400	BLW 1919	2

Notes:

1. 2401-2402, 2406-2408 equipped with disc-type main drivers permitting maximum speed of 40 mph. Remainder of class restricted to 30 mph. Most scrapped 1949–50.
2. B-1 class engines were USRA light 2-10-2's; retired 1950–53.

R CLASS 2-6-6-4

No.	Class	Cyl.	Driv.	WT	Pres.	T.E.	Builder/Date	Note
2500-2504	R-1	22x30	69	480,000	230	69,230	BLW 1935	1
2505-2509	R-2	22x30	69	480,000	230	69,230	BLW 1937	2

Notes:

1. To Baltimore & Ohio class KB-1 7700-7704 in July 1947.
2. To Baltimore & Ohio class KB-1a 7705-7709 in July 1947.

GAINESVILLE & MIDLAND (1959)

No.	Type	Class	Cyl.	Driv.	WT	Pres.	T.E.	Builder/Date	Note
116	2-8-0		20x28	57	163,390	200	34,000	BLW 1907	1
203	2-10-0		24x28	56	213,000	200	49,400	BLW 1923	2
205	2-10-0		25x28	52	207,700	180	51,500	Alco-R 1918	3
206	2-10-0	D4	25x28	52	207,200	180	51,500	BLW 1918	4
207	2-10-0	D2	24x28	56	212,000	190	46,510	BLW 1924	5
208	2-10-0	D3	24x28	56	212,000	190	46,510	BLW 1930	6
209	2-10-0	D3	24x28	56	212,000	190	46,510	BLW 1930	6
301	2-8-0		21x28	54	177,000	180	35,000	BLW 1920	7

Notes:

1. Ex-Central of Georgia 215. On display at Jefferson, Ga.
2. Ex-Alabama, Tennessee & Northern Ry. 402. Preserved at Tennessee Valley Railroad Museum, Chattanooga, Tenn.
3. "Russian" Decapod. Ex-Macon, Dublin & Savannah 518, nee-SAL 518.
4. "Russian" Decapod built as USA 1088. Ex-MD&S 544, previously SAL 544, originally DT&I 310. Preserved as SAL 544 at Historic Spencer Shops, Spencer, N.C.
5. Ex-SAL 524, originally GF&A 401.
6. Ex-SAL 530, 533. 208 on display Winder, Ga.; 209 preserved at Gainesville, Ga.
7. Acquired by GM in 1951; ex-SAL 930; originally CH&N 72. Built as oil burner and converted to coal after sale to SAL. On display Charlotte, N.C.

JACKSONVILLE, GAINESVILLE & GULF (1938–1943)

No.	Type	Cyl.	Driv.	Pres.	T.E.	Builder	Date
60	4-6-0	18x24	57	170	19,710	BLW	1911
70	4-6-0	16x24	57	170	15,575	BLW	1909
71	4-6-0	16x24	59	165	14,605	BLW	1914

MACON, DUBLIN & SAVANNAH (1938–1951)

No.	Type	Cyl.	Driv.	WT	Pres.	T.E.	Builder/Date	Note
34	2-8-0	22x28	53				Alco-B 1908	1
46	2-10-0	25x28	52	207,700	180	51,200	Alco-R 1918	2
47	2-10-0	25x28	52	207,700	180	51,200	BLW 1918	2
48	2-10-0	25x28	52	207,700	180	51,200	BLW 1918	2
50	0-6-0	18x24	50	104,000	180	24,000	BLW 1906	
110	4-6-0	18x26	56	136,500	185	24,000	BLW 1920	3
518	2-10-0	25x28	52	207,700	180	51,500	Alco-R 1918	4
537	2-10-0	25x28	52	207,700	180	51,500	Alco-B 1918	5
544	2-10-0	25x28	52	207,700	180	51,500	Alco-B 1918	5
875	4-6-2	23x28	68	201,700	200	37,030	BLW 1911	6
993	2-8-0	21x30	57	178,940	200	39,500	BLW 1904	7
998	2-8-0	21x30	57	178,940	200	39,500	BLW 1904	7

Notes:

1. Ex-Birmingham & Southern 34; acquired Dec. 1938.
2. Ex-Erie "Russian" Decapods 2468, 2483 and 2486.
3. Built for J.F. Darby Lumber Co.
4. "Russian" Decapod, ex-SAL 518. Acquired Dec. 1949; to Gainesville Midland 205.
5. "Russian" Decapods. Ex-Detroit, Toledo & Ironton 303 and 310; to SAL 537 and 544 in 1935; to MD&S in 1949. 544 to Gainesville Midland 206; preserved as SAL 544 at Historic Spencer Shops, Spencer, N.C.
6. Ex-SAL class P-4 875; originally Western Maryland 157. Purchased by SAL in 1943; acquired by MD&S in March 1946.
7. Ex-SAL 993 and 998; acquired in 1937.

TAVARES & GULF (1938–1953)

No.	Type	Cyl.	Driv.	WT	Pres.	T.E.	Builder/Date	Note
100	2-6-2	16x24	46	103,000	180	20,400	BLW 1916	
104	2-6-2	16x24	46	111,000	180	20,400	Alco 1916	
105	2-6-2	16x24	46	111,000	180	20,400	Alco 1916	
106	4-6-0	18x26	54	116,500	180	23,900	BLW 1912	
661	4-6-0	19x28	60	172,000	200	28,640	BLW 1910	1
874	4-6-2	23x28	68	201,700	200	37,030	BLW 1911	2

Notes:

1. Ex-SAL L-4S 661; acquired in 1942.
2. Ex-SAL class P-4 874; originally Western Maryland 156. Purchased by SAL in 1943; acquired by T&G in April 1946.

Roster sources: *Railroad* magazine; Seaboard Air Line; *Trains* magazine; W.H.N. Rossiter.

APPENDIX II
SEABOARD AIR LINE DIESEL LOCOMOTIVE ROSTER

This roster covers all diesel locomotives rostered by the Seaboard Air Line and its subsidiaries. Seaboard Coast Line road numbers are given for those locomotives on the roster at the time of the merger.

BUILDERS

ACF	American Car & Foundry
Alco	American Locomotive Co., Schenectady, N.Y.
Alco-GE	American Locomotive Co., Schenectady, N.Y.
BLW	Baldwin Locomotive Works, Eddystone, Pa.
Brill	J.G. Brill Co.
EMC	Electro-Motive Corp., La Grange, Ill.
EMC/St.L	St. Louis Car Co., to design of Electro-Motive Corp., St. Louis, Mo.
EMD	Electro-Motive Division, General Motors Corp., La Grange, Ill.
GE	General Electric Co., Erie, Pa.
GE-Wason	General Electric-Wason

SAL	SCL	Model	Builder	Serial	Built	Notes
100-106	1202-1208	RS11	Alco	83588-83594	6/60	
107-109	1209-1211	RS11	Alco	83681-83683	6/60	
110-125	1212-1227	C420	Alco	3418-1 to -16	5/65–6/65	
126		C420	Alco	3418-17	6/65	1
127	1228	C420	Alco	3418-18	6/65	
128-135	1229-1236	C420	Alco	3418-19 to -26	8/65	
136	1237	C420	Alco	3459-01	5/66	1
400-409	1056-1065	GP18	EMD	26114-26123	8/60–9/60	
500-533	1309-1342	GP30	EMD	27928-27961	11/62–1/63	
534	1343	GP30	EMD	27462	3/62	2
535-544	1406-1415	GP35	EMD	30628-30637	6/65	
600-614	1515-1529	GP40	EMD	31767-31781	5/66	
615-629	1530-1544	GP40	EMD	31784-31798	5/66–8/66	
630-644	1545-1559	GP40	EMD	32609-32623	1/67	
645-650	1560-1565	GP40	EMD	32958-32963	2/67	
800-814	1704-1718	U30B	GE	36121-36135	12/66–1/67	
1100-1113	601-614	SDP35	EMD	29339-29352	7/64–9/64	
1114-1119	615-620	SDP35	EMD	29353-29358	11/64	6
1200		SW1	EMC	802	3/39	3
1201	26	S1	Alco-GE	69406	1/41	4
1202	27	VO660	BLW	62490	2/41	5
1400	28	VO1000	BLW	64209	9/41	5
1401-1402	29-30	VO1000	BLW	64256-64257	11/41	5
1403-1405		S2	Alco-GE	69657-69659	2/42–4/42	3
1406-1407	31-32	NW2	EMD	1595-1596	3/42	
1408		NW2	EMD	1873	6/42	7
1409-1412	33-36	NW2	EMD	1874-1877	6/42	
1413-1416	37-40	VO1000	BLW	71979-71982	12/44–1/45	5
1417		DS-4-4-1000	BLW	72233	6/46	3
1418-1419		DS-4-4-1000	BLW	72791-72792	7/46	3
1420-1424		DS-4-4-1000	BLW	72803-72807	9/46–10/46	3
1425-1427	41-43	S2	Alco-GE	74659-74661	8/46	
1428	44	S2	Alco-GE	74665	8/46	
1429	45	S2	Alco-GE	74786	8/46	
1430-1431	46-47	S2	Alco-GE	74791-74792	9/46	
1432-1434	48-50	S2	Alco-GE	75907-75909	6/48	
1435-1437		DS-4-4-1000	BLW	74760-74762	2/50	3
1438		DS-4-4-1000	BLW	74793	8/50	3
1439-1443	51-55	DS-4-4-1000	BLW	74794-74798	8/50	
1444-1451	56-63	DS-4-4-1000	BLW	74883-74890	8/50	
1452-1461	64-73	DS-4-4-1000	BLW	75098-75107	10/50–1/51	
1462-1465	203-206	S12	BLW	75142-75145	1/52	
1466-1471	207-212	RS12	BLW	75475-75480	5/52	8
1472-1475	213-216	RS12	BLW	75765-75768	1/53	8
1476-1481	217-222	S12	BLW	75759-75764	1/53	
1482-1486	74-78	S4	Alco-GE	79820-79824	4/53	
1487-1491	79-83	S4	Alco-GE	80457-80461	4/53–5/53	
1492	84	VO1000	BLW	62475	2/42	9
1500-1501		RSC2	Alco-GE	75397-75398	10/47	10, 11
1502-1503	1100-1101	RSC2	Alco-GE	75399-75400	11/47	10
1504-1512		RSC2	Alco-GE	76806-76814	4/49	10, 11
1513	1102	RSC2	Alco-GE	76815	5/49	10
1514-1516		RSC2	Alco-GE	76816-76818	5/49	11
1517-1523		RSC2	Alco-GE	77176-77182	8/49	11
1524	1103	RSC2	Alco-GE	77183	8/49	
1525		RSC2	Alco-GE	77184	8/49	11
1526	1104	RSC2	Alco-GE	77408	9/49	
1527-1530		RSC2	Alco-GE	77409-77412	9/49	11
1531	1105	RSC2	Alco-GE	77413	9/49	
1532-1535	1106-1109	RSC2	Alco-GE	77967-77970	4/50	12
1536	1110	RSC2	Alco-GE	77966	4/50	12
1537-1540	1111-1114	RSC3	Alco-GE	78427-78430	11/50–12/50	
1541-1543	1115-1117	RSC3	Alco-GE	78539-78541	1/51	
1600-1603		RS2	Alco-GE	77869-77872	12/49	3
1604	1118	RS2	Alco-GE	77887	12/49	
1605-1608	1119-1122	RS2	Alco-GE	77922-77925	3/50	13
1609-1627	1123-1141	RS2	Alco-GE	77946-77964	3/50–4/50	
1628		RS2	Alco-GE	77965	4/50	3
1629-1647	1142-1160	RS3	Alco-GE	78431-78449	11/50	
1648-1656	1161-1169	RS3	Alco-GE	78467-78475	11/50–12/50	
1657-1664	1170-1177	RS3	Alco-GE	78531-78538	12/50–1/51	
1665-1672	1178-1185	RS3	Alco-GE	79419-79426	12/51	
1673-1674	1186-1187	RS3	Alco-GE	79592-79593	12/51	
1675-1679	1188-1192	RS3	Alco-GE	80214-80218	10/52	
1680-1684	1193-1197	RS3	Alco-GE	79825-79829	10/52	
1685-1687		RS2	Alco-GE	77538-77540	10/49	3, 14
1688	1198	RS3	Alco-GE	79361	11/51	14
1689-1690	1199-1200	RS3	Alco-GE	78360-78361	10/50	14
1691	1201	RS3	Alco-GE	81850	2/56	14
1700-1703	880-883	GP7	EMD	11503-11506	5/50	
1704-1711	884-891	GP7	EMD	11495-11502	4/50	8
1712-1729	892-909	GP7	EMD	11588-11605	5/50–6/50	
1730-1744	910-924	GP7	EMD	11588-11605	5/50–6/50	
1745-1752	925-932	GP7	EMD	11341-11348	11/50	8
1753-1775	933-955	GP7	EMD	13366-13388	12/50–1/51	15, 16
1776-1782	956-962	GP7	EMD	13389-13395	3/51	
1783-1789	963-969	GP7	EMD	15527-15533	1/52	
1790-1797	970-977	GP7	EMD	15534-15541	2/52	
1798-1822	978-1002	GP7	EMD	17370-17394	9/52	15
1900-1902	1053-1055	GP9	EMD	21069-21071	11/55	
1903-1909	1003-1009	GP9	EMD	21072-21078	11/55	
1910	1010	GP9	EMD	21512	10/55	
1911		GP9	EMD	21513	10/55	17
1912-1921	1011-1020	GP9	EMD	21514-21523	10/55–11/55	
1922-1925	1021-1024	GP9	EMD	23095-23098	9/56	
1926	1025	GP9	EMD	23778	11/57	
1927		GP9	EMD	23779	11/57	17
1928-1929	1026-1027	GP9	EMD	23780-23781	11/57	
1954-1962	1028-1036	GP9	EMD	22625-22633	10/56	
1963		GP9	EMD	22634	10/56	17
1964-1970	1037-1043	GP9	EMD	22635-22641	10/56	
1971		GP9	EMD	22642	10/56	17
1972-1978	1044-1050	GP9	EMD	22643-22649	10/56	
1979		GP9	EMD	25717	10/59	17, 30
2000-2001		Motor Car	GE-Wason	3793-3794	5/17	18
2002-2003		Motor Car	EMC/St.L	137-138	11/25	19
2012		Motor Car	Brill		1922	20
2013-2021		Motor Car	Brill		1927	21
2022-2023		Motor Car	EMC/St.L	261-262	2/28	22
2024-2026		Motor Car	ACF		1935	23
2027		AA	EMC/St.L	523	4/36	24
2028	4900	AA	EMC/St.L	524	4/36	24
2700-2702		DR-6-4-1500	BLW	73396-73398	11/47–1/48	25
3000-3005		E4A	EMC	832-837	10/38–12/38	26
3006		E4A	EMC	807	1/39	26
3007-3012		E4A	EMC	960-965	11/39–12/39	26
3013		E4A	EMC	851	12/39	26
3014		E6A	EMD	974	11/39	27
3015-3016		E6A	EMD	1593-1594	12/41	25, 28
3017-3020	544-547	E7A	EMD	1929-1932	3/45	
3021-3026	548-553	E7A	EMD	2875-2880	8/45–9/45	
3027		E7A	EMD	2881	/45	29
3028-3030	554-556	E7A	EMD	2882-2884	5/45–9/45	
3031-3034	557-560	E7A	EMD	3611-3614	9/46	
3035	561	E7A	EMD	4444	9/46	
3036-3040	562-566	E7A	EMD	6028-6032	2/48	
3041	567	E7A	EMD	6149	7/48	
3042		E7A	EMD	6150	7/48	30
3043-3044	568-569	E7A	EMD	6151-6152	7/48	
3045-3048	570-573	E7A	EMD	8259-8262	4/49	
3049-3054	588-593	E8A	EMD	13274-13279	10/50	
3055-3059	594-598	E8A	EMD	17339-17343	11/52–12/52	
3060	599	E9A	EMD	28524	12/63	
3100-3102		E4B	EMC	838-840	10/38–11/38	31
3103-3104		E4B	EMC	966, 852	12/39, 11/39	31

3105-3107	667B-669B	E7B	EMD	6153-6155	7/48	
4000-4005		FTA	EMD	1570-1575	6/42	32
4006-4009		FTA	EMD	1865-1868	6/43–10/43	32
4010-4011		FTA	EMD	2156-2157	11/43	32
4012-4021		FTA	EMD	2318-2327	1/44–10/44	32
4022-4027		F3A	EMD	4737-4742	3/48	17, 33
4028-4032		F3A	EMD	5657-5661	3/48	33
4100-4105		FTB	EMD	1576-1581	6/42	32
4106-4109		FTB	EMD	1869-1872	8/43–10/43	32
4110-4111		FTB	EMD	2158-2159	11/43	32
4112-4121		FTB	EMD	2328-2337	1/44–10/44	32
4200-4202		FA1	Alco-GE	75974-75976	5/48	3
4300-4302		FB1	Alco-GE	75772-75774	5/48	3
4500		DR-12-8-3000	BLW	71579	12/45	34, 35
4501-4505		DR-12-8-3000	BLW	73141-73145	3/47–5/47	35
4506-4509		DR-12-8-3000	BLW	73388-73391	6/47–9/47	35
4510-4513		DR-12-8-3000	BLW	73392-73395	9/47–12/47	35

GAINESVILLE & MIDLAND

GM	SBD	Model	Builder	Serial	Built	Notes
10	010	SD40	EMD	31799	6/66	36

MACON, DUBLIN & SAVANNAH

MD&S	SAL	Model	Builder	Serial	Built	Notes
1000	1492	VO1000	BLW	62475	2/42	9
1700-1702	1685-87	RS2	Alco-GE	77538-77540	10/49	3
1703-1704	1689-1690	RS3	Alco-GE	78360-78361	10/50	
1705	1688	RS3	Alco-GE	79361	11/51	
1706	1691	RS3	Alco-GE	81850	2/56	

Notes:

1. SAL 126 wrecked in 1966 and traded in to Alco on replacement C420 136.
2. Ex-EMD GP30 demonstrator 5639, purchased by SAL in 1964.
3. Traded in to EMD 1966–67 on GP40's and scrapped at Pielet Bros., McCook, Ill.
4. 1201 re-powered with 1000 hp 539 engine in 1957.
5. 1202, 1400-1402, 1413-1416 re-powered 1962–63 with 1000 hp EMD 12-567 engines.
6. SAL 1100-1113 first SDP35's built. SAL SDP35 1114 restored and displayed at Hamlet, N.C.
7. 1408 wrecked in collision with DS-4-4-1000 1459 and runaway cut of cars at Hamlet, N.C., 9/5/64 and traded in to EMD on GP35.
8. Equipped with steam generators.
9. Ex-Macon, Dublin & Savannah 1000. Re-powered in 1964 with 1000 hp 12-567 engine.
10. 1501-1511, 1513-1519, 1522, 1524-1526, 1528-1531 converted to B-B in 1954–55 by removing center wheel set and modifying trucks with single drop equalizer. 1502, 1503, 1513, 1524, 1526 and 1531 restored to A1A-A1A in 1965.
11. 1532-1536 are 1600 hp RSC2's; Alco spec E1661C.
12. 1500-1501, 1504-1512, 1514-1523, 1525, 1527-1530 traded in to Alco in 1965 on C420's.
13. 1605-1628 are 1600 hp RS2's; Alco spec E1661C.
14. Ex-Macon, Dublin & Savannah 1700-1702, 1705, 1703-1704 and 1706.
15. 1771, 1798, 1801 wrecked at Matthews, N.C., 1955. Units returned to EMD, with some components used in construction of replacement locomotives. SAL 1771 outshopped by EMD 4/56 with GP9 frame/GP7 carbody. Components and equipment from 1798 and 1801 combined with new frames and carbodies to build 1500 hp GP9m's 1798 and 1801. Units outshopped from La Grange in March 1956 under new order number 8040.
16. 1753-1769 equipped with steam generators.
17. GP9's 1911, 1927, 1963, 1971, 1979 and F3A 4027 wrecked in head-on collision at Cherryville, N.C., July 13, 1966, and scrapped; several units cut up on spot.
18. 2000-2001 GE class CRE-70-B-10 1/2; 175 hp. Baggage/48-seat coach. 2000 retired 12/32, 2001 retired 5/23.
19. 175 hp. Combine: baggage/44-seat coach. 2002 sold to Sperry Rail Service 4/43. 2003 sold to Sperry Rail Service 1/42 and rebuilt to self-powered rail defect detector car SRS 132.
20. 2012 Brill Model 55; 68 hp. Baggage/30-seat coach. Retired by 1941.
21. 2013-2021 Brill baggage/mail motor car; 250 hp. 2017 converted to trailer 2045. All retired.
22. 275 hp. 2022-2023 sold to Sperry Rail Service in 1945 and rebuilt to self-powered rail defect detector cars SRS 134-135.
23. Lightweight, 61-foot cars with baggage/Jim Crow coach configuration, built by American Car & Foundry. Powered by 176 hp Scott-Hall Model 180 engines. 2024-2025 to NS in 1944, later sold to Cuba. 2026 to Aberdeen & Rockfish 106, then to Salt Lake, Garfield & Western; finally sold to California & Western M-300.
24. Model AA "power cars" with 8-cylinder, 660 hp Winton 201A engine; RPO and baggage sections behind engine room. 2028 rebuilt with 600-hp 6-567A engine in 1948. 2027 retired in 1957, still with Winton engine. 2028 to SCL 4900, retired 7/71.
25. Traded in to EMD in 1964 on SDP35's.
26. SAL 3000 first production unit built with 567 engine. 3003 and 3012 wrecked at Hypoluxo, Fla., 2/19/42 and scrapped. 3013 wrecked at Kollocks, S.C., in collision between the southbound *Silver Meteor* and the *Sun Queen* in 1943 and scrapped. 3000-3002, 3004-3011 traded in to EMD in 1964 on SDP35's.
27. 3014 built as E4A as part of SAL order, but displayed at 1939–40 New York World's Fair as GM 1939. After display, unit returned to EMD La Grange, upgraded to E6A and outshopped as SAL 3014; the first E6. Retired 1964 after running 4.6 million miles and traded in to EMD on SDP35. EMD displayed 3014 at 1964 New York World's Fair, then shipped to La Grange and scrapped at Pielet Bros.
28. 3016 wrecked in 1962 and traded in to EMD on E9A 3060.
29. 3027 wrecked on No. 4 at Raleigh, N.C., April 8, 1961, and scrapped. Some components shipped to EMD for use in E9A 3060.
30. 3042 wrecked in 1958 and traded in to EMD on wreck replacement GP9 1979, which was also wrecked.
31. 3101 wrecked in 1962 and scrapped at West Jacksonville. 3100, 3102-3104 traded in to EMD in 1964 on SDP35's.
32. Operated in semi-permanently coupled A-B sets with matched 4000 and 4100 series road numbers. 4001-4003, 4007, 4009, 4012-4014, 4018-4019 and FTB's 4101-4103, 4107, 4109, 4112-4114, 4118-4119 traded in to EMD in 1955–57 on GP9's. FTA's 4000, 4004-4006, 4008, 4010-4011, 4015-4017, 4020-4021 and FTB's 4100, 4104-4106, 4108, 4110-4111, 4115-4117, 4120-4121 traded in to EMD in 1962–63 on GP30's.
33. 4022-4026, 4028-4032 traded in to GE in 1966.
34. Running gear from Baldwin DR-12-8-3000 demonstrator 6000 utilized in construction of SAL 4500.
35. 4500, 4502-4504, 4508, 4511, 4513 retired in 1957 and scrapped. 4501, 4505-4507, 4509-4510, 4512 retired in 1961 and scrapped.
36. Gainesville Midland 10 renumbered SBD 0010 in 1983; to SBD 8300 in 1985.

Roster sources: EMD Product Reference Guide; Extra 2200 South; Seaboard Air Line; W.L. Calloway and Paul Withers; *Trains* magazine.

LEFT:
Wearing Seaboard's handsome black-and-red switcher scheme, Alco S4 1490 works

RIGHT:
Still in full Seaboard dress, C420 118 stands at Hialeah with SCL GP9 1009,

SELECTED BIBLIOGRAPHY

BOOKS

Beebe, Lucius and Clegg, Charles, *The Trains We Rode*, Vol. I. Berkeley, California: Howell-North, 1965.

Black, Robert C., III, *The Railroads of the Confederacy*. Chapel Hill: The University of North Carolina Press, 1952.

Bramson, Seth H., *Speedway to Sunshine*. Erin, Ontario, Canada: The Boston Mills Press, 1984.

Brown, Alexander Crosby, *The Old Bay Line*. Richmond: The Dietz Press, 1940.

Bush, Donald J., *The Streamlined Decade*. New York: George Braziller, 1975.

Calloway, Warren L. and Withers, Paul K., *Seaboard Air Line Railroad Company Motive Power*. Halifax, Pennsylvania: Withers Publishing, 1988.

Dolzall, Gary W. and Stephen F., *Diesels From Eddystone: The Story of Baldwin Diesel Locomotives*. Milwaukee: Kalmbach Publishing Co., 1984.

Dozier, Howard D., *A History of the Atlantic Coast Line Railroad*. Boston: Houghton Mifflin Co., 1920. Reprinted, New York: Augustus M. Kelley, 1971.

Drury, George H., *The Historical Guide to North American Railroads*. Milwaukee: Kalmbach Publishing Co., 1985.

Dubin, Arthur D., *Some Classic Trains*. Milwaukee: Kalmbach Publishing Co., 1964.

———, *More Classic Trains*. Milwaukee: Kalmbach Publishing Co., 1974.

Farrell, Jack W. and Pearsall, Mike, *North American Steam Locomotives: The Mountains*. Edmonds, Washington: Pacific Fast Mail, 1977.

Farrington, S. Kip, Jr., *Railroading the Modern Way*. New York: Coward-McCann, Inc., 1951.

Fetters, Thomas, *Logging Railroads of South Carolina*. Forest Park, Illinois: Heimburger House, 1990.

Griffin, William E., Jr., *All Lines North of Raleigh: A History of the Seaboard Air Line Railway's Virginia Division*. Richmond: William E. Griffin, Jr., 1991.

Hilton, George W., *American Narrow Gauge Railroads*. Stanford, California: Stanford University Press, 1990.

———, *The Night Boat*. Berkeley, California: Howell-North Books, 1968.

Holbrook, Stewart H., *The Story of American Railroads*. New York: Crown Publishers, 1947.

Keilty, Edmund, *Doodlebug Country*. Glendale, California: Interurban Press, 1982.

Kratville, William W., *Steam, Steel and Limiteds*. Omaha: William W. Kratville, 1962.

Langley, Albert M., Jr.; Beckum, W. Forrest, Jr.; and Tidwell, C. Ronnie, *Seaboard Air Line Railway Album*. North Augusta, South Carolina: Union Station Publishing, 1988.

Lewis, Edward A., *American Short Line Railway Guide*. Strasburg, Pennsylvania: The Baggage Car, 1975.

Mann, Robert W., *Rails 'Neath the Palms*. Burbank, California: Darwin Publications, 1983.

Mulhearn, Daniel J. and Taibi, John R., *General Motors' F-Units: The Locomotives That Revolutionized Railroading*. New York: Quadrant Press, Inc., 1982.

Our GM Scrapbook. Milwaukee: Kalmbach Publishing Co., 1971.

Pettengill, George W., Jr., *The Story of the Florida Railroads 1834–1903, Railway & Locomotive Histrorical Society Bulletin No. 86*. Boston: The Railway & Locomotive Historical Society, 1952.

Prince, Richard E., *Atlantic Coast Line Railroad Steam Locomotives, Ships and History*. Green River, Wyoming: Richard E. Prince, 1966.

———, *Central of Georgia Railway and Connecting Lines*. Millard, Nebraska: Richard E. Prince, 1976.

———, *The Richmond-Washington Line and Related Railroads*. Millard, Nebraska: Richard E. Prince, 1973.

———, *Seaboard Air Line Railway Steam Boats, Locomotives and History*. Green River, Wyoming: Richard E. Prince, 1969.

———, *Southern Railway System Steam Locomotives and Boats*. Green River, Wyoming: Richard E. Prince, 1970.

Randall, W. David and Lind, Alan R., *From Zephyr to Amtrak*. Park Forest, Illinois: Prototype Publications, 1972.

Reed, Robert C., *The Streamline Era*. San Marino, California: Golden West Books, 1975.

Sagle, Lawrence W., *B. & O. Power*. Medina, Ohio: Alvin F. Staufer, 1964.

Stover, John F., *The Railroads of the South 1865–1900*. Chapel Hill: The University of North Carolina Press, 1955.

Westcott, Linn H., Editor, *Steam Locomotives: Model Railroader Cyclopedia*–Vol. 1. Milwaukee: Kalmbach Publishing Co., 1960.

White, John H., *The Great Yellow Fleet*. San Marino, California: Golden West Books, 1986.

UNPUBLISHED DISSERTATIONS AND THESES

Johnson, Dudley Sady, *The Railroads of Florida, 1865–1900*. Ph.D. Dissertation, Florida State University, 1965.

Joubert, William Henry, *A History of the Seaboard Air Line Railway Co*. Master's Thesis, University of Florida, 1935.

Lord, Mills M., Jr., *David Levy Yulee, Statesman and Railroad Builder*. Master's Thesis, University of Florida, 1940.

Patterson, William Herman, *Through the Heart of the South*. Ph.D. Dissertation, University of South Carolina, 1951.

GOVERNMENT AGENCY DECISIONS

Gainesville Midland Ry. Valuation 84 I.C.C. 381.

Georgia, Florida & Alabama Ry. Valuation 122 I.C.C. 419.

Seaboard Air Line Ry. Co. 35 I.C.C. Valuation Reports 337.

Seaboard Air Line R. Co., Discontinuance of Trains 330 I.C.C. 171 (1966).

Seaboard Air Line R. Co. - Merger - Atlantic Coast Line 320 I.C.C. 122 (1963).

Seaboard Air Line Ry. Receivers Abandonment 202 I.C.C. 543 (1934).

Tavares & Gulf R. Co. Valuation 35 I.C.C. Valuation Reports 870.

ARTICLES

Appleby, Sam, Jr., "Through the Heart of the South," *Trains*, February 1949.

Boyd, Jim, "Atlanta Before Amtrak," *Railfan Magazine*, Fall 1975.

———, "Dutchland Decapod," *Railfan Magazine*, September 1978.

———, "Richmond's Triple Crossing," *Railfan Magazine*, November 1983.

Brockmeyer, Joe, et al, "Seaboard Coast Line RR. Roster," *Extra 2200 South*, July 1968.

Bryan, Wiley M., "There Was Just Something About the Smell of Coal Smoke," *Trains*, February 1974.

———, "Twin Stacks," *Trains*, August 1979.

Davis, T. Frederick, "Pioneer Florida," *Florida Historical Quarterly*, Vol. 23, January 1945.

Doherty, Herbert J., Jr., "Jacksonville As a Nineteenth Century Railroad Center," *Florida Historical Quarterly*, Vol. 58.

"The 'E' in Evolution," *Lines South*, March 1984.

Edson, William D., "The U.S.R.A. Locomotives," *Railway & Locomotive Historical Society Bulletin*, No. 93.

Fenlon, Paul E., "The Florida, Atlantic & Gulf Central R.R.," *Florida Historical Quarterly*, Vol. 32.

———, "The Notorious Swepson-Littlefield Fraud," *Florida Historical Quarterly*, Vol. 32, April 1954.

Fisher, Charles E., "Moncure Robinson," *Railway & Locomotive Historical Society Bulletin*, No. 53.

———, "The United States Military Railroads," *Railway & Locomotive Historical Society Bulletin*, No. 108.

"Florida Streamliners," *Lines South*, January 1984.

Frazier, R.B., "From Merger to Merger," *Rail Classics*, May 1982.

"Hamlet Yard," *Lines South*, March 1987, June 1987.

Hundman, Robert L., "U.S.R.A. Light 2-10-2," *Mainline Modeler*, October 1983.

Johnson, Dudley S., "The Florida Railroad After the Civil War," *Florida Historical Quarterly*, Vol. 47.

King, E.W., Jr., "Decapods and Red Clay," *Trains*, August 1988.

Lamb, J.P., Jr. "A Tale of Two Freight Trains," *Trains*, May 1963.

"Locomotives of the Seaboard Air Line," *Railroad Magazine*, September 1948.

"Locomotives of the Seaboard Air Line Railway," *Railroad Stories Magazine*, May 1935.

McBride, H.A., "The Seaboard Railroad," *Railroad Magazine*, April 1953.

Morgan, David P., "Jacksonville Terminal, Mr. Wilkes, and Me," *Trains*, June 1978.

———, "The Rare and Wonderful Gainesville Midland," *Trains*, October 1957.

Oates, J.L., "The SDP35's," *Lines South*, October 1988.

Pinkepank, Jerry A., "Wet Rock, Dry Rock and the Seaboard," *Trains*, October 1984.

"Robinson, Moncure," *Dictionary of American Biography*, Vol. 16.

"Robinson, Moncure," *The National Cyclopedia of American Biography*, Vol. III.

"Ryan, Thomas Fortune," *Dictionary of American Biography*, Vol. 16.

"Seaboard Air Line's Classic Mountains," *Locomotive Quarterly*, Vol. VII, No. 1, Fall 1983.

"Seaboard Air Line Diesel-Powered Rail Cars," *Lines South*, December 1985.

"Seaboard's Mountains: Comparable to the Best," *Trains*, December 1952.

Smiley, Tom, "Seaboard Air Line F3's," *Prototype Modeler*, May/June 1989.

"This $3 3/4 Million Terminal...," *Railway Age*, November 30, 1953.

"Threshold to Florida," *Trains*, May 1949.

"Trains That Are Making Good: The Orange Blossom Special," *Railroad Magazine*, April 1938.

"Trains That Are Making Good: The Silver Meteor," *Railroad Magazine*, May 1939.

"Warfield, Solomon Davies," *Dictionary of American Biography*, Vol. 19.

Watkins, Caroline, "Some Early Railroads in Alachua County, " *Florida Historical Quarterly*, Vol. 45.

Yulee, C. Wicliffe, "Senator David L. Yulee," *Florida Historical Society Quarterly*, July 1909.

PERIODICALS

Moody's Steam Railroads. New York: Moody's Investors Service (various years, 1941–1967).

The Official Guide of Railways. New York: National Railway Publications Co. (various issues, 1870–1967).

Poor's Manual of the Railroads of the United States. New York: H.V. & H.W. Poor (various years, 1868–1940).

COMPANY DOCUMENTS

A Brief History of the Seaboard Air Line Railway.

Brief History of the Seaboard Air Line Railway System in the State of Florida.

Corporate History of the Seaboard-All Florida Railway.

History of Construction of Lines Forming Present Seaboard Air Line Railway in Alabama.

Seaboard Air Line Annual Reports (various years, 1900–1966).

Seaboard Air Line Condensed Roster (various years).

Seaboard Air Line Railroad Company Corporate History.

Seaboard Air Line Employee Timetables (various issues).

Seaboard Air Line Public Timetables (various issues).

INDEX